Air Fryer Cookbook

Top 500 Healthy & Delicious Air Fryer Recipes
for Your Family

By Kathy Robins

Table of Content

Fries

Rings

Skewer Recipes 191

Dessert & Snacks Recipes 239

PART I

Your Ultimate Guide to Air Fryer Accessories

An air fryer is a kitchen appliance that has a lot to offer. It is a popular choice for people who want to make low-fat meals using hot air circulation, allowing the food to cook with virtually no oil. With an air fryer, healthier foods can be made while keeping the mess and unpleasant aromas to a minimum.

Many air fryers come with a recipe book so that you can get started with this appliance right away. However, if you have been using an air fryer for quite some time, you might find yourself bored and looking for new ideas. This is where air fryer accessories come into play.

The Benefits of Air Fryer Accessories

Air fryer accessories offer a variety of different functions. Accessories can take your air fryer cooking to the next level by allowing you to prepare all kinds of foods in an assortment of novel ways. There are many types of air fryer accessories that you can purchase, and they will help you to create items that you would not think are possible to make in an air fryer. These include baked goodies, grilled foods, and even barbecued meats.

There are many accessory options available to help maximize the use you are getting from your air fryer. While a simple air fryer can help you to cook your favorite fried foods without oil, the accessories can transform your air fryer into another kitchen appliance such as a grill or an oven. With the right accessories, you may not need to buy other kitchen equipment, especially if you only cook for a few people on a regular basis. Air fryer accessories transform the basic air fryer into a whole kitchen's worth of appliances.

Accessory users are not only saving money on kitchen appliance purchases, they are also able to save a lot of space on their kitchen counters. This will benefit foodies who have small kitchens in their homes, college students living in cramped dormitories, single employees living in apartments, and practical moms looking to reduce their household spending.

Using Air Fryer Accessories

There are many types of air fryer accessories that are available but only a few that are necessary in order to expand the way that the air fryer can be used. These include the air fryer baking dish, the air fryer grill pan, and the air fryer double layer rack with skewers. Continue reading to learn more about the different types of air fryer accessories that are available.

Air Fryer Baking Dish

The air fryer baking dish allows home cooks to use the air fryer as an oven to bake cakes, muffins, and breads. While some people use heat-proof dishes in their air fryers, using a baking dish that was made for the air fryer better enables foods to be cooked properly. The baking dish accessory helps to ensure that the right amount of air flow is distributed within the air fryer to evenly cook the food.

The right air fryer baking dish or pan not only aids in making baked goodies such as cakes and breads, however. This accessory can also be used to cook quiche, lasagna, shepherd's pie, and other deep-dish recipes that would typically be baked in an oven. The air fryer baking dish comes with a non-stick surface, making the cleanup really easy. The non-stick surface also ensures that cooked foods release easily, giving you the perfect results every time. The baking dish is also dishwasher safe.

As there are so many brands of air fryers available in the market, it is important to choose a baking dish that will be compatible with your air fryer. Thus, it is crucial to check with the store to learn whether the air fryer baking dish that you want to buy is appropriate to use with the brand and model of air fryer that you have.

Air Fryer Grill Pan

As previously mentioned, air fryers are not only good for frying food without oil. The air fryer grill pan accessory allows the user to make perfectly grilled fish, meat, and vegetables. It can also be used for the searing and browning of foods. The grill pan comes with a rapid air technology design (thanks to the perforated surface) that makes it ideal for the air to flow throughout the food while grilling.

The perforations on the surface of the grill pan allow the extra fat to drip away, perfectly grilling the meat to tender perfection. Like the air fryer baking dish, the grill pan also has a non-stick coating so that foods can be removed easily. Want some surf and turf? The surface of the grill pan is large enough for a big steak, a whole fillet of fish, and a generous amount of vegetables. Since the grill pan is placed at the bottom of the air fryer, it comes with an easy click removable handle to help position the grill pan in the air fryer and also take it out to be cleaned.

The grill pan is compatible with most air fryers, but it is still crucial to ask the store if it will work with your particular air fryer model. This is the easiest way to make sure that you can use this accessory without any problems.

Air Fryer Double Layer Rack with Skewers

The double layer rack accessory allows you to maximize the cooking space within the fryer. You can bake, fry, or grill meats on the bottom rack while cooking another type of food on the upper rack. This accessory also comes with four skewers so that you can make kabobs if the whim strikes you. Simply put the food on the rack and place the entire thing (rack, food, and all) into the fryer. Cook according to the recipe instructions. That really is all there is to it! This is a great accessory for expanding the usefulness of your air fryer and it is perfect for making multiple types of food in a shorter amount of time. You will be surprised at how much food will fit into your air fryer using this accessory.

The rack is dishwasher safe making cleanup a breeze. It is also compatible with most air fryer models but again make sure that you ask the store where you are making your purchase whether it will work with the brand and model of air fryer that you have.

PART II

Air Fryer Recipes

Vegetable Recipes

Crispy Kale Chips

(Servings: 3, Cooking Time: 7 minutes)

Ingredients:
- 3 cups kale leaves, stems removed
- 1 tablespoon olive oil
- Salt and pepper, to taste

Directions for Cooking:
1) In a bowl, combine all of the ingredients. Toss to coat the kale leaves with oil, salt, and pepper.
2) Arrange the kale leaves on the double layer rack and insert inside the air fryer.
3) Close the air fryer and cook for 7 minutes at 370°F.
4) Allow to cool before serving.

Nutrition Information:
Calories: 48; Carbs: 1.4g; Protein: 0.7g; Fat: 4.8g

Grilled Buffalo Cauliflower

(Servings: 1, Cooking Time: 5 minutes)

Ingredients:
- 1 cup cauliflower florets
- Cooking oil spray
- Salt and pepper, to taste
- ½ cup buffalo sauce

Directions for Cooking:
1) Place the cauliflower florets in a bowl and spray with cooking oil. Season with salt and pepper.
2) Toss to coat.
3) Place the grill pan in the air fryer and add the cauliflower florets.
4) Close the lid and cook for 5 minutes at 390°F.
5) Once cooked, place in a bowl and pour the buffalo sauce over the top. Toss to coat.

Nutrition Information:
Calories: 25; Carbs: 5.3g; Protein: 2g; Fat: 0.1g

Faux Fried Pickles

(Servings: 1, Cooking Time: 5 minutes)

Ingredients:
- 1 cup pickle slices
- 1 egg, beaten
- ½ cup grated Parmesan cheese
- ½ cup almond flour
- ¼ cup pork rinds, crushed
- Salt and pepper, to taste

Directions for Cooking:
1) Place the pickles in a bowl and pour the beaten egg over the top. Allow to soak.
2) In another dish or bowl, combine the Parmesan cheese, almond flour, pork rinds, salt, and pepper.
3) Dredge the pickles in the Parmesan cheese mixture and place on the double layer rack.
4) Place the rack with the pickles inside of the air fryer.
5) Close the lid and cook for 5 minutes at 390°F.

Nutrition Information:
Calories: 664; Carbs: 17.9g; Protein: 42g; Fat: 49.9g

Greatest Green Beans

(Servings: 1, Cooking Time: 5 minutes)

Ingredients:
- 1 cup green beans, trimmed
- ½ teaspoon oil
- Salt and pepper, to taste

Directions for Cooking:
1) Place the green beans in a bowl and add in oil, salt, and pepper.
2) Toss to coat the beans.
3) Place the grill pan in the air fryer and add the green beans in a single layer.
4) Close the lid and cook for 5 minutes at 390°F.

Nutrition Information:
Calories: 54; Carbs: 7.7g; Protein: 2g; Fat: 2.5g

Summer Grilled Corn

(Servings: 2, Cooking Time: 6 minutes)

Ingredients:
- 2 corn on the cob, cut into halves widthwise
- ½ teaspoon oil
- Salt and pepper, to taste

Directions for Cooking:
1) Brush the corn cobs with oil and season with salt and pepper.
2) Place the grill pan accessory into the air fryer.
3) Place the corn cobs on the grill pan.
4) Close the lid and cook for 3 minutes at 390°F.
5) Open the air fryer and turn the corn cobs.
6) Cook for another 3 minutes at the same temperature.

Nutrition Information:
Calories: 173; Carbs: 29g; Protein: 4.5 g; Fat: 4.5g

Air Fried Green Tomatoes

(Servings: 1, Cooking Time: 7 minutes)

Ingredients:
- ½ cup panko breadcrumbs
- 3 tablespoons cornstarch
- ½ teaspoon dried basil, ground
- ½ teaspoon dried oregano, ground
- ½ teaspoon granulated onion
- Salt and pepper, to taste
- 1 medium-sized green tomato, sliced
- ½ teaspoon cooking oil

Directions for Cooking:
1) In a mixing bowl, combine the panko breadcrumbs, cornstarch, basil, oregano, onion, salt, and pepper.
2) Dredge the tomato slices in the breadcrumb mixture.
3) Brush with oil and arrange on the double layer rack.
4) Place the rack with the dredged tomato slices in the air fryer.
5) Close the lid and cook for 7 minutes at 350°F.

Nutrition Information:
Calories: 254; Carbs: 53.1g; Protein: 4.8g; Fat: 3.1g

Not-So-Plain Grilled Plantains

(Servings: 2, Cooking Time: 8 minutes)

Ingredients:
- 2 ripe plantains, sliced
- A pinch of salt to taste
- Oil for brushing

Directions for Cooking:
1) Place the grill pan accessory in the air fryer.
2) Arrange the plantain slices on the grill pan.
3) Sprinkle with salt and brush with oil on both sides.
4) Close the air fryer and cook for 8 minutes at 300°F.

Nutrition Information:
Calories: 218; Carbs: 57.1g; Protein: 2.3g; Fat: 0.7g

Baked Potato for One

(Servings: 1, Cooking Time: 35 minutes)

Ingredients:
- 1 medium russet potato
- 1 teaspoon canola oil
- ¼ teaspoon onion powder
- Salt and pepper, to taste
- 1 tablespoon cream cheese
- 1 tablespoon chopped chives

Directions for Cooking:
1) Scrub the potato under running water to remove debris.
2) Place the baking dish in the air fryer and add the potato.
3) Brush with oil over entire surface and season with onion powder, salt, and pepper.
4) Close the air fryer and cook for 35 minutes at 350°F.
5) Once cooked, slice through the potato and serve with cream cheese and chives.

Nutrition Information:
Calories: 262; Carbs: 38.3g; Protein: 5.6g; Fat: 9.9g

Sweet Potato Fries with Avocado Dipping Sauce

(Servings: 2, Cooking Time: 15 minutes)

Ingredients:
- 2 large sweet potatoes, peeled and cut into thick strips
- 2 tablespoons olive oil
- 1 teaspoon paprika
- 1 teaspoon garlic powder
- Salt and pepper, to taste
- 1 ripe avocado, flesh scooped out
- 2 tablespoons sour cream
- 2 tablespoons fresh cilantro, chopped
- Juice from ½ lime
- ½ teaspoon garlic, minced

Directions for Cooking:
1) Place the sweet potatoes in a bowl and season with oil, paprika, garlic powder, salt, and pepper.
2) Toss to coat. Place the baking dish in the air fryer and add the sweet potato.
3) Close the air fryer and cook for 15 minutes at 350°F.
4) Halfway through the cooking time, give the baking dish a shake.
5) Meanwhile, prepare the avocado dip by combining the rest of the ingredient in a food processor.
6) Dip the sweet potato fries in the avocado dressing.

Nutrition Information:
Calories: 395; Carbs: 35.5g; Protein: 4.4g; Fat: 27.8g

Garlic Parmesan French Fries

(Servings: 2, Cooking Time: 15 minutes)

Ingredients:
- 2 russet potatoes, scrubbed and julienned
- 1 tablespoon olive oil
- 1 tablespoon salt
- ¼ cup Parmesan cheese, grated
- ½ teaspoon garlic powder
- 2 tablespoons chopped parsley

Directions for Cooking:
1) Place the potatoes in a bowl and add in the rest of the ingredients.
2) Toss to combine all ingredients.
3) Place the grill pan accessory in the air fryer.
4) Place the seasoned potatoes on the grill pan.
5) Close the air fryer and cook for 15 minutes.
6) Halfway through the cooking time, give it a good shake.

Nutrition Information:
Calories: 409; Carbs: 65.4g; Protein: 12.9g; Fat: 11g

Best Roasted Broccoli

(Servings: 2, Cooking Time: 15 minutes)

Ingredients:

- 2 cups broccoli florets
- 2 tablespoons yogurt
- 1 tablespoon chickpea flour
- ¼ teaspoons turmeric powder
- ½ teaspoon salt
- ¼ teaspoon chaat masala

Directions for Cooking:

1) Place all ingredients in a bowl and toss to combine.
2) Place the baking dish accessory into the air fryer and place the food into the dish.
3) Close the air fryer and cook for 15 minutes at 350°F.
4) Halfway through the cooking time, give the baking dish a good shake.

Nutrition Information:

Calories: 52; Carbs: 8.6g; Protein: 3.8g; Fat: 1g

Tater Tots for Two

(Servings: 2, Cooking Time: 20 minutes)

Ingredients:

- 2 cups frozen tater tots
- ½ teaspoon cooking oil

Directions for Cooking:

1) Place all ingredients into the air fryer baking dish. Toss to coat the tater tots in the oil.
2) Close the air fryer and cook for 20 minutes at 350°F.
3) Halfway through the cooking time, give the baking dish a good shake.

Nutrition Information:

Calories: 245; Carbs: 30g; Protein: 3g; Fat: 12.6g

Air Fried Vegetable Tempura

(Servings: 3, Cooking Time: 20 minutes)

Ingredients:

- 1 cup broccoli florets
- 1 red bell pepper, cut into strips
- 1 small sweet potato, peeled and cut into thick slices
- 1 small zucchini, cut into thick slices
- ⅔ cup cornstarch
- ⅓ cup all-purpose flour
- 1 egg, beaten
- ¾ cup club soda
- 1½ cups panko breadcrumbs
- Non-stick cooking spray

Directions for Cooking:

1) Mix the cornstarch and all-purpose flour. Dredge the vegetables in this mixture.
2) Mix egg and club soda. Dip each flour-coated vegetable into this mixture soda before dredging in bread crumbs.
3) Place the vegetables on the double layer rack accessory and spray with cooking oil.
4) Place inside the air fryer.
5) Close and cook for 20 minutes at 350°F.

Nutrition Information:
Calories: 357; Carbs: 74.3g; Protein: 8.9g; Fat: 2.6g

Easiest Air Fried Falafel

(Servings: 3, Cooking Time: 20 minutes)

Ingredients:

- 1 can chickpeas, rinsed and allowed to drain
- ⅓ cup fresh parsley
- 4 garlic cloves, minced
- 2 shallots, minced
- 2 tablespoons sesame seeds, raw
- 1½ teaspoons cumin powder
- ¼ teaspoon salt
- 3 tablespoons flour
- 3 tablespoons avocado oil
- 1 cup panko breadcrumbs

Directions for Cooking:

1) In a food processor, combine the chickpeas, parsley, garlic, shallots, sesame seeds, cumin powder, salt, and flour. Pulse until smooth.
2) Form balls of the mixture using your hands.
3) Brush with avocado oil and roll in panko breadcrumbs.
4) Arrange balls on the double layer rack and place the rack into the air fryer.
5) Cook for 20 minutes at 350°F.

Nutrition Information:
Calories: 416; Carbs: 49.6g; Protein: 11.6g; Fat: 20.1g

Vegan Crab Cakes

(Servings: 4, Cooking Time: 20 minutes)

Ingredients:
- 4 cups diced potatoes
- 1 bunch green onions
- 1 lime, zest and juice
- 1½-inch knob of fresh ginger
- 1 tablespoon soy sauce
- 4 tablespoons Thai red curry paste
- 1 can hearts of palm, drained and chopped
- ¾ cup canned artichoke hearts, drained and chopped
- Salt and pepper, to taste
- 4 sheets of nori
- 2 tablespoons oil for frying

Directions for Cooking:

1) Place all Ingredients in a food processor except for the nori and oil. Pulse until smooth and combined.
2) Form small cakes using your hands. Allow to rest in the fridge for at least 30 minutes.
3) Wrap the sides of the crab cakes with nori sheets.
4) Brush the crab cakes with oil.
5) Place the crab cakes on the grill pan accessory.
6) Close the air fryer and cook for 20 minutes at 350°F, making sure to flip the crab cakes over halfway through the cooking time.

Nutrition Information:
Calories: 243; Carbs: 35.2g; Protein: 6.9g; Fat: 7.6g

Zippy Zucchini Wedges

(Servings: 2, Cooking Time: 8 minutes)

Ingredients:
- ½ cup panko breadcrumbs
- 4 tablespoons Parmesan cheese
- ¼ teaspoon basil
- ¼ teaspoon oregano
- ¼ teaspoon cayenne pepper
- ¼ cup egg whites
- 2 zucchinis, sliced

Directions for Cooking:
1) Place all ingredients into a mixing bowl.
2) Toss to coat the zucchini with the breading.
3) Arrange zucchini wedges on the double layer rack and place inside of the air fryer.
4) Close the air fryer and cook for eight minutes at 390°F.

Nutrition Information:
Calories: 158; Carbs: 19.7g; Protein: 12.1g; Fat: 4.3g

Almond Crusted Cauliflower

(Servings: 3, Cooking Time: 7 minutes)

Ingredients:

- 1 large head cauliflower, chopped into florets
- ½ cup unsweetened non-dairy milk
- 6 tablespoons vegan mayo
- ¼ cup chickpea flour
- ¾ cup almond meal
- ¼ cup cornmeal
- 1 teaspoon garlic powder
- 1 teaspoon onion powder
- Salt and pepper, to taste
- 1 cup mashed avocado
- 2 tablespoons non-dairy milk
- 1 tablespoon white vinegar
- 1 tablespoon lemon juice
- ½ teaspoon onion powder
- ½ teaspoon dried parsley
- ½ teaspoon nutritional yeast
- ¼ teaspoon garlic powder
- ¼ teaspoon agave nectar

Directions for Cooking:

1) In a mixing bowl, combine the cauliflower, ½ cup non-dairy milk, vegan mayo, chickpea flour, almond meal, cornmeal, 1 teaspoon garlic powder, 1 teaspoon onion powder, salt, and pepper.
2) Toss until well combined.
3) Place the baking pan accessory in the air fryer and add in the cauliflower florets.
4) Close the air fryer and cook for seven minutes at 350°F.
5) Meanwhile, prepare the avocado dip by placing the rest of the ingredients into a food processor.
6) Pulse until smooth.
7) Serve the cauliflower florets with the avocado dip.

Nutrition Information:
Calories: 566; Carbs: 43.5g; Protein: 18.1g; Fat: 39g

Air Fried Courgetti

(Servings: 2, Cooking Time: 5 minutes)

Ingredients:

- 1 large zucchini, sliced
- 1 tablespoon olive oil
- 1 teaspoon thyme
- A pinch of mixed spices
- Salt and pepper, to taste

Directions for Cooking:

1) Place all ingredients into a mixing bowl.
2) Toss to coat the zucchini.
3) Arrange coated zucchini on the double layer rack and place inside of the air fryer.
4) Close the air fryer and cook for five minutes at 390°F.

Nutrition Information:
Calories: 77; Carbs: 3.6g; Protein: 1.3g; Fat: 7.2g

Simplest Spring Rolls

(Servings: 8, Cooking Time: 8 minutes)

Ingredients:

- 1 tablespoon extra-virgin olive oil
- 4 garlic cloves, minced
- 1 onion, minced
- 2 carrots, peeled and julienned
- 4 cabbage leaves, torn into pieces
- ½ cup soybean sprouts
- 2 tablespoons soy sauce
- 8 sheets spring roll wrappers
- Water
- 2 tablespoons oil

Directions for Cooking:

1) In a mixing bowl, combine all of the ingredients except for the spring roll wrappers, water, and oil.
2) Place the spring roll wrapper on a flat surface and put two tablespoons of vegetable mixture along the middle of it.
3) Fold the spring roll wrapper and wet the edge with water to hold it in. Brush the filled wrappers with oil.
4) Place the spring rolls on the double layer rack and place inside of the air fryer.
5) Close the air fryer and cook for eight minutes at 350°F.

Nutrition Information:
Calories: 101; Carbs: 11.6g; Protein: 1.1g; Fat: 5.6g

Herbed Sweet Potato Fries

(Servings: 2, Cooking Time: 10 minutes)

Ingredients:

- 1 tablespoon olive oil
- 1 teaspoon chopped fresh thyme
- ¼ teaspoon sea salt
- ¼ teaspoon garlic powder
- 2 sweet potatoes, peeled and cut into thick strips

Directions for Cooking:

1) Place all ingredients into a mixing bowl.
2) Toss to coat the sweet potatoes.
3) Arrange fries on the double layer rack and place inside of the air fryer.
4) Close the air fryer and cook for 10 minutes at 350°F.

Nutrition Information:
Calories: 173; Carbs: 26.5g; Protein: 2.1g; Fat: 7.1g

Sweetened Carrot Fries

(Servings: 2, Cooking Time: 5 minutes)

Ingredients:

- 2 large carrots, peeled and cut into thick strips
- 1 tablespoon olive oil
- Salt and pepper, to taste
- ¾ cup honey
- 1 teaspoon thyme

Directions for Cooking:

1) Place all ingredients in a mixing bowl.
2) Toss to coat the carrots.
3) Arrange carrots on the double layer rack and place inside of the air fryer.
4) Close the air fryer and cook for five minutes at 390°F.

Nutrition Information:
Calories: 445; Carbs: 107.9g; Protein: 0.6g; Fat: 7.2g

Jackfruit Rangoon for A Pair

(Servings: 2, Cooking Time: 10 minutes)

Ingredients:

- 1 can green jackfruit in brine
- 2 cups vegetable broth
- 1 cup vegan cream cheese
- ¾ tablespoon Thai curry paste
- 1 scallion, chopped
- 2 teaspoons sesame oil
- Salt and pepper, to taste

Directions for Cooking:

1) Place the baking pan accessory into the air fryer.
2) Place all ingredients into the pan and give them a good stir.
3) Close the air fryer and cook for 10 minutes at 390°F.

Nutrition Information:
Calories: 465; Carbs: 17.7g; Protein: 4.5g; Fat: 40.5g

Vegan Popcorn Chicken

(Servings: 4, Cooking Time: 10 minutes)

Ingredients:

- 2 cups dried TVP or soy chunks, soaked and drained
- 3¾ cups vegetable broth
- 2 garlic cloves, mashed
- 1 teaspoon salt
- 1-inch knob of fresh ginger, grated
- ½ cup flour
- ½ cup cornstarch
- 1 cup breadcrumbs
- 1 tablespoon garlic powder
- 1 tablespoon lemon pepper

Directions for Cooking:

1) Place all ingredients into a mixing bowl and blend until well-combined.
2) Use your hands to form small balls of the mixture.
3) Place the grill pan accessory into the air fryer and add the vegan popcorn chicken.
4) Close the air fryer and cook for 10 minutes at 390°F.

Nutrition Information:

Calories: 406; Carbs: 65.8g; Protein: 31g; Fat: 1.3g

Crispy Cauliflower Bites

(Servings: 2, Cooking Time: 5 minutes)

Ingredients:

- 2 cups cauliflower florets, sliced ½-inch thick
- 1 tablespoon olive oil
- Salt and pepper, to taste

Directions for Cooking:

1) Place all ingredients into a mixing bowl.
2) Toss to combine everything.
3) Place the grill pan accessory into the air fryer and arrange the cauliflower slices on the pan.
4) Close the air fryer and cook for five minutes at 390°F.

Nutrition Information:

Calories: 85; Carbs: 5.3g; Protein: 2g; Fat: 7.1g

Cheesy Potato Wedges

(Servings: 2, Cooking Time: 15 minutes)

Ingredients:

- 1-pound fingerling potatoes, washed and cut lengthwise
- 1 teaspoon extra virgin olive oil
- 1 teaspoon salt
- 1 teaspoon black pepper
- ½ teaspoon garlic powder
- ½ cup raw cashews, soaked overnight and rinsed
- ½ teaspoon ground turmeric
- ½ teaspoon paprika
- 2 tablespoons nutritional yeast
- 1 teaspoon fresh lemon juice
- 2 tablespoons water

Directions for Cooking:

1) Place the potatoes, olive oil, salt, pepper, and garlic powder into a bowl. Toss to combine everything.
2) Place the baking dish accessory into the air fryer.
3) Arrange the potato wedges on the baking dish.
4) Close the air fryer and cook for 15 minutes at 390°F.
5) While it cooks, place the cashews, turmeric, paprika, nutritional yeast, lemon juice, and water into a food processor. Pulse until smooth.
6) Serve the fries with the vegan cheese sauce.

Nutrition Information:

Calories: 461; Carbs: 71.6g; Protein: 15.3g; Fat: 14.9g

Bow Tie Pasta Chips

(Servings: 2, Cooking Time: 10 minutes)

Ingredients:

- 2 cups whole wheat bow tie pasta, cooked for ½ time recommended on package
- 1 tablespoon olive oil
- 1 tablespoon nutritional yeast
- 1½ teaspoons Italian seasoning blend
- ½ teaspoon salt

Directions for Cooking:

1) Place the baking dish accessory into the air fryer.
2) Add all ingredients and give it a good stir.
3) Close the air fryer and cook for 10 minutes at 390°F.

Nutrition Information:

Calories: 270; Carbs: 43g; Protein: 8.5g; Fat: 8g

Cauliflower Steaks with Creamy Bourbon Sauce

(Servings: 4, Cooking Time: 10 minutes)

Ingredients:

- 1 large head cauliflower, sliced into steaks
- Salt and pepper, to taste
- 1 stick vegan butter
- 1½ cups all-purpose flour
- ⅓ cup cornstarch
- 1 tablespoon garlic powder
- 1 tablespoon onion powder
- 1 tablespoon salt
- 1 tablespoon paprika
- 2 teaspoon cayenne pepper
- 1 cup soy milk
- 2 tablespoon vegan egg powder
- 2 tablespoons bourbon

Directions for Cooking:

1) Season the cauliflower with salt and pepper to taste.
2) Place the grill pan accessory into the air fryer.
3) Place the cauliflower steaks on the grill pan.
4) Close the air fryer and cook for 10 minutes at 350°F.
5) While it cooks, prepare the sauce by melting the butter in a skillet over a medium flame.
6) Stir in the flour, cornstarch, garlic powder, onion powder, salt, paprika, and cayenne pepper. Continue stirring until lightly golden.
7) Pour in the soy milk, vegan egg powder, and bourbon.
8) Keep stirring until the sauce thickens.
9) Serve the steaks with the sauce.

Nutrition Information:
Calories: 531; Carbs: 63.2g; Protein: 11.3g; Fat: 24.4g

Garlic and Herb Roasted Chickpeas

(Servings: 4, Cooking Time: 5 minutes)

Ingredients:

- 2 cans of chickpeas, drained
- 1 tablespoon olive oil
- 1 tablespoon nutritional yeast
- 2 teaspoons garlic powder
- 1 tablespoon mixed herbs
- Salt and pepper, to taste

Directions for Cooking:

1) Place all ingredients into a mixing bowl. Toss to combine everything.
2) Place the baking dish accessory into the air fryer and pour in the seasoned chickpeas.
3) Close the air fryer and cook for five minutes at 390°F.

Nutrition Information:
Calories: 250; Carbs: 36.8g; Protein: 11.8g; Fat: 7.3g

Garlicky Air Fryer Potatoes

(Servings: 2, Cooking Time: 15 minutes)

Ingredients:

- 3 medium red potatoes, washed and halved
- 1 teaspoon garlic powder
- 4 garlic cloves, minced
- 1 teaspoon onion powder
- ¼ teaspoon chili powder
- ¼ teaspoon paprika
- ¼ teaspoon basil
- Salt to taste

Directions for Cooking:

1) Place all ingredients into a mixing bowl. Toss to combine everything.
2) Place the baking dish accessory into the air fryer and pour in the seasoned potatoes.
3) Close the air fryer and cook for 15 minutes at 350°F.

Nutrition Information:

Calories: 251; Carbs: 55.1g; Protein: 6.8g; Fat: 0.5g

Healthy Onion Rings

(Servings: 3, Cooking Time: 10 minutes)

Ingredients:

- 3 large yellow onions, sliced into rings
- ½ cup all-purpose flour
- ⅔ cup milk alternative beverage
- ½ teaspoon paprika
- ¼ teaspoon turmeric
- Salt to taste
- 1 cup panko breadcrumbs

Directions for Cooking:

1) Separate the onions into individual rings.
2) In a mixing bowl, combine the all-purpose flour, milk alternative, paprika, turmeric, and salt.
3) Place the panko breadcrumbs in another bowl.
4) Coat the onion rings in the wet mixture and dredge in the panko breadcrumbs.
5) Arrange onion rings on the double layer rack and place into the air fryer.
6) Close the air fryer and cook for 10 minutes at 350°F.

Nutrition Information:

Calories: 215; Carbs: 45.2g; Protein: 5.9g; Fat: 1.4g

Vegan Baked Ravioli

(Servings: 2, Cooking Time: 10 minutes)

Ingredients:

- 8 ounces vegan ravioli
- 1 teaspoon dried basil
- 1 teaspoon dried oregano
- 1 teaspoon garlic powder
- Salt and pepper, to taste
- ½ cup marinara sauce
- ½ cup panko breadcrumbs
- 2 teaspoons nutritional yeast

Directions for Cooking:

1) Place the baking dish accessory into the air fryer.
2) Add in the ravioli, dried basil, oregano, garlic powder, salt, and pepper.
3) Stir in the marinara sauce.
4) In a bowl, combine the panko breadcrumbs and the nutritional yeast.
5) Pour on top of the ravioli.
6) Close the air fryer and cook for 10 minutes at 350°F.

Nutrition Information:

Calories: 296; Carbs: 58.2g; Protein: 12g; Fat: 3.8g

Grilled Simple Black Bean Burger

(Servings: 3, Cooking Time: 20 minutes)

Ingredients:

- 1½ cups rolled oats
- 1 can black beans, rinsed and drained
- ¾ cup salsa
- 1 tablespoon soy sauce
- 1¼ teaspoon chili powder
- ½ teaspoon chipotle powder
- ½ teaspoon garlic powder
- ½ cup corn kernels
- Oil for brushing, if desired

Directions for Cooking:

1) Put all ingredients except the oil into a mixing bowl and combine using your hands.
2) Form small patties using your hands and set aside.
3) Brush patties with oil, if desired.
4) Put the grill pan into the air fryer and place the patties on the pan.
5) Close the lid and cook for 20 minutes at 350°F.
6) Halfway through the cooking time, flip the patties to brown the other side evenly.

Nutrition Information:

Calories: 329; Carbs: 57.7g; Protein: 14.2g; Fat: 3.5g

Terrific Tofu Buddha Bowl

(Servings: 4, Cooking Time: 10 minutes)

Ingredients:

- 1 block extra firm tofu, sliced
- 2 tablespoons sesame oil
- Salt and pepper, to taste
- ¼ cup soy sauce
- 3 tablespoons molasses
- 2 tablespoons lime juice
- 1 tablespoon sriracha
- 2 cups quinoa, cooked according to package instructions
- 1-pound fresh broccoli florets, blanched
- 3 medium carrots, peeled and thinly sliced
- 1 red bell pepper, sliced
- 8 ounces spinach, blanched

Directions for Cooking:

1) Season tofu with sesame oil, salt, and pepper.
2) Place the grill pan accessory in the air fryer.
3) Place the seasoned tofu on the grill pan accessory.
4) Close the air fryer and cook for 10 minutes at 350°F.
5) Stir the tofu to brown all sides evenly.
6) Set aside and arrange the Buddha bowl.
7) In a mixing bowl, combine the soy sauce, molasses, lime juice, and sriracha. Set aside.
8) Place quinoa in bowls and top with broccoli, carrots, red bell pepper, and spinach.
9) Add the tofu and drizzle with the sauce last.

Nutrition Information:
Calories: 616; Carbs: 88.2g; Protein: 27.6g; Fat: 18.7g

Butternut Squash with a Crunchy Kick

(Servings: 2, Cooking Time: 10 minutes)

Ingredients:

- 1-pound butternut squash, seeded and sliced
- 1 tablespoon cooking oil
- Salt and pepper, to taste

Directions for Cooking:

1) Place the grill pan accessory into the air fryer.
2) In a bowl, place all Ingredients. Toss to coat and season the squash.
3) Arrange squash on the grill pan.
4) Close the air fryer and cook for 10 minutes at 350°F.

Nutrition Information:
Calories: 162; Carbs: 26.5g; Protein: 2.3g; Fat: 7.2g

Very Veggie Wontons

(Servings: 4, Cooking Time: 10 minutes)

Ingredients:

- ¾ cup grated cabbage
- ½ cup grated white onion
- ½ cup grated carrots
- ½ cup chopped mushrooms
- ¾ cup chopped red pepper
- 1 tablespoon chili sauce
- 1 teaspoon garlic powder
- ½ teaspoon white pepper
- Salt to taste
- 28 wonton wrappers
- Water for sealing wontons
- 2 tablespoons olive oil

Directions for Cooking:

1) In a skillet over medium heat, place all the vegetables. Cook until all of the moisture has been released from the vegetables.
2) Remove from the heat and season with the chili sauce, garlic powder, white pepper, and salt.
3) Put the wonton wrappers on a working surface and add a tablespoon of the vegetable mixture to the middle of each wrapper. Wet the edges of the wonton wrapper with water and fold the wrapper to close.
4) Brush the wontons with oil and arrange them on the double layer rack.
5) Place the rack in the air fryer.
6) Close the air fryer and cook for 10 minutes at 350°F.

Nutrition Information:
Calories: 234; Carbs: 34.6g; Protein: 6.5g; Fat: 8.1g

Portobello Mushrooms for Two

(Servings: 2, Cooking Time: 10 minutes)

Ingredients:

- 1-pound Portobello mushrooms, sliced
- 1 tablespoon cooking oil
- Salt and pepper, to taste

Directions for Cooking:

1) Place the grill pan accessory into the air fryer.
2) Put all ingredients into a bowl. Toss to coat and season the mushrooms.
3) Arrange seasoned mushrooms on the grill pan.
4) Close the air fryer and cook for 10 minutes at 350°F.

Nutrition Information:
Calories: 117; Carbs: 6.9g; Protein: 4.6g; Fat: 7g

Sweet and Savory Apple Chips

(Servings: 1, Cooking Time: 6 minutes)

Ingredients:
- 1 apple, cored and sliced thinly
- ½ teaspoon ground cumin
- 1 tablespoon sugar
- A pinch of salt

Directions for Cooking:
1) Place all ingredients in a bowl and toss to coat everything.
2) Put the grill pan accessory into the air fryer. Arrange the sliced apples on the grill pan.
3) Close the air fryer and cook for six minutes at 390°F.

Nutrition Information:
Calories: 129; Carbs: 34.5g; Protein: 0.2g; Fat: 0.3g

Grilled Avocado Fries

(Servings: 2, Cooking Time: 10 minutes)

Ingredients:
- ½ cup panko breadcrumbs
- ½ teaspoon salt
- Liquid from 1 can chickpeas (aquafaba)
- 1 Haas avocado, peeled, pitted, and sliced

Directions for Cooking:
1) In a small bowl, combine the breadcrumbs and salt. Set aside.
2) Place the aquafaba in another bowl.
3) Dip the avocado in the aquafaba first then dredge in the breadcrumbs.
4) Place the grill pan accessory into the air fryer.
5) Place the avocado slices into the grill pan.
6) Close the air fryer and cook for 10 minutes at 390°F.
7) Halfway through the cooking time, flip the avocado slices to brown evenly.

Nutrition Information:
Calories: 190; Carbs: 20.9g; Protein: 4g; Fat: 10.9g

Herb and Cheese Stuffed Burger Patties

(Servings: 2, Cooking Time: 25 minutes)

Ingredients:
- 2 green onions, sliced thinly
- 2 tablespoons chopped parsley
- 3 tablespoons Dijon mustard
- 3 tablespoons dry breadcrumbs
- 2 tablespoons ketchup
- Salt and pepper to taste
- ½ teaspoon dried rosemary, crushed
- 1-pound lean ground beef
- ¼ cup cheddar cheese

Directions for Cooking:
1) In a mixing bowl, combine all Ingredients: except for the cheddar cheese.
2) Mix using your hands. Use your hands to make burger patties.
3) At the center of each patty, place a tablespoon of cheese and cover with the meat mixture.
4) Preheat the air fryer at 375°F.
5) Place the grill pan accessory and cook the patties for 25 minutes. Flip the patties halfway through the cooking time.

Nutrition information:
Calories:369; Carbs: 29g; Protein: 29g; Fat: 14g

Air Fried Beef Strips

(Servings: 3, Cooking Time: 25 minutes)

Ingredients:
- 1 ½ pounds stir fry steak slices
- 3 tablespoons soy sauce
- 6 tablespoons cornstarch
- 1 tablespoon olive oil
- 3 cloves of garlic, minced
- 1 teaspoon grated ginger
- 1 navel oranges, segmented
- 3 tablespoons molasses
- 1 tablespoon rice vinegar
- 1 ½ teaspoon sesame oil
- 2 scallions, chopped

Directions for Cooking:
1) Preheat the air fryer at 350°F.
2) Season the steak slices with soy sauce and dust with cornstarch.
3) Place in the air fryer basket and cook for 25 minutes.
4) Meanwhile, place in the skillet oil and heat over medium flame.
5) Sauté the garlic and ginger until fragrant.
6) Stir in the oranges, molasses, and rice vinegar. Season with salt and pepper to taste.
7) Once the meat is cooked, place in the skillet and stir to coat the sauce.
8) Drizzle with sesame oil and garnish with scallions.

Nutrition information:
Calories: 289; Carbs: 43.6g; Protein: 9.4g; Fat: 10.4g

Air Fryer Moroccan Meat Balls with Mint Yogurt

(Servings: 2, Cooking Time: 25 minutes)

Ingredients:
- 1-pound ground beef
- 1 teaspoon ground cumin
- 1 teaspoon ground coriander
- 1 teaspoon cayenne pepper
- 1 teaspoon red chili paste
- 2 cloves of garlic, minced
- 2 tablespoon flat leaf parsley, chopped
- 1 tablespoon mint, chopped
- 1 egg, beaten
- ¼ cup bread crumbs
- Salt and pepper to taste
- ½ cup Greek yogurt
- ¼ cup sour cream
- 2 tablespoons buttermilk
- 2 tablespoons mint
- 1 clove of garlic, minced
- 2 tablespoons honey

Directions for Cooking:

1) In a mixing bowl, combine the ground beef, cumin, coriander, cayenne pepper, red chili paste, minced garlic, parsley, chopped mint, egg, and bread crumbs. Season with salt and pepper to taste. Use your hands and form small balls. Set aside and allow to rest in the fridge for at least 30 minutes.
2) Preheat the air fryer at 350°F.
3) Place the meatballs in the air fryer basket and cook for 25 minutes. Give the air fryer basket a shake to cook evenly.
4) Meanwhile, mix the Greek yogurt, sour cream, buttermilk, mint, garlic, and honey in a bowl. Season with salt and pepper.
5) Serve the meatballs with the yogurt sauce.

Nutrition information:
Calories: 789; Carbs: 28.5g; Protein: 65g; Fat: 45g

Cheesy Chili Polenta Bake

(Servings: 3, Cooking Time: 10 minutes)

Ingredients:
- 1 commercial polenta roll, sliced
- 1 tablespoon chili powder
- 1 cup cheddar cheese sauce

Directions for Cooking:
1) Place the baking dish accessory into the air fryer.
2) Arrange the polenta slices in the baking dish.
3) Top with the chili powder and cheddar cheese sauce.
4) Close the air fryer and cook for 10 minutes at 390°F.

Nutrition Information:
Calories: 263; Carbs: 34.1g; Protein: 5.3g; Fat: 11.7g

Crunchy Beet Chips

(Servings: 2, Cooking Time: 6 minutes)

Ingredients:
- 1-pound beets, peeled and sliced
- 1 tablespoon cooking oil
- Salt and pepper, to taste

Directions for Cooking:
1) Place all ingredients in a bowl and toss to coat the beets.
2) Place the sliced beets on the double layer rack.
3) Place the rack with the beets into the air fryer.
4) Close the air fryer and cook for six minutes at 390°F.

Nutrition Information:
Calories: 94; Carbs: 7.6g; Protein: 1.3g; Fat: 7.1g

Crispy Curry Chickpeas

(Servings: 2, Cooking Time: 7 minutes)

Ingredients:
- 1 can chickpeas, rinsed and drained
- 1 tablespoon garam masala
- 1 tablespoon lemon juice
- Salt and pepper, to taste
- 1 teaspoon ground cumin

Directions for Cooking:
1) Place all ingredients into a bowl and toss to coat the chickpeas.
2) Place the grill pan into the air fryer.
3) Arrange the seasoned chickpeas on the grill pan
4) Close the air fryer and cook for seven minutes at 390°F.
5) Give them a good shake halfway through the cooking time.

Nutrition Information:
Calories: 207; Carbs: 36g; Protein: 11g; Fat: 2.3g

Grilled Vegetables Air Fryer Recipes

Grilled Mediterranean Vegetables
(Servings: 4, Cooking Time: 15 minutes)

Ingredients:
- ½ cup cherry tomatoes
- 1 large zucchini, sliced
- 1 green pepper, seeded and sliced
- 1 large parsnips, peeled and sliced
- 1 carrot, peeled and sliced
- 1 teaspoon mixed herbs
- 2 tablespoons honey
- 1 teaspoon mustard
- 2 teaspoons garlic puree
- 6 tablespoons olive oil
- Salt and pepper to taste

Directions for Cooking:
1) Preheat the air fryer at 375°F.

2) Place the grill pan accessory in the air fryer.
3) In a mixing bowl, toss all Ingredients until well combined.
4) Place on the grill pan and cook for 15 minutes.

5) Give a good shake halfway through the cooking time.

Nutrition information:
Calories: 280; Carbs: 21g; Protein: 2g; Fat:21 g

Perfectly Roasted Veggies

(Servings: 5, Cooking Time: 20 minutes)

Ingredients:
- 2/3 pounds parsnips, peeled and sliced
- 2/3 pounds celeriac root, peeled and sliced
- 2 red onions, chopped
- 2/3 pounds butternut squash
- 1 tablespoon thyme
- 1 tablespoon olive oil
- Salt and pepper to taste

Directions for Cooking:

1) Preheat the air fryer at 375ºF.
2) Place the grill pan accessory in the air fryer.
3) In a mixing bowl, combine all Ingredients: and place on the grill pan.
4) Cook for 20 minutes and make sure to stir the veggies halfway through the cooking time.

Nutrition information:
Calories:124; Carbs: 24g; Protein: 2.5g; Fat: 3.1g

Air Fried Roasted Potatoes

(Servings: 6, Cooking Time: 25 minutes)

Ingredients:
- 3 pounds potatoes, scrubbed and halved
- 1 teaspoon oil
- Salt and pepper to taste

Directions for Cooking:
1) Preheat the air fryer at 375ºF.
2) Place the grill pan accessory in the air fryer.

3) Combine all ingredients, in a mixing bowl and place on the grill accessory.
4) Cook for 25 minutes while giving the air fryer a shake every now and then for even cooking.

Nutrition information:
Calories:184; Carbs: 40.3g; Protein:4.7 g; Fat: 0.9g

Air Fried Indian Grilled Broccoli

(Servings: 2, Cooking Time: 15 minutes)

Ingredients:
- 1-pound broccoli florets
- 2 tablespoons yogurt
- 1 tablespoon chickpea flour
- ¼ teaspoon turmeric powder
- ½ teaspoon salt
- ½ teaspoon red chili powder
- ¼ teaspoon masala chat

Directions for Cooking:
1) Preheat the air fryer at 375°F.
2) Place the grill pan accessory in the air fryer.
3) Put all ingredients in a Ziploc bag and shake to combine.
4) Place all ingredient on the grill pan accessory and cook for 15 minutes.
5) Give a good shake to cook the broccoli evenly.

Nutrition information:
Calories: 96; Carbs: 16.9g; Protein: 7.1g; Fat: 1.3g

Air Fryer Roasted Brussels Sprouts

(Servings: 2, Cooking Time: 20 minutes)

Ingredients:
- 1-pound Brussels sprouts
- 1 ½ tablespoons olive oil
- ½ teaspoon salt
- ½ teaspoon black pepper

Directions for Cooking:
1) Preheat the air fryer at 375°F.
2) Place the grill pan accessory in the air fryer.
3) Put the Brussels sprouts in a mixing bowl and toss the remaining ingredients.
4) Place the Brussels sprouts on the grill pan and cook for 20 minutes.
5) Give a good shake to cook the Brussels sprouts immediately.

Nutrition information:
Calories: 189; Carbs: 20.7g; Protein: 7.7g; Fat: 10.8g

Air Fried Grilled Asparagus

(Servings: 1, Cooking Time: 15 minutes)

Ingredients:
- ½ bunch asparagus spears, trimmed
- Salt and pepper to taste
- 1 tablespoon olive oil

Directions for Cooking:
1) Preheat the air fryer at 375°F.
2) Place the grill pan accessory in the air fryer.
3) Season the asparagus with salt and pepper. Drizzle with oil.
4) Place on the grill pan and cook for 15 minutes.
5) Give the air fryer a good shake to cook evenly.

Nutrition information:
Calories: 138; Carbs: 4.3g; Protein: 0.9g; Fat: 13.5g

Grilled Hasselback Potatoes

(Servings: 1, Cooking Time: 25 minutes)

Ingredients:
- 1 large potato
- 1 tablespoon butter
- ½ tablespoon oil
- Salt and pepper to taste

Directions for Cooking:
1) Preheat the air fryer at 375°F.
2) Place the grill pan accessory in the air fryer.
3) Place the potato on a cutting board. Place chopsticks on each side of the potato and slice until where the cut marks are.
4) Brush potato with butter and oil.
5) Season with salt and pepper to taste.
6) Place on the grill pan and cook for20 to 25 minutes

Nutrition information:
Calories: 464; Carbs: 68.7g; Protein: 8.7g; Fat: 18.6g

Air Fryer Roasted Vegetables

(Servings: 4, Cooking Time: 15 minutes)

Ingredients:
- 1 teaspoon olive oil
- 1 bunch asparagus spears, trimmed
- 1 yellow squash, seeded and cut in circles
- 1 zucchini, seeded and cut in circles
- 1 cup button mushrooms, quartered
- Salt and pepper to taste
- 1 teaspoon basil powder
- 1 teaspoon thyme

Directions for Cooking:
1) Preheat the air fryer at 375°F.
2) Place the grill pan accessory in the air fryer.
3) Mix all vegetables in a bowl and toss to coat everything with the seasoning.
4) Place on the grill pan and cook for 15 minutes.
5) Make sure to stir the vegetables halfway through the cooking time.

Nutrition information:
Calories: 38; Carbs: 5.8g; Protein: 1.8g; Fat: 1.5g

Air Fried Roasted Summer Squash

(Servings: 2, Preparation Time: 5 minutes, Cooking Time: 15 minutes)

Ingredients:
- 1-pound zucchini, sliced into rounds or circles
- 2 tablespoons extra virgin olive oil
- 1 teaspoon salt
- ½ teaspoon black pepper
- 1 teaspoon garlic powder

Directions for Cooking:
1) Preheat the air fryer at 375°F.
2) Place the grill pan accessory in the air fryer.

3) In a mixing bowl, toss all Ingredients: until well-combined.
4) Place on the grill pan and cook for 15 minutes.
5) Stir the vegetables halfway through the cooking time.

Nutrition information:
Calories:109; Carbs: 8.6g; Protein: 6.9g; Fat: 6.5g

Grilled Cauliflower Bites

(Servings: 1, Cooking Time: 15 minutes)

Ingredients:
- 1 ½ cups cauliflower florets
- 1 tablespoon olive oil
- 2 tablespoons nutritional yeast
- Salt and pepper to taste

Directions for Cooking:
1) Preheat the air fryer at 375°F.
2) Place the grill pan accessory in the air fryer.
3) In a mixing bowl, toss all Ingredients: until well-combined.
4) Dump the vegetables on to the grill pan and cook for 10 to 15 minutes.

Nutrition information:
Calories: 81; Carbs: 6.5g; Protein: 4.2g; Fat: 4.9g

Roasted Air Fried Vegetables

(Servings: 4, Cooking Time: 15 minutes)

Ingredients:
- 12 small red potatoes, scrubbed and halved
- 1 cup chopped carrots
- 1 cup butternut squash, peeled and chopped
- 1 cup red onion, diced
- 1 red pepper, chopped
- 1 tablespoon olive oil
- 1 teaspoon thyme
- 1 teaspoon basil
- 1 teaspoon Italian seasoning
- ½ teaspoon garlic powder
- Salt and pepper to taste

Directions for Cooking:
1) Preheat the air fryer at 375°F.
2) Place the grill pan accessory in the air fryer.
3) In a mixing bowl, toss all Ingredients: until well-combined.
4) Place on the grill pan and cook for 15 minutes.
5) Stir the vegetables halfway through the cooking time to grill evenly.

Nutrition information:
Calories: 127; Carbs: 22.4g; Protein: 2.6g

Air Fryer Grilled Mexican Corn

(Servings: 4, Cooking Time: 15 minutes)

Ingredients:
- 4 pieces fresh corn on the cob
- ¼ teaspoon chili powder
- ½ teaspoon stone house seasoning
- ¼ cup chopped cilantro
- 1 lime cut into wedge
- ¼ cup cojita or feta cheese

Directions for Cooking:
1) Preheat the air fryer at 375°F.
2) Place the grill pan accessory in the air fryer.
3) Season the corn with chili powder and stone house seasoning.
4) Place on the grill pan and cook for 15 minutes while flipping the corn halfway through the cooking time.
5) Serve the corn with cilantro, lime, and feta cheese.

Nutrition information:
Calories:102; Carbs: 17g; Protein: 4g; Fat: 3g

Crispy and Spicy Grilled Broccoli in Air Fryer

(Servings: 1, Cooking Time: 15 minutes)

Ingredients:
- 1 head of broccoli, cut into florets
- 2 tablespoons yogurt
- 1 tablespoon chickpea flour
- Salt and pepper to taste
- ½ teaspoon red chili flakes
- 1 tablespoon nutritional yeast

Directions for Cooking:
1) Preheat the air fryer at 375°F.
2) Place the grill pan accessory in the air fryer.
3) Put all Ingredients in a Ziploc bag and shake until well combined.
4) Dump the Ingredients: on the grill pan and cook for 15 minutes until crispy.

Nutrition information:
Calories: 96; Carbs: 16.9g; Protein: 7.1g; Fat: 1.3g

Easy Grilled Corn in The Air Fryer

(Servings: 4, Cooking Time: 20 minutes)

Ingredients:
- 2 ears of corn
- Salt and pepper to taste
- 2 teaspoons vegetable oil

Directions for Cooking:
1) Preheat the air fryer at 375°F.
2) Place the grill pan accessory in the air fryer.
3) Season the corn with salt and pepper. Brush with oil.
4) Place on the grill pan and cook for 20 minutes making sure to flip the corn every 5 minutes to brown evenly.

Nutrition information:
Calories: 86; Carbs: 14.6g; Protein:2.5 g; Fat: 3.1g

Grilled Pineapple and Peppers

(Servings: 2, Cooking Time: 10 minutes)

Ingredients:
- 1 medium-sized pineapple, peeled and sliced
- 1 red bell pepper, seeded and julienned
- 2 teaspoons melted butter
- 1 teaspoon brown sugar
- Salt to taste

Directions for Cooking:

1) Preheat the air fryer at 390ºF.
2) Place the grill pan accessory in the air fryer.
3) Mix all Ingredients: in a Ziploc bag and give a good shake.
4) Dump onto the grill pan and cook for 10 minutes making sure that you flip the pineapples every 5 minutes.

Nutrition information:
Calories:295; Carbs: 57g; Protein: 1g; Fat: 8g

Grilled Onion Potatoes

(Servings: 4, Cooking Time: 25 minutes)

Ingredients:
- 2 pounds baby red potatoes, scrubbed and halved
- 2 tablespoons olive oil
- 1 envelop onion soup mix

Directions for Cooking:
1) Preheat the air fryer at 390ºF.
2) Place the grill pan accessory in the air fryer.
3) Mix all ingredients: in a Ziploc bag and give a good shake to coat the potatoes with the onion soup mix.
4) Dump on to the grill pan and cook for 20 to 25 minutes.
5) Make sure to give the potatoes a stir every 5 minutes to grill evenly.

Nutrition information:
Calories: 218; Carbs: 36.1g; Protein: 4.2g; Fat: 7.1g

Grilled Frozen Vegetables

(Servings: 4, Cooking Time: 35 minutes)

Ingredients:
- 2 bags frozen vegetable mix of your choice
- 1 tablespoon salt and pepper to taste
- 2 tablespoon coconut oil
- 2 tablespoon balsamic vinegar

Directions for Cooking:
1) Preheat the air fryer at 390ºF.
2) Place the grill pan accessory in the air fryer.
3) Season the vegetables with salt, pepper, oil, and balsamic vinegar.
4) Dump the vegetables on the grill pan and cook for 35 minutes.
5) Give the grill pan a good shake to grill the vegetables evenly.

Nutrition information:
Calories: 160; Carbs: 20.5g; Protein: 4.2g; Fat: 7.1g

Simple Grilled Vegetables

(Servings: 4, Cooking Time: 20 minutes)

Ingredients:
- 1 tablespoon rosemary, chopped
- 1 clove of garlic, minced
- 1 tablespoon fresh basil, chopped
- 1 tablespoon fresh parsley
- 1 medium eggplant, sliced
- 1 zucchini, sliced
- 1 yellow squash, seeded and sliced
- 1 red onion, sliced
- Salt and pepper to taste
- 3 tablespoons nutritional yeast

Directions for Cooking:

1) Preheat the air fryer at 390°F.
2) Place the grill pan accessory in the air fryer.
3) Place all ingredients: in a bowl and toss the vegetables until all vegetables are seasoned well.
4) Dump the vegetables on to the grill pan and cook for 15 to 20 minutes.
5) Make sure to give the vegetables a shake to grill evenly on all sides.

Nutrition information:
Calories:68; Carbs: 12.6g; Protein: 5.1g; Fat: 0.5g

Italian Grilled Vegetables

(Servings: 4, Cooking Time:15 minutes)

Ingredients:
- 8-ounce baby bella mushrooms, sliced
- 12 ounces baby potatoes, scrubbed and halved
- 12 ounces cherry tomatoes, halved
- 2 zucchinis, sliced
- 12 garlic cloves, peeled and grated
- 2 tablespoon extra-virgin olive oil
- ½ tablespoon dried oregano
- 1 teaspoon dried thyme
- Salt and pepper to taste
- 3 tablespoons grated parmesan cheese
- A pinch of crushed red pepper flakes

Directions for Cooking:

1) Preheat the air fryer at 390°F.
2) Place the grill pan accessory in the air fryer.
3) Place all Ingredients: in a bowl and toss the vegetables until all vegetables are seasoned well.
4) Dump the seasoned vegetables on the grill pan and cook for 15 minutes.
5) Give a good shake every 5 minutes to evenly grill the vegetables.

Nutrition information:
Calories: 353; Carbs: 77g; Protein: 10.3g; Fat: 4.9g

Balsamic Grilled Vegetables

(Servings: 6, Cooking Time: 20 minutes)

Ingredients:
- 2 small zucchinis, sliced
- 1 yellow squash, seeded and sliced
- 1 large yellow onion, cut into rings
- 1 small head broccoli, cut into florets
- ½ head cauliflower, cut into florets
- 1 carrot, peeled and sliced
- Salt and pepper to taste
- ½ cup balsamic vinegar
- 2 tablespoons olive oil

Directions for Cooking:
1) Preheat the air fryer at 350°F.
2) Place the grill pan accessory in the air fryer.
3) Put all vegetables in a Ziploc bag and season with salt, pepper, balsamic vinegar, and olive oil.
4) Shake to season all vegetables.
5) Dump on to the grill pan and cook for 15 to 20 minutes.
6) Make sure to give the vegetables a good shake every 5 minutes.

Nutrition information:
Calories: 124; Carbs: 24g; Protein: 6g; Fat: 1g

Grilled Vegetables with Lemon Herb Vinaigrette

(Servings: 4, Cooking Time: 15 minutes)

Ingredients:
- 1 cup sliced carrots
- 1 zucchini, sliced
- 1 red bell pepper, seeded and julienned
- 1 cup snow peas
- Salt and pepper to taste
- 1 tablespoon olive oil
- 2 tablespoons nutritional yeast
- 1/8 cup red wine vinegar
- 1 teaspoon Dijon mustard
- 2 cloves of garlic, minced
- 1 tablespoon lemon juice
- 2 tablespoons honey

Directions for Cooking:
1) Preheat the air fryer at 350°F.
2) Place the grill pan accessory in the air fryer.
3) In a Ziploc bag, combine the carrots, zucchini, bell pepper, and snow peas. Season with salt, pepper, olive oil, and nutritional yeast. Give a good shake to combine everything.
4) Dump on to the grill pan and cook for 15 minutes.
5) Meanwhile, combine the red wine vinegar, Dijon mustard, garlic, lemon juice, and honey. Season with salt and pepper to taste.
6) Drizzle the grilled vegetables with the sauce.

Nutrition information:
Calories: 93; Carbs: 13.5g; Protein: 2.8g; Fat: 2.5g

Grilled Zucchini with Mozzarella

(Servings: 6, Cooking Time: 20 minutes)

Ingredients:
- 3 medium zucchinis, sliced lengthwise
- 3 tablespoons extra virgin olive oil
- Salt and ground black pepper
- 18-ounce mozzarella ball, pulled into large pieces
- 2 tablespoons fresh dill
- ¼ crushed red pepper
- 1 tablespoon lemon juice

Directions for Cooking:
1) Preheat the air fryer at 350°F.
2) Place the grill pan accessory in the air fryer.
3) Drizzle the zucchini with olive oil and season with salt and pepper to taste.
4) Place on the grill pan and cook for 15 to 20 minutes.
5) Serve the zucchini with mozzarella, dill, red pepper and lemon juice.

Nutrition information:
Calories:182; Carbs: 18.3g; Protein: 11.4g; Fat: 7.1g

Grilled Vegetables with Garlic

(Servings: 4, Cooking Time: 15 minutes)

Ingredients:
- 1 package frozen chopped vegetables
- 1 red onion, sliced
- 1 cup baby Portobello mushrooms, chopped
- Salt and pepper to taste
- 4 cloves of garlic, minced
- 3 tablespoon red wine vinegar
- ¼ cup chopped fresh basil
- 1 ½ tablespoons honey1 teaspoon Dijon mustard
- 1/3 cup olive oil

Directions for Cooking:
1) Preheat the air fryer at 350°F.
2) Place the grill pan accessory in the air fryer.
3) In a Ziploc bag, combine the vegetables and season with salt, pepper, and garlic. Give a good shake to combine everything.
4) Dump on to the grill pan and cook for 15 minutes.
5) Meanwhile, combine the rest of the Ingredients in a bowl and season with more salt and pepper.
6) Drizzle the grilled vegetables with the sauce. Serve and enjoy.

Nutrition information:
Calories: 200; Carbs: 8.3g; Protein: 2.1g; Fat: 18.2g

Grilled Tomato Melts

(Servings: 3, Cooking Time: 20 minutes)

Ingredients:
- 3 large tomatoes
- 4 ounces Monterey Jack cheese
- 1 yellow red bell pepper, chopped
- ¼ cup toasted almonds
- Salt and pepper to taste

Directions for Cooking:
1) Preheat the air fryer at 350°F.
2) Place the grill pan accessory in the air fryer.
3) Slice the tops of the tomatoes and remove the seeds to create hollow "cups."
4) In a mixing bowl, combine the cheese, bell pepper, and almonds. Season with salt and pepper to taste.
5) Stuff the tomatoes with the cheese filling.
6) Place the stuffed tomatoes on the grill pan and cook for 15 to 20 minutes.

Nutrition information:
Calories: 125; Carbs: 13g; Protein: 10g; Fat: 14g

Grilled Asparagus with Hollandaise Sauce

(Servings: 6, Cooking Time: 15 minutes)

Ingredients:
- 3 pounds asparagus spears, trimmed
- 2 tablespoons olive oil
- ½ teaspoon salt
- ¼ teaspoon black pepper
- 3 egg yolks
- ½ lemon juice
- ½ teaspoon salt
- A pinch of mustard powder
- A punch of ground white pepper
- ½ cup butter, melted
- 1 teaspoon chopped tarragon leaves

Directions for Cooking:
1) Preheat the air fryer at 350°F.
2) Place the grill pan accessory in the air fryer.
3) In a Ziploc bag, combine the asparagus, olive oil, salt and pepper. Give a good shake to combine everything.
4) Dump on to the grill pan and cook for 15 minutes.
5) Meanwhile, on a double boiler over medium flame, whisk the egg yolks, lemon juice, and salt until silky. Add in the mustard powder, white pepper and melted butter. Keep whisking until the sauce is smooth. Garnish with tarragon leaves.
6) Drizzle the sauce over asparagus spears.

Nutrition information:
Calories: 253; Carbs: 10.2g; Protein: 6.7g; Fat: 22.4g

Air Fryer Grilled Mushrooms

(Servings: 2, Cooking Time: 20 minutes)

Ingredients:
- 6 large Portobello mushrooms, sliced
- ½ cup Italian vinaigrette
- ½ teaspoon black pepper
- 4 eggplants, sliced
- 4 onion, sliced
- 2 yellow bell peppers, seeded and sliced
- 5 ounces shredded mozzarella cheese

Directions for Cooking:

1) Preheat the air fryer at 350°F.
2) Place the grill pan accessory in the air fryer.
3) In a Ziploc bag, put all Ingredients, except for the cheese. Shake to combine.
4) Dump on the grill pan and cook for 20 minutes.
5) While still hot, garnish with mozzarella cheese.

Nutrition information:
Calories: 212; Carbs: 23g; Protein: 13g; Fat: 14g

Grilled Asparagus and Arugula Salad

(Servings: 4, Cooking Time: 15 minutes)

Ingredients:
- 1-pound fresh asparagus, trimmed
- 2 tablespoons olive oil
- Salt and pepper to taste
- ¼ cup olive oil
- 2 teaspoons lemon zest
- 3 tablespoons lemon juice
- 3 tablespoons balsamic vinegar
- 4 cups arugula leaves
- 1 cup parmesan cheese, grated

Directions for Cooking:

1) Preheat the air fryer at 350°F.
2) Place the grill pan accessory in the air fryer.
3) In a Ziploc bag, combine the asparagus, olive oil, salt and pepper. Give a good shake to combine everything. Dump on to the grill pan and cook for 15 minutes.
4) Meanwhile, prepare the sauce by mixing together the olive oil, lemon, zest, lemon juice, and balsamic vinegar. Season with salt and pepper to taste. Set aside.
5) Assemble the salad by mixing the asparagus, arugula, and parmesan cheese. Drizzle with sauce on top.

Nutrition information:
Calories: 231; Carbs: 14g; Protein: 10g; Fat: 29g

Spicy Thai –Style Veggies

(Servings: 4, Cooking Time: 15 minutes)

Ingredients:
- 1 ½ cups packed cilantro leaves
- 8 cloves of garlic, minced
- 2 tablespoons fish sauce
- 1 tablespoon black pepper
- 1 tablespoon chili garlic sauce
- 1/3 cup vegetable oil
- 2 pounds vegetable of your choice, sliced into cubes

Directions for Cooking:

1) Preheat the air fryer at 350°F.
2) Place the grill pan accessory in the air fryer.
3) Place all ingredients: in a mixing bowl and toss to coat all ingredients.
4) Put in the grill pan and cook for 15 minutes.

Nutrition information:
Calories: 340; Carbs: 34.44g; Protein:8.8 g; Fat: 19.5g

Grilled Vegetables with Smokey Mustard Sauce

(Servings: 5, Cooking Time: 15 minutes)

Ingredients:
- 2 medium zucchinis, cut into ½ inch thick slices
- 2 large yellow squash, cut into ½ inch thick slices
- 1 large red bell pepper, sliced
- 3 tablespoons olive oil
- 1 teaspoon salt
- 1 teaspoon black pepper
- ¼ cup yellow mustard
- ¼ cup honey
- 2 teaspoons smoked paprika
- 2 teaspoons creole seasoning

Directions for Cooking:
1) Preheat the air fryer at 350°F.
2) Place the grill pan accessory in the air fryer.
3) In a Ziploc bag, put the zucchini, squash, red bell pepper, olive oil, salt and pepper. Give a shake to season all vegetables.
4) Place on the grill pan and cook for 15 minutes.
5) Meanwhile, prepare the sauce by combining the mustard, honey, paprika, and creole seasoning. Season with salt to taste.
6) Serve the vegetables with the sauce.

Nutrition information:
Calories: 164; Carbs: 21.5g; Protein: 2.6g; Fat: 8.9g

Indian Grilled Vegetables

(Servings: 6, Cooking Time: 20 minutes)

Ingredients:
- ½ cup yogurt
- 6 cloves of garlic, minced
- 2-inch fresh ginger, minced
- 3 tablespoons Tandoori spice blend
- 2 tablespoons canola oil
- 2 small onions, cut into wedges
- 1 small zucchini, cut into thick slices
- 1 carrot, peeled and shaved to 1/8-inch thick
- 1 yellow sweet pepper, seeded and chopped
- ½ head cauliflower, cut into florets
- 1 handful sugar snap peas
- 1 cup young ears of corn

Directions for Cooking:
1) Preheat the air fryer at 350°F.
2) Place the grill pan accessory in the air fryer.
3) In a Ziploc bag, put all ingredients: and give a shake to season all vegetables.
4) Dump all Ingredients: on the grill pan and cook for 20 minutes.
5) Make sure to give the vegetables a shake halfway through the cooking time.

Nutrition information:
Calories:126; Carbs: 17.9g; Protein: 2.9g; Fat: 6.1g

Grilled Sweet Potato Wedges with Dipping Sauce

(Servings: 3, Cooking Time: 20 minutes)

Ingredients:
- 3 medium sweet potatoes, peeled and sliced
- 2 tablespoons olive oil
- Salt and pepper to taste
- ½ cup sour cream
- ½ cup mayonnaise
- 2 tablespoons fresh chives, chopped
- 3 tablespoons Asiago cheese, grated
- 2 tablespoons parmesan cheese

Directions for Cooking:
1) Preheat the air fryer at 350°F.
2) Place the grill pan accessory in the air fryer.
3) Brush the potatoes with olive oil and drizzle with salt and pepper to taste.
4) Place on the grill pan and cook for 20 minutes.
5) Meanwhile, mix the sour cream, mayonnaise, fresh chives, Asiago cheese, and parmesan cheese in a bowl. Season with salt and pepper to taste.
6) Serve the potatoes with the sauce.

Nutrition information:
Calories: 625; Carbs: 50.5g; Protein: 12.7g; Fat: 42.3g

Grilled Green Beans with Shallots

(Servings: 6, Cooking Time: 25 minutes)

Ingredients:
- 1-pound fresh green beans, trimmed
- 2 large shallots, sliced
- 1 tablespoon vegetable oil
- 1 teaspoon soy sauce
- 2 tablespoons fresh basil, chopped
- 1 tablespoon fresh mint, chopped
- 1 tablespoon sesame seeds, toasted
- 2 tablespoons pine nuts

Directions for Cooking:
1) Preheat the air fryer at 350°F.
2) Place the grill pan accessory in the air fryer.
3) In a mixing bowl, combine the green beans, shallots, vegetable oil, and soy sauce.
4) Dump in the air fryer and cook for 25 minutes.
5) Once cooked, garnish with basil, mints, sesame seeds, and pine nuts.

Nutrition information:
Calories:307; Carbs: 11.2g; Protein: 23.7g; Fat: 19.7g

Grille Tomatoes with Garden Herb Salad

(Servings: 4, Cooking Time: 20 minutes)

Ingredients:
- 3 large green tomatoes
- 1 clove of garlic, minced
- 5 tablespoons olive oil
- Salt and pepper to taste
- ¾ cup fresh parsley, chopped
- ¾ cup cilantro leaves, chopped
- ½ cup chopped chives
- 4 leaves iceberg lettuce
- ¼ cup hazelnuts, toasted and chopped
- ¼ cup pistachios, toasted and chopped
- ¼ cup golden raisins
- 2 tablespoons white balsamic vinegar

Directions for Cooking:
1) Preheat the air fryer at 350°F.
2) Place the grill pan accessory in the air fryer.
3) In a mixing bowl, season the tomatoes with garlic, oil, salt and pepper to taste.
4) Place on the grill pan and grill for 20 minutes.
5) Once the tomatoes are done, toss in a salad bowl together with the rest of the ingredients.

Nutrition information:
Calories: 287; Carbs: 12.2g; Protein: 4.8g; Fat: 25.9g

Grilled Potato Packets

(Servings: 3, Cooking Time: 40 minutes)

Ingredients:
- 2 large russet potatoes, peeled and sliced
- 2 medium red sweet potatoes, sliced
- 1 onion, sliced
- 2 tablespoons olive oil
- 1 ½ teaspoons seasoning blend
- Salt and pepper to taste

Directions for Cooking:
1) Preheat the air fryer at 350°F.
2) Place the grill pan accessory in the air fryer.
3) Take a large piece of foil and place all ingredients in the middle. Give a good stir. Fold the foil and crimp the edges.
4) Place the foil on the grill pan.
5) Cook for 40 minutes.

Nutrition information:
Calories: 362; Carbs: 68.4g; Protein: 6.3g; Fat: 9.4g

Grilled Sweet Onions

(Servings: 2, Cooking Time: 30 minutes)

Ingredients:
- 2 large sweet onions, sliced
- ½ cup ranch salad dressing
- 2 tablespoons Worcestershire sauce
- 1 teaspoon salad seasoning

Directions for Cooking:
1) Preheat the air fryer at 350°F.
2) Place the grill pan accessory in the air fryer.
3) Place all ingredients in a mixing bowl and give a good stir. Allow the onions to marinate in the fridge for at least 30 minutes.
4) Dump on the grill pan and cook for 30 minutes.

Nutrition information:
Calories:342; Carbs: 20.8g; Protein: 2.5g; Fat: 4g

Roasted Dill Potato Medley

(Servings: 3, Cooking Time: 30 minutes)

Ingredients:
- 3 Yukon gold potatoes, scrubbed and cut into 1-inch pieces
- 1 ½ cups peeled baby carrots, peeled and sliced
- 1 cup frozen pearl onions, peeled and sliced
- 4 tablespoons olive oil
- 2 tablespoons snipped fresh dill, chopped
- 1 teaspoon salt
- ½ teaspoon black pepper
- 1 lemon, juiced

Directions for Cooking:
1) Preheat the air fryer at 350°F.
2) Place the grill pan accessory in the air fryer.
3) Season the vegetables with the rest of the ingredients.
4) Place on the grill pan and cook for 30 minutes.
5) Be sure to shake the vegetables every 5 minutes to cook evenly.

Nutrition information:
Calories: 480; Carbs: 72.4g; Protein: 8.7g; Fat: 19.1g

Grilled Squash

(Servings: 3, Cooking Time: 20 minutes)

Ingredients:
- 3 zucchinis, cut into quarters
- 1 onion, sliced
- 8 ounces fresh mushrooms, stems removed and sliced
- 1 tablespoon oil
- Salt and pepper to taste
- ½ cup Italian salad dressing

Directions for Cooking:
1) Preheat the air fryer at 350°F.
2) Place the grill pan accessory in the air fryer.
3) Season the zucchini, onion, and mushrooms with oil, salt, and pepper.
4) Place on the grill pan and cook for 20 minutes.
5) Serve with Italian salad dressing.

Nutrition information:
Calories: 367; Carbs: 63.7g; Protein:8.1 g; Fat: 13.6g

Air Fryer Grilled Fennel

(Servings: 2, Cooking Time: 20 minutes)

Ingredients:
- 2 medium fennel bulbs, peeled and sliced
- 2 tablespoons olive oil
- 3 tablespoons lemon juice
- Salt and pepper to taste
- 4 cloves of garlic, minced

Directions for Cooking:
1) Preheat the air fryer at 350°F.
2) Place the grill pan accessory in the air fryer.
3) Place all ingredients: in a mixing bowl until the fennel slices are well-seasoned.
4) Dump on the grill pan and cook for 20 minutes.

Nutrition information:
Calories:215; Carbs: 22.7g; Protein: 3.8g; Fat: 14.1g

Grilled Corn Kabobs

(Servings: 2, Cooking Time: 25 minutes)

Ingredients:
- 2 ears of corn
- 2 medium green peppers, cut into large chunks
- 1-pound apricots, halved
- Salt and pepper to taste
- 2 teaspoons prepared mustard

Directions for Cooking:
1) Preheat the air fryer at 350°F.
2) Place the grill pan accessory in the air fryer.
3) On the double layer rack with the skewer accessories, skewer the corn, green peppers, and apricots. Season with salt and pepper to taste.
4) Place skewered corn on the double layer rack and cook for 25 minutes.
5) Once cooked, brush with prepared mustard.

Nutrition information:
Calories: 341; Carbs: 82.5g; Protein: 7.43g; Fat: 2.2g

Grill Smoked Mushrooms

(Servings: 4, Cooking Time: 30 minutes)

Ingredients:
- 4 cups sliced mushrooms
- ¼ cup butter
- 1 teaspoon liquid smoke
- 1 teaspoon poultry seasoning
- Salt and pepper to taste

Directions for Cooking:
1) Preheat the air fryer at 350°F.
2) Place the grill pan accessory in the air fryer.
3) Place all ingredients in a large piece of aluminum foil and mix until well-combined.
4) Close the foil and crimp the edges.
5) Place on the grill pan and cook for 30 minutes.

Nutrition information:
Calories: 109; Carbs:1.5 g; Protein: 0.5g; Fat: 11.6g

Grilled Poultry Recipes

Sticky Grilled Chicken

(Servings: 2, Cooking Time: 40 minutes)

Ingredients:
- ½ cup soy sauce
- ½ cup balsamic vinegar
- 3 tablespoons honey
- 2 cloves of garlic, minced
- 1-pound chicken drumsticks
- 2 tablespoons sesame seeds
- 2 green onion, sliced thinly

Directions for Cooking:
1) In a Ziploc bag, combine the soy sauce, balsamic vinegar, honey, garlic, and chicken. Allow to marinate in the fridge for at least 30 minutes.
2) Preheat the air fryer at 350°F.
3) Place the grill pan accessory in the air fryer.
4) Place on the grill and cook for 30 to 40 minutes. Make sure to flip the chicken every 10 minutes to cook evenly.
5) Meanwhile, use the remaining marinade and put it in a saucepan. Simmer until the sauce thickens.
6) Once the chicken is cooked, brush with the thickened marinade and garnish with sesame seeds and green onions.

Nutrition information:
Calories: 603; Carbs: 43.7g; Protein: 48.7g; Fat: 24.9g

Sweet Chili Lime Grilled Chicken

(Servings: 2, Cooking Time: 40 minutes)

Ingredients:
- 1 cup sweet chili sauce
- Juice from 2 limes, freshly squeezed
- ¼ cup soy sauce
- 1-pound chicken breasts

Directions for Cooking:
1) In a Ziploc bag, combine all ingredients and give a good shake. Allow to marinate for at least 2 hours in the fridge.
2) Preheat the air fryer at 375°F.
3) Place the grill pan accessory in the air fryer.
4) Place chicken on the grill and cook for 30 to 40 minutes. Make sure to flip the chicken every 10 minutes to cook evenly.
5) Meanwhile, use the remaining marinade and put it in a saucepan. Simmer until the sauce thickens.
6) Once the chicken is cooked, brush with the thickened marinade.

Nutrition information:
Calories: 547; Carbs: 39.2g; Protein: 43.6g; Fat: 25.7g

Copycat Grilled Chipotle Chicken

(Servings: 2, Cooking Time: 30 minutes)

Ingredients:
- ½ red onion, chopped
- 2 cloves of garlic, minced
- 1 chipotle pepper in adobo sauce
- 3 tablespoons vegetable oil
- 1 teaspoon dried oregano
- 1/2 teaspoon ground cumin
- Salt and pepper to taste
- 1-pound chicken breasts

Directions for Cooking:
1) In a Ziploc bag, combine all ingredients and give a good shake. Allow to marinate for at least 2 hours in the fridge.
2) Preheat the air fryer at 375°F.
3) Place the grill pan accessory in the air fryer.
4) Place chicken on the grill and cook for 30 to 40 minutes. Make sure to flip the chicken every 10 minutes to cook evenly.
5) Serve chicken with rice, salsa, or guacamole.

Nutrition information:
Calories: 636; Carbs: 38.6g; Protein: 53.4g; Fat: 27.1g

Chicken, Tomatoes, And Corn Foil Packs

(Servings: 4, Cooking Time: 45 minutes)

Ingredients:
- 4 boneless chicken breasts
- 2 cups grape tomatoes, halved
- 2 ears of corn, halved
- 2 cloves of garlic, minced
- 2 tablespoons butter
- Salt and pepper to taste
- Fresh basil for garnish

Directions for Cooking:
1) Preheat the air fryer at 375°F.
2) Place the grill pan accessory in the air fryer.
3) On a large piece of tin foil, combine all ingredients. Fold the foil and crimp the edges.
4) Place on the grill and cook to 40 to 45 minutes.

Nutrition information:
Calories: 459; Carbs: 18.1g; Protein: 64.5g; Fat: 13.9g

Pineapple Salsa Grilled Chicken

(Servings: 2, Cooking Time: 45 minutes)

Ingredients:
- 1-pound boneless chicken breasts
- Juice from 1 lime
- ¼ cup extra virgin olive oil
- 2 teaspoons honey
- Salt and pepper to taste
- 2 cups canned pineapples
- ¼ cup freshly chopped cilantro
- 1 avocado, diced

Directions for Cooking:
1) Preheat the air fryer at 375°F.
2) Place the grill pan accessory in the air fryer.
3) Season the chicken breasts with lime juice, olive oil, honey, salt, and pepper.
4) Place on the grill pan and cook for 45 minutes.
5) Flip the chicken every 10 minutes to grill all sides evenly.
6) Once the chicken is cooked, serve with pineapples, cilantro, and avocado.

Nutrition information:
Calories: 723; Carbs: 57.4g; Protein: 54.7g; Fat: 32.8g

Honey Balsamic Grilled Chicken Thighs

(Servings: 8, Cooking Time: 40 minutes)

Ingredients:
- 8 bone-in chicken thighs
- Salt and pepper to taste
- 2 tablespoons butter
- 2 tablespoons balsamic vinegar
- 1/3 cup honey
- 3 cloves of garlic, minced
- Chopped chives for garnish
- Lemon wedges for garnish

Directions for Cooking:
1) In a mixing bowl, season the chicken with salt and pepper to taste. Add in the butter, balsamic vinegar, honey, and garlic. Allow to marinate for2 hours in the fridge.
2) Preheat the air fryer at 375°F.
3) Place the grill pan accessory in the air fryer.
4) Put the chicken on the grill pan and cook for 40 minutes. Flip the chicken every 10 minutes to grill evenly.
5) Meanwhile, place the remaining marinade in a saucepan and allow to simmer until thickened.
6) Once cooked, brush the chicken with the sauce and garnish with chives and lemon wedges.

Nutrition information:
Calories: 521; Carbs: 32.4g; Protein: 25.1g; Fat: 32.7g

Best Grilled Chicken Breast

(Servings: 4, Cooking Time: 40 minutes)

Ingredients:

- ¼ cup balsamic vinegar
- 3 tablespoons extra virgin olive oil
- 2 tablespoons brown sugar
- 3 cloves of garlic, minced
- 1 teaspoon dried thyme
- 1 teaspoon dried rosemary
- 4 chicken breasts
- Salt and pepper to taste

Directions for Cooking:

1) In a Ziploc bag, combine all ingredients and allow to marinate in the fridge for at least 2 hours.
2) Preheat the air fryer at 375°F.
3) Place the grill pan accessory in the air fryer.
4) Put the chicken on the grill pan and cook for 40 minutes.
5) Flip the chicken every 10 minutes to grill all sides evenly.

Nutrition information:
Calories: 562; Carbs: 4.6g; Protein: 60.9g; Fat: 31.3g

California Grilled Chicken

(Servings: 4, Cooking Time: 40 minutes)

Ingredients:

- ¾ cup balsamic vinegar
- 1 teaspoon garlic powder
- 2 tablespoons honey
- 2 tablespoons extra virgin olive oil
- 2 teaspoons Italian seasoning
- Salt and pepper to taste
- 4 boneless chicken breasts
- 4 slices mozzarella
- 4 slices of avocado
- 4 slices tomato
- Balsamic vinegar for drizzling

Directions for Cooking:

1) In a Ziploc bag, mix together the balsamic vinegar, garlic powder, honey, olive oil, Italian seasoning, salt, pepper, and chicken. Allow to marinate in the fridge for at least 2 hours.
2) Preheat the air fryer at 375°F.
3) Place the grill pan accessory in the air fryer.
4) Put the chicken on the grill and cook for 40 minutes.
5) Flip the chicken every 10 minutes to grill all sides evenly.
6) Serve the chicken with mozzarella, avocado, and tomato. Drizzle with balsamic vinegar.

Nutrition information:
Calories: 838; Carbs: 43.2g; Protein:69.4 g; Fat: 44.7g

Grilled Salsa Verde

(Servings: 2, Cooking Time: 40 minutes)

Ingredients:

- 1 jar salsa verde, divided
- 2 tablespoons extra virgin olive oil
- Juice from ½ lime
- 2 cloves of garlic, minced
- ½ teaspoon chili powder
- 1-pound boneless skinless chicken breasts
- 4 slices Monterey Jack cheese
- 1 jalapeno thinly sliced
- ½ red onion, chopped
- 2 tablespoons chopped cilantro
- Lime wedges for serving

Directions for Cooking:

1) In a Ziploc bag, add half of the salsa verde, olive oil, lime juice, garlic, chili powder and chicken. Allow to marinate in the fridge for at least 2 hours.
2) Preheat the air fryer at 375°F.
3) Place the grill pan accessory in the air fryer.
4) Grill the chicken for 40 minutes.
5) Flip the chicken every 10 minutes to cook evenly.
6) Serve the chicken with the cheese, jalapeno, red onion, cilantro, and lime wedges.

Nutrition information:

Calories: 550; Carbs: 4.5g; Protein: 65.3g; Fat: 29.1g

Grilled Hawaiian Chicken

(Servings: 2, Cooking Time: 40 minutes)

Ingredients:

- ½ cup barbecue sauce
- 1/3 cup soy sauce
- 1 tablespoon rice wine vinegar
- 2 teaspoons sesame oil
- 1 cup pineapple juice
- 2 cloves of garlic, minced
- 1 tablespoon ginger, minced
- Salt and pepper to taste
- 2 chicken breasts

Directions for Cooking:

1) In a Ziploc bag, mix all ingredients and allow to marinate for at least 2 hours in the fridge.
2) Preheat the air fryer at 375°F.
3) Place the grill pan accessory in the air fryer.
4) Grill the chicken on the grill pan for 40 minutes.
5) Flip the chicken every 10 minutes for even cooking.

Nutrition information:

Calories:876; Carbs: 62.8g; Protein: 65.3g; Fat: 39.7g

BBQ Chicken with Peach Glaze

(Servings: 4, Cooking Time: 40 minutes)

Ingredients:
- 5 peaches, pitted and halved
- Juice and zest from 1 lime
- 2 tablespoons extra virgin olive oil
- Salt and pepper to taste
- 2 pounds chicken breasts

Directions for Cooking:
1) In a food processor or blender, put the peaches, lime juice, lime zest, and olive oil. Season with salt and pepper to taste.
2) Put the chicken in a Ziploc bag and pour over the sauce. Allow to marinate in the fridge for at least 2 hours.
3) Preheat the air fryer at 375ºF.
4) Place the grill pan accessory in the air fryer.
5) Grill the chicken for 40 minutes making sure to flip every 10 minutes for even grilling.
6) Meanwhile, place the marinade in a saucepan over medium flame. Allow to simmer until it thickens.
7) Brush the chicken with the glaze before serving.

Nutrition information:
Calories: 521; Carbs: 28.1g; Protein: 48.2g; Fat: 24.1g

Air Fried Balsamic Chicken

(Servings: 3, Cooking Time: 40 minutes)

Ingredients:
- ½ cup honey
- ½ cup balsamic vinegar
- 1 tablespoon orange zest
- 1 teaspoon fresh oregano, chopped
- Salt and pepper to taste
- 1 ½ pounds boneless chicken breasts, pounded
- 2 tablespoons extra virgin olive oil

Directions for Cooking:
1) Put the chicken in a Ziploc bag and pour over the rest of the ingredients. Shake to combine everything. Allow to marinate in the fridge for at least 2 hours.
2) Preheat the air fryer at 375ºF.
3) Place the grill pan accessory in the air fryer.
4) Grill the chicken for 40 minutes.

Nutrition information:
Calories: 527; Carbs: 56.1g; Protein: 51.8g; Fat: 9.9g

Crack BBQ Chicken

(Servings: 2, Cooking Time: 40 minutes)

Ingredients:
- 1-pound boneless chicken breasts
- 2 cups water
- 2 tablespoons salt
- ¼ cup brown sugar
- Ground pepper to taste
- 1 cup barbecue sauce
- 2 cloves of garlic, minced
- Juice from 2 limes, freshly squeezed

Directions for Cooking:
1) Put the chicken in a Ziploc bag and pour over the rest of the ingredients. Shake to combine everything. Allow to marinate in the fridge for at least 2 hours.
2) Preheat the air fryer at 375°F.
3) Place the grill pan accessory in the air fryer.
4) Grill for 40 minutes.
5) Meanwhile, pour the rest of the marinade in a saucepan and heat over medium heat. Allow to simmer until you reach desired thickness.
6) Before serving, brush the chicken with the glaze.

Nutrition information:
Calories: 647; Carbs: 92.1g; Protein:53.1 g; Fat: 6.9g

Hawaiian Chicken with Pineapple Skewers

(Servings: 4, Cooking Time: 25 minutes)

Ingredients:
- ¼ cup pineapple juice
- ¼ cup soy sauce
- 2 pounds chicken breasts, cut into cubes
- 3 teaspoons brown sugar
- 1 teaspoon ketchup
- 2 cloves of garlic, minced
- 1 ½ cups cubed pineapples
- 2 large bell peppers, cut into large pieces
- 1 onion, cut into pieces

Directions for Cooking:
1) In a Ziploc bag, combine the pineapple juice, soy sauce, chicken breasts, sugar, ketchup, and garlic. Marinate in the fridge for at least 2 hours.
2) Preheat the air fryer at 375°F.
3) Place the grill pan accessory in the air fryer.
4) Using a bamboo stick, skewer the chicken with pineapple, bell pepper, and onions.
5) Place on the grill and cook for 25 minutes making sure to flip the chicken skewers every 5 minutes for even grilling.

Nutrition information:
Calories: 538; Carbs:30 g; Protein: 49.7g; Fat: 24.1g

Barbecue Chicken with Chili Lime Corn

(Servings: 4, Cooking Time: 40 minutes)

Ingredients:
- 2 chicken breasts
- 2 chicken thighs
- Salt and pepper to taste
- 2 cups barbecue sauce
- 2 teaspoon grated lime zest
- 1 tablespoon lime juice
- 1 teaspoon chili powder
- ½ teaspoon cumin
- 4 ears of corn, cleaned

Directions for Cooking:
1) Place all Ingredients: in a Ziploc bag except for the corn. Allow to marinate in the fridge for at least 2 hours.
2) Preheat the air fryer at 375°F.
3) Place the grill pan accessory in the air fryer.
4) Grill the chicken and corn for 40 minutes.
5) Meanwhile, pour the marinade in a saucepan over medium heat until it thickens.
6) Before serving, brush the chicken and corn with the glaze.

Nutrition information:
Calories:841; Carbs: 87.7g; Protein: 52.3g; Fat: 32.1g

Italian Air Fryer Grilled Chicken

(Servings: 2, Cooking Time: 40 minutes)

Ingredients:
- 1-pound boneless chicken breasts
- Salt and pepper to taste
- 2 tablespoons tomato paste
- 1 tablespoon minced garlic
- 1 tablespoon fresh Italian parsley

Directions for Cooking:
1) Place all ingredients in a Ziploc bag except for the corn. Allow to marinate in the fridge for at least 2 hours.
2) Preheat the air fryer at 375°F.
3) Place the grill pan accessory in the air fryer.
4) Grill the chicken for 40 minutes.

Nutrition information:
Calories: 301; Carbs: 6.6g; Protein: 52.6g; Fat: 6.1g

Grilled Chicken with Sriracha Sauce

(Servings: 4, Cooking Time: 40 minutes)

Ingredients:
- ¼ cup Thai fish sauce
- Juice from 1 lime, freshly squeezed
- 2 garlic cloves, minced
- 2 pounds chicken breasts
- ½ cup rice vinegar
- 1 tablespoons sugar
- ¼ cups sriracha sauce
- Salt and pepper to taste

Directions for Cooking:
1) Place all ingredients in a Ziploc bag except for the corn. Allow to marinate in the fridge for at least 2 hours.
2) Preheat the air fryer at 375°F.
3) Place the grill pan accessory in the air fryer.
4) Grill the chicken for 40 minutes and make sure to flip the chicken to grill evenly.
5) Meanwhile, place the marinade in a saucepan and heat over medium heat until it reaches desired thickness.
6) Brush the chicken with the glaze and serve with cucumbers if desired.

Nutrition information:
Calories:441; Carbs: 6.7g; Protein: 49.1g; Fat: 22.6g

Grilled Chicken with Kale Salad

(Servings: 4, Cooking Time: 30 minutes)

Ingredients:
- ¼ cup parmesan cheese, grated
- ¼ cup Greek yogurt
- Juice from 2 lemons, divided
- ½ teaspoon Worcestershire sauce
- 1 clove of garlic, minced
- 3 tablespoons extra virgin olive oil
- Salt and pepper to taste
- 4 large chicken breasts, pounded
- 1 large bunch Tuscan kale, cleaned and torn
- ½ cup cherry tomatoes, halved

Directions for Cooking:
1) Place all ingredients in a bowl except for the kale and tomatoes. Allow to marinate in the fridge for at least 2 hours.
2) Preheat the air fryer at 375°F.
3) Place the grill pan accessory in the air fryer.
4) Grill the chicken for 30 minutes.
5) Once cooked, slice the chicken and toss together with the kale and tomatoes.

Nutrition information:
Calories: 507; Carbs: 5.9g; Protein: 82.3g; Fat: 16.3g

Garlic Cilantro-Lime Chicken

(Servings: 4, Cooking Time: 40 minutes)

Ingredients:

- 4 chicken breasts, halved
- 1 tablespoon lime zest
- 1/3 cup fresh lime juice
- 2 tablespoons olive oil
- 1 ½ teaspoon honey
- 1 teaspoon liquid smoke
- 1/3 cup chopped cilantro
- 3 cloves of garlic, minced
- Salt and pepper to taste

Directions for Cooking:

1) Place all ingredients in a bowl and allow to marinate in the fridge for at least 2 hours.
2) Preheat the air fryer at 375°F.
3) Place the grill pan accessory in the air fryer.
4) Grill in the chicken for 40 minutes and make sure to flip the chicken every 10 minutes for even grilling.

Nutrition information:
Calories: 581; Carbs: 6.1g; Protein: 60.9g; Fat: 33.6g

Grilled Chicken Stuffed with Cheese

(Servings: 4, Cooking Time: 30 minutes)

Ingredients:

- 1 tablespoon creole seasoning
- 1 teaspoon garlic powder
- 1 teaspoon onion powder
- 4 chicken breasts, butterflied and pounded
- 4 slices pepper jack cheese
- 4 slices Colby cheese
- 1 tablespoon olive oil

Directions for Cooking:

1) Preheat the air fryer at 375°F.
2) Place the grill pan accessory in the air fryer.
3) Create the dry rub by mixing in a bowl the creole seasoning, garlic powder, and onion powder. Season with salt and pepper if desired.
4) Rub the seasoning on to the chicken.
5) Place the chicken on a working surface and place a slice each of pepper jack and Colby cheese.
6) Fold the chicken and secure the edges with toothpicks.
7) Brush chicken with olive oil.
8) Grill for 30 minutes and make sure to flip the meat every 10 minutes.

Nutrition information:
Calories:742; Carbs:5.4 g; Protein: 73.1g; Fat: 45.9g

Southwest Chicken Foil Packets

(Servings: 4, Cooking Time: 40 minutes)

Ingredients:

- 4 chicken breasts
- Salt and pepper to taste
- 1 cup corn kernels, frozen
- 1 cup salsa
- 1 can black beans, rinsed and drained
- 4 teaspoons taco seasoning
- 1 cup Mexican cheese blend, shredded
- 1 cup cilantro, chopped
- 4 lime wedges

Directions for Cooking:

1) Preheat the air fryer at 375°F.
2) Place the grill pan accessory in the air fryer.
3) On a piece of big aluminum foil, place the chicken breasts and season with salt and pepper to taste.
4) Add in the corn, commercial salsa, beans, and taco seasoning.
5) Close the foil and crimp the edges.
6) Place on the grill pan and cook for 40 minutes.
7) Before serving, top with cheese, cilantro, and lime wedges.

Nutrition information:
Calories: 838; Carbs: 47.5g; Protein: 80.1g; Fat: 36.2g

Teriyaki Grilled Chicken

(Servings: 3, Cooking Time: 40 minutes)

Ingredients:

- ½ cup soy sauce
- ½ cup water
- 3 tablespoons brown sugar
- 3 tablespoon honey
- 3 cloves of garlic, minced
- 1 tablespoon minced ginger
- 1 tablespoons rice vinegar
- 3 tablespoons olive oil
- 1 ½ pounds boneless skinless chicken breasts

Directions for Cooking:

1) Place all ingredients in a Ziploc bag and give a good shake. Allow to marinate in the fridge for at least 2 hours.
2) Preheat the air fryer at 375°F.
3) Place the grill pan accessory in the air fryer.
4) Grill the chicken for 40 minutes making sure to flip the chicken every 10 minutes.
5) Meanwhile, prepare the teriyaki glaze by pouring the marinade on a saucepan and allow to simmer over medium flame until the sauce thickens.
6) Before serving, brush the chicken with the teriyaki glaze.

Nutrition information:
Calories: 603; Carbs: 33.7g; Protein: 54.4g; Fat: 27.3g

Sweet and Spicy Grilled Chicken

(Servings: 4, Cooking Time: 35 minutes)

Ingredients:

- ½ cup brown sugar
- 2 tablespoons chili powder
- 1 teaspoon salt
- ½ teaspoon garlic powder
- 1 teaspoon liquid smoke seasoning
- 4 boneless chicken breasts

Directions for Cooking:

1) Place all ingredients in a Ziploc bag and give a good shake. Allow to marinate in the fridge for at least 2 hours.
2) Preheat the air fryer at 375°F.
3) Place the grill pan accessory in the air fryer.
4) Grill the chicken for 35 minutes.
5) Make sure to flip the chicken every 10 minute to grill evenly.

Nutrition information:
Calories: 446; Carbs: 29.6g; Protein: 61.8g; Fat: 7.7g

Honey Lime Grilled Chicken

(Servings: 4, Cooking Time: 40 minutes)

Ingredients:

- 2 pounds boneless chicken breasts
- ¼ cup lime juice, freshly squeezed
- ½ cup honey
- 2 tablespoons soy sauce
- 1 tablespoon olive oil
- 2 cloves of garlic, minced
- ½ cup cilantro, chopped finely
- Salt and pepper to taste

Directions for Cooking:

1) Place all ingredients in a Ziploc bag and give a good shake. Allow to marinate in the fridge for at least 2 hours.
2) Preheat the air fryer at 375°F.
3) Place the grill pan accessory in the air fryer.
4) Grill the chicken for 40 minutes making sure to flip the chicken every 10 minutes to grill evenly on all sides.

Nutrition information:
Calories:467; Carbs: 38.9g; Protein:52.5 g; Fat: 10.2g

Grilled Jerk Chicken

(Servings: 8, Cooking Time: 60 minutes)

Ingredients:
- 4 habanero chilies
- 5 cloves of garlic, minced
- ¾ malt vinegar
- ¾ soy sauce
- 2 tablespoons rum
- 2 tablespoon salt
- 2 ½ teaspoons ground allspice
- 1 ½ teaspoons ground nutmeg
- ¾ ground cloves
- 8 pieces chicken legs

Directions for Cooking:

1) Place all ingredients in a Ziploc bag and give a good shake. Allow to marinate in the fridge for at least 2 hours.
2) Preheat the air fryer at 375°F.
3) Place the grill pan accessory in the air fryer.
4) Grill the chicken for 60 minutes and flip the chicken every 10 minutes for even grilling.

Nutrition information:
Calories: 204; Carbs: 1.2g; Protein:28.7 g; Fat: 8.1g

Butterflied Chicken with Herbs

(Servings: 4, Cooking Time: 1 hour)

Ingredients:
- 2 pounds whole chicken, backbones removed and butterflied
- Salt and pepper to taste
- 6 cloves of garlic, minced
- ¼ cup Aleppo-style pepper
- 1 and 1/4 cup chopped rosemary
- ¼ cup fresh lemon juice
- ¼ cup oregano
- 1 cup green olives, pitted and cracked

Directions for Cooking:
1) Place the chicken breast side up and slice through the breasts. Using your palms, press against the breastbone to flatten the breasts or you may remove the bones altogether.
2) Once the bones have been removed, season the chicken with salt, pepper, garlic, pepper, rosemary, lemon juice, and oregano.
3) Allow to marinate in the fridge for at least 12 hours.
4) Preheat the air fryer at 375°F.
5) Place the grill pan accessory in the air fryer.
6) Place the chicken on the grill pan and place the olives around the chicken.
7) Grill for 1 hour and make sure to flip the chicken every 10 minutes for even grilling.

Nutrition information:
Calories: 492; Carbs:50.4 g; Protein:37.6 g; Fat: 16.6g

4-Ingredient Garlic Herb Chicken Wings

(Servings: 4, Cooking Time: 35 minutes)

Ingredients:
- 2 pounds chicken wings
- 6 medium garlic cloves, grated
- ¼ cup chopped rosemary
- Salt and pepper to taste

Directions for Cooking:
1) Season the chicken with garlic, rosemary, salt, and pepper.
2) Preheat the air fryer at 375°F.
3) Place the grill pan accessory in the air fryer.
4) Grill for 35 minutes and make sure to flip the chicken every 10 minutes.

Nutrition information:
Calories:299; Carbs: 2.9g; Protein: 50.4g; Fat: 8.2g

Pesto Grilled Chicken

(Servings: 8, Cooking Time: 30 minutes)

Ingredients:
- 1 ¾ cup of your favorite pesto
- 8 chicken thighs
- Salt and pepper to taste

Directions for Cooking:
1) Place all ingredients in the Ziploc bag and allow to marinate in the fridge for at least 2 hours.
2) Preheat the air fryer at 375°F.
3) Place the grill pan accessory in the air fryer.
4) Grill the chicken for at least 30 minutes.
5) Make sure to flip the chicken every 10 minutes for even grilling.

Nutrition information:
Calories: 481; Carbs: 3.8g; Protein: 32.6g; Fat: 36.8g

Chili and Yogurt Marinated Chicken

(Servings: 3, Cooking Time: 40 minutes)

Ingredients:
- 7 dried chilies, seeds removed and broken into pieces
- 1-inch ginger, peeled and chopped
- 4 cloves of garlic, minced
- ½ cup whole milk yogurt
- 3 tablespoons fresh lime juice
- 2 tablespoons prepared mustard
- 1 tablespoon ground coriander
- 1 tablespoon smoked paprika
- 1 ½ teaspoon garam masala
- ½ teaspoon ground cumin
- 1 ½ pounds skinless chicken thighs
- Salt and pepper to taste

Directions for Cooking:

1) Place all ingredients in a Ziploc bag and give a good shake to combine everything.
2) Allow to marinate for at least 2 hours in the fridge.
3) Preheat the air fryer at 375°F.
4) Place the grill pan accessory in the air fryer.
5) Grill for at least 40 minutes.
6) Make sure to flip the chicken every 10 minutes.

Nutrition information:
Calories: 583; Carbs: 25.5g; Protein:54.6 g; Fat: 29.8g

Grilled Chicken with Bold Dressing

(Servings: 8, Cooking Time: 40 minutes)

Ingredients:
- 1 dried Mexican chili, shredded
- ½ teaspoon crushed red pepper flakes
- ¾ cup fresh cilantro
- ¼ cup chopped oregano
- 1 teaspoon lime zest
- Salt and pepper to taste
- 4 pounds chicken breasts

Directions for Cooking:
1) Place all ingredients in a Ziploc bag and give a good shake.
2) Allow to marinate in the fridge for at least 2 hours.
3) Preheat the air fryer at 375°F.
4) Place the grill pan accessory in the air fryer.
5) Grill for at least 40 minutes making sure to flip the chicken every 10 minutes for even grilling.

Nutrition information:
Calories: 394; Carbs:0.9 g; Protein: 47.4g; Fat: 21g

Indian Spiced Chicken, Eggplant, and Tomato Skewers

(Servings: 4, Cooking Time: 25 minutes)

Ingredients:
- 4 cloves of garlic, minced
- 1-inch ginger, grated
- 1 can coconut milk
- 3 teaspoons lime zest
- 2 tablespoons fresh lime juice
- 2 tablespoons tomato paste
- Salt and pepper to taste
- 1 ½ teaspoon ground turmeric
- ¼ teaspoon cayenne pepper
- ¼ teaspoon ground cardamom
- 2 pounds boneless chicken breasts, cut into cubes
- 1 medium eggplant, cut into cubes
- 1 onion, cut into wedges
- 1 cup cherry tomatoes

Directions for Cooking:
1) In a bowl, place the garlic, ginger, coconut milk, lime zest, lime juice, tomato paste, salt, pepper, turmeric, cayenne pepper, cardamom, and chicken breasts. Allow to marinate in the fridge for at least for 2 hours.
2) Preheat the air fryer at 375°F.
3) Place the grill pan accessory in the air fryer.
4) Skewer the chicken cubes with eggplant, onion, and cherry tomatoes on bamboo skewers.
5) Place on the grill pan and cook for 25 minutes making sure to flip the skewers every 5 minutes for even cooking.

Nutrition information:
Calories: 479; Carbs:19.7 g; Protein: 55.2g; Fat: 20.6g

Easy Curry Grilled Chicken Wings

(Servings: 4, Cooking Time: 35 minutes)

Ingredients:
- 2 pounds chicken wings
- ½ cup plain yogurt
- 1 tablespoons curry powder
- Salt and pepper to taste

Directions for Cooking:
1) Season the chicken wings with yogurt, curry powder, salt, and pepper. Toss to combine everything.
2) Allow to marinate in the fridge for at least 2 hours.
3) Preheat the air fryer at 375°F.
4) Place the grill pan accessory in the air fryer.
5) Grill the chicken for 35 minutes and make sure to flip the chicken halfway through the cooking time.

Nutrition information:
Calories:314; Carbs: 3.3g; Protein: 51.3g; Fat: 9.2g

Spicy Chicken with Lemon and Parsley in A Packet

(Servings: 4, Cooking Time: 45 minutes)

Ingredients:
- 2 pounds chicken thighs
- ¼ cup smoked paprika
- ½ teaspoon liquid smoke seasoning
- Salt and pepper to taste
- 1 ½ tablespoon cayenne pepper
- 4 lemons, halved
- ½ cup parsley leaves

Directions for Cooking:
1) Preheat the air fryer at 375°F.
2) Place the grill pan accessory in the air fryer.
3) In a large piece of foil, place the chicken and season with paprika, liquid smoke seasoning, salt, pepper, and cayenne pepper.
4) Top with lemon and parsley.
5) Place on the grill and cook for 45 minutes.

Nutrition information:
Calories: 546; Carbs: 10.4g; Protein: 39.2g; Fat: 39.1g

Korean Grilled Chicken

(Servings: 4, Cooking Time: 30 minutes)

Ingredients:
- 2 pounds chicken wings
- 1 teaspoon salt
- ½ teaspoon fresh ground black pepper
- ½ cup gochujang
- 1 scallion, sliced thinly

Directions for Cooking:
1) Place in a Ziploc bag the chicken wings, salt, pepper, and gochujang sauce.
2) Allow to marinate in the fridge for at least 2 hours.
3) Preheat the air fryer at 375°F.
4) Place the grill pan accessory in the air fryer.
5) Grill the chicken wings for 30 minutes making sure to flip the chicken every 10 minutes.
6) Top with scallions and serve with more gochujang.

Nutrition information:
Calories: 289; Carbs: 0.8g; Protein: 50.1g; Fat: 8.2g

Grilled Chicken with Shishito Peppers

(Servings: 6, Cooking Time: 30 minutes)

Ingredients:

- 3 pounds chicken wings
- Salt and pepper to taste
- 2 tablespoons sesame oil
- 1 ½ cups shishito peppers, pureed

Directions for Cooking:

1) Place all ingredients in a Ziploc bag and allow to marinate for at least 2 hours in the fridge.
2) Preheat the air fryer at 375°F.
3) Place the grill pan accessory in the air fryer.
4) Grill for at least 30 minutes flipping the chicken every 5 minutes and basting with the remaining sauce.

Nutrition information:
Calories: 333; Carbs: 1.7g; Protein: 50.2g; Fat: 12.6g

Grilled Chicken with Scallions

(Servings: 4, Cooking Time: 1 hour)

Ingredients:

- 2 pounds whole chicken
- Salt and pepper to taste
- 4 sprigs rosemary
- 2 cloves of garlic, peeled and crushed
- 2 bunches scallions

Directions for Cooking:

1) Season the whole chicken with salt and pepper.
2) Place inside the chicken cavity the rosemary, garlic, and scallions.
3) Preheat the air fryer at 375°F.
4) Place the grill pan accessory in the air fryer.
5) Grill the chicken for 1 hour.

Nutrition information:
Calories: 470; Carbs: 46.2g; Protein: 37.2g; Fat: 15.9g

Piri Piri Chicken

(Servings: 6, Cooking Time: 45 minutes)

Ingredients:
- 3 pounds chicken breasts
- ½ cup piri piri sauce
- ¼ cup fresh lemon juice
- Salt and pepper to taste
- 1-inch fresh ginger, peeled, and sliced thinly
- 1 large shallot, quartered
- 3 cloves of garlic, minced

Directions for Cooking:

1) Preheat the air fryer at 375°F.
2) Place the grill pan accessory in the air fryer.
3) On a large piece of foil, place the chicken and top with the rest of the ingredients.
4) Fold the foil and crimp the edges.
5) Grill for 45 minutes.

Nutrition information:
Calories:404; Carbs: 3.4g; Protein: 47.9g; Fat: 21.1g

Grilled Turmeric and Lemongrass Chicken

(Servings: 6, Cooking Time: 40 minutes)

Ingredients:
- 3 shallots, chopped
- 3 cloves of garlic, minced
- 2 lemongrass stalks
- 1 teaspoon turmeric
- Salt and pepper to taste
- 2 tablespoons fish sauce
- 3 pounds whole chicken

Directions for Cooking:

1) Place all ingredients in a Ziploc bag and allow to marinate for at least 2 hours in the fridge.
2) Preheat the air fryer at 375°F.
3) Place the grill pan accessory in the air fryer.
4) Grill the chicken for 40 minutes making sure to flip every 10 minutes for even grilling.

Nutrition information:
Calories: 486; Carbs: 49.1g; Protein: 38.5g; Fat: 16.1g

Peruvian Grilled Chicken

(Servings: 4, Cooking Time: 40 minutes)

Ingredients:
- 1/3 cup soy sauce
- 2 tablespoons fresh lime juice
- 5 cloves of garlic, minced
- 2 teaspoons ground cumin
- 1 teaspoon paprika
- ½ teaspoon dried oregano
- 2 ½ pounds chicken, quartered

Directions for Cooking:
1) Place all ingredients in a Ziploc bag and shake to mix everything.
2) Allow to marinate for at least 2 hours in the fridge.
3) Preheat the air fryer at 375°F.
4) Place the grill pan accessory in the air fryer.
5) Grill the chicken for 40 minutes making sure to flip the chicken every 10 minutes for even grilling.

Nutrition information:
Calories:389; Carbs: 7.9g; Protein: 59.7g; Fat: 11.8g

Air Fryer Grilled Moroccan Chicken

(Servings: 4, Cooking Time: 40 minutes)

Ingredients:
- 2 pounds of boneless chicken thighs
- 4 cloves of garlic, chopped
- Salt and pepper to taste
- 2 teaspoons paprika
- ¼ teaspoons crushed red pepper flakes
- 2 teaspoons ground cumin

Directions for Cooking:
1) In a dish, season the chicken with garlic, salt, pepper, paprika, crushed red pepper flakes, and ground cumin.
2) Preheat the air fryer at 375°F.
3) Place the grill pan accessory in the air fryer.
4) Grill the chicken for 40 minutes.
5) Flip the chicken every 10 minutes to cook evenly.

Nutrition information:
Calories:755; Carbs: 35.6g; Protein: 43.1g; Fat: 51.3g

Rotisserie Chicken with Herbes De Provence

(Servings: 6, Cooking Time: 1 hour)

Ingredients:
- 3 pounds chicken, whole
- 2 tablespoons dried herbes de Provence
- 1 tablespoon salt

Directions for Cooking:
1) Season the whole chicken with dried herbes de Provence and salt. Rub all the seasoning on the chicken including the cavity.
2) Preheat the air fryer at 375°F.
3) Place the grill pan accessory in the air fryer.
4) Place the chicken and grill for 1 hour.

Nutrition information:
Calories: 256; Carbs:1.1 g; Protein: 46.2g; Fat: 6.2g

Grilled Oregano Chicken

(Servings: 6, Cooking Time: 40 minutes)

Ingredients:
- 3 pounds chicken breasts
- 2 tablespoons oregano, chopped
- 4 cloves of garlic, minced
- 1 tablespoon grated lemon zest
- 2 tablespoons fresh lemon juice
- Salt and pepper to taste

Directions for Cooking:
1) Preheat the air fryer at 375°F.
2) Place the grill pan accessory in the air fryer.
3) Season the chicken with oregano, garlic, lemon zest, lemon juice, salt and pepper.
4) Grill for 40 minutes and flip every 10 minutes to cook evenly.

Nutrition information:
Calories: 398; Carbs: 1.9g; Protein: 47.5g; Fat: 21.2g

Honey Sriracha Chicken

(Servings: 4, Cooking Time: 40 minutes)

Ingredients:
- 3 tablespoons rice vinegar
- 2 tablespoons sriracha
- 1 tablespoon honey
- 1 teaspoon Dijon mustard
- 4 chicken breasts
- ½ teaspoon paprika
- ½ teaspoon garlic powder
- Salt and pepper to taste

Directions for Cooking:

1) Place all ingredients in a Ziploc bag and allow to marinate for at least 2 hours in the fridge.
2) Preheat the air fryer at 375°F.
3) Place the grill pan accessory in the air fryer.
4) Grill the chicken for at least 40 minutes and flip the chicken every 10 minutes for even cooking.

Nutrition information:
Calories: 525; Carbs: 6.1g; Protein: 60.8g; Fat: 26.9g

Tequila Glazed Chicken

(Servings: 6, Cooking Time: 40 minutes)

Ingredients:
- 2 tablespoons whole coriander seeds
- Salt and pepper to taste
- 3 pounds chicken breasts
- 1/3 cup orange juice
- ¼ cup tequila
- 2 tablespoons brown sugar
- 2 tablespoons honey
- 3 cloves of garlic, minced
- 1 shallot, minced

Directions for Cooking:
1) Place all ingredients in a Ziploc bag and allow to marinate for at least 2 hours in the fridge.
2) Preheat the air fryer at 375°F.
3) Place the grill pan accessory in the air fryer.
4) Grill the chicken for at least 40 minutes.
5) Flip the chicken every 10 minutes for even cooking.
6) Meanwhile, pour the marinade in a saucepan and simmer until the sauce thickens.
7) Brush the chicken with the glaze before serving.

Nutrition information:
Calories: 449; Carbs: 11.2g; Protein: 48.1g; Fat: 22.5g

Grilled Sambal Chicken

(Servings: 3, Cooking Time: 25 minutes)

Ingredients:

- ½ cup light brown sugar
- ½ cup rice vinegar
- 1/3 cup hot chili paste
- ¼ cup fish sauce
- ¼ cup sriracha
- 2 teaspoons grated and peeled ginger
- 1 ½ pounds chicken breasts, pounded

Directions for Cooking:

1) Place all ingredients in a Ziploc bag and allow to marinate for at least 2 hours in the fridge.
2) Preheat the air fryer at 375°F.
3) Place the grill pan accessory in the air fryer.
4) Grill the chicken for 25 minutes.
5) Flip the chicken every 10 minutes for even grilling.
6) Meanwhile, pour the marinade in a saucepan and heat over medium heat until the sauce thickens.
7) Before serving the chicken, brush with the sriracha glaze.

Nutrition information:
Calories: 434; Carbs: 5.4g; Protein: 49.3g; Fat: 21.8g

Smoked Chicken Wings

(Servings: 8, Cooking Time: 30 minutes)

Ingredients:

- 3 tablespoons paprika
- 4 teaspoons salt
- 1 tablespoon chili powder
- 1 tablespoon garlic powder
- 1 teaspoon chipotle chili powder
- 1 teaspoon mustard powder
- 4 pounds chicken wings
- ½ cup barbecue sauce
- 1 tablespoon liquid smoke seasoning

Directions for Cooking:

1) Place all ingredients in a Ziploc bag.
2) Allow to marinate for at least 2 hours in the fridge.
3) Preheat the air fryer at 375°F.
4) Place the grill pan accessory in the air fryer.
5) Grill the chicken for 30 minutes.
6) Flip the chicken every 10 minutes for even grilling.
7) Meanwhile, pour the marinade in a saucepan and heat over medium heat until the sauce thickens.
8) Before serving the chicken, brush with the glaze.

Nutrition information:
Calories: 353; Carbs: 10.8g; Protein: 50.7g; Fat: 8.6g

Sweet and Sour Grilled Chicken

(Servings: 6, Cooking Time: 40 minutes)

Ingredients:
- 6 chicken drumsticks
- 1 cup water
- ¼ cup tomato paste
- 1 cup soy sauce
- 1 cup white vinegar
- ¾ cup sugar
- ¾ cup minced onion
- ¼ cup minced garlic
- Salt and pepper to taste

Directions for Cooking:
1) Place all ingredients in a Ziploc bag
2) Allow to marinate for at least 2 hours in the fridge.
3) Preheat the air fryer at 375°F.
4) Place the grill pan accessory in the air fryer.
5) Grill the chicken for 40 minutes.
6) Flip the chicken every 10 minutes for even grilling.
7) Meanwhile, pour the marinade in a saucepan and heat over medium flame until the sauce thickens.
8) Before serving the chicken, brush with the glaze.

Nutrition information:
Calories: 416; Carbs:29.6 g; Protein: 27.8g; Fat: 19.7g

Lemon Grilled Chicken Breasts

(Servings: 6, Cooking Time: 40 minutes)

Ingredients:
- 3 tablespoons fresh lemon juice
- 2 tablespoons olive oil
- 2 cloves of garlic, minced
- 6 boneless chicken breasts, halved
- Salt and pepper to taste

Directions for Cooking:
1) Place all ingredients in a Ziploc bag
2) Allow to marinate for at least 2 hours in the fridge.
3) Preheat the air fryer at 375°F.
4) Place the grill pan accessory in the air fryer.
5) Grill for 40 minutes and make sure to flip the chicken every 10 minutes for even cooking.

Nutrition information:
Calories: 372; Carbs: 1.5g; Protein: 61.5g; Fat: 11.7g

Spicy Peach Glazed Grilled Chicken

(Servings: 4, Cooking Time: 40 minutes)

Ingredients:
- 2 cups peach preserves
- 2 pounds chicken thighs
- 3 tablespoons olive oil
- 2 tablespoons soy sauce
- 1 tablespoons Dijon mustard
- 1 tablespoon chili powder
- 1 tablespoon minced garlic
- 1 jalapeno chopped
- Salt and pepper to taste

Directions for Cooking:
1) Place all ingredients in a Ziploc bag and allow to rest in the fridge for at least 2 hours.
2) Preheat the air fryer at 375°F.
3) Place the grill pan accessory in the air fryer.
4) Grill for 40 minutes while flipping the chicken every 10 minutes.
5) Meanwhile, pour the marinade in a saucepan and allow to simmer for 5 minutes until the sauce thickens.
6) Brush the chicken with the glaze before serving.

Nutrition information:
Calories: 726; Carbs: 31.7g; Protein: 39.4g; Fat: 49.5g

Chinese Style Chicken

(Servings: 4, Cooking Time: 40 minutes)

Ingredients:
- 2 teaspoons brown sugar
- 1 ½ teaspoon five spice powder
- Salt and pepper to taste
- 2 chicken breasts, halved
- 3 ½ teaspoon grated ginger
- ¼ cup hoisin sauce
- 2 tablespoons rice vinegar
- 3 ½ teaspoons honey
- 1 ¼ teaspoons sesame oil
- 3 cucumbers, sliced

Directions for Cooking:
1) Place all ingredients, except for the cucumber, in a Ziploc bag.
2) Allow to rest in the fridge for at least 2 hours.
3) Preheat the air fryer at 375°F.
4) Place the grill pan accessory in the air fryer.
5) Grill for 40 minutes and make sure to flip the chicken often for even cooking.
6) Serve chicken with cucumber once cooked.

Nutrition information:
Calories:336; Carbs:16.7 g; Protein: 31.2g; Fat: 15.4g

Garlic Cilantro-Lime Chicken

(Servings: 4, Cooking Time: 40 minutes)

Ingredients:
- 4 chicken breasts, halved
- 1 tablespoon lime zest
- 1/3 cup fresh lime juice
- 2 tablespoons olive oil
- 1 ½ teaspoon honey
- 1 teaspoon liquid smoke
- 1/3 cup chopped cilantro
- 3 cloves of garlic, minced
- Salt and pepper to taste

Directions for Cooking:

1) Place all ingredients in a bowl and allow to marinate in the fridge for at least 2 hours.
2) Preheat the air fryer at 390°F.
3) Place the grill pan accessory in the air fryer.
4) Grill in the chicken for 40 minutes and make sure to flip the chicken every 10 minutes for even grilling.

Nutrition information:
Calories: 581; Carbs: 6.1g; Protein: 60.9g; Fat: 33.6g

Grilled Chicken Stuffed with Cheese

(Servings: 4, Cooking Time: 30 minutes)

Ingredients:
- 1 tablespoon creole seasoning
- 1 teaspoon garlic powder
- 1 teaspoon onion powder
- 4 chicken breasts, butterflied and pounded
- 4 slices pepper jack cheese
- 4 slices Colby cheese
- 1 tablespoon olive oil

Directions for Cooking:
1) Preheat the air fryer at 390°F.
2) Place the grill pan accessory in the air fryer.
3) Create the dry rub by mixing in a bowl the creole seasoning, garlic powder, and onion powder. Season with salt and pepper if desired.
4) Rub the seasoning on to the chicken.
5) Place the chicken on a working surface and place a slice each of pepper jack and Colby cheese.
6) Fold the chicken and secure the edges with toothpicks.
7) Brush chicken with olive oil.
8) Grill for 30 minutes and make sure to flip the meat every 10 minutes.

Nutrition information:
Calories:742 ; Carbs:5.4 g; Protein: 73.1g; Fat: 45.9g

Southwest Chicken Foil Packets

(Servings: 4, Cooking Time: 40 minutes)

Ingredients:

- 4 chicken breasts
- Salt and pepper to taste
- 1 cup corn kernels, frozen
- 1 cup commercial salsa
- 1 can black beans, rinsed and drained
- 4 teaspoons taco seasoning
- 1 cup Mexican cheese blend, shredded
- 1 cup cilantro, chopped
- 4 lime wedges

Directions for Cooking:

1) Preheat the air fryer at 390°F.
2) Place the grill pan accessory in the air fryer.
3) On a big aluminum foil, place the chicken breasts and season with salt and pepper to taste.
4) Add the corn, commercial salsa beans, and taco seasoning.
5) Close the foil and crimp the edges.
6) Place on the grill pan and cook for 40 minutes.
7) Before serving, top with cheese, cilantro and lime wedges.

Nutrition information:

Calories: 838; Carbs: 47.5g; Protein: 80.1g; Fat: 36.2g

Teriyaki Grilled Chicken

(Servings: 3, Cooking Time: 40 minutes)

Ingredients:

- ½ cup soy sauce
- ½ cup water
- 3 tablespoons brown sugar
- 3 tablespoon honey
- 3 cloves of garlic, minced
- 1 tablespoon minced ginger
- 1 tablespoons rice vinegar
- 3 tablespoons olive oil
- 1 ½ pounds boneless skinless chicken breasts

Directions for Cooking:

1) Place all ingredients in a Ziploc bag and give a good shake. Allow to marinate in the fridge for at least 2 hours.
2) Preheat the air fryer at 390°F.
3) Place the grill pan accessory in the air fryer.
4) Grill the chicken for 40 minutes making sure to flip the chicken every 10 minutes.
5) Meanwhile, prepare the teriyaki glaze by pouring the marinade on a saucepan and allow to simmer over medium flame until the sauce thickens.
6) Before serving, brush the chicken with the teriyaki glaze.

Nutrition information:

Calories: 603; Carbs: 33.7g; Protein: 54.4g; Fat: 27.3g

Sweet and Spicy Grilled Chicken

(Servings: 4, Cooking Time: 35 minutes)

Ingredients:
- ½ cup brown sugar
- 2 tablespoons chili powder
- 1 teaspoon salt
- ½ teaspoon garlic powder
- 1 teaspoon liquid smoke seasoning
- 4 boneless chicken breasts

Directions for Cooking:
1) Place all ingredients in a Ziploc bag and give a good shake. Allow to marinate in the fridge for at least 2 hours.
2) Preheat the air fryer at 390°F.
3) Place the grill pan accessory in the air fryer.
4) Grill the chicken for 35 minutes.
5) Make sure to flip the chicken every 10 minute to grill evenly.

Nutrition information:
Calories: 446; Carbs: 29.6g; Protein: 61.8g; Fat: 7.7g

Hone, Lime, And Lime Grilled Chicken

(Servings: 4, Cooking Time: 40 minutes)

Ingredients:
- 2 pounds boneless chicken breasts
- ¼ cup lime juice, freshly squeezed
- ½ cup honey
- 2 tablespoons soy sauce
- 1 tablespoon olive oil
- 2 cloves of garlic, minced
- ½ cup cilantro, chopped finely
- Salt and pepper to taste

Directions for Cooking:
1) Place all ingredients in a Ziploc bag and give a good shake. Allow to marinate in the fridge for at least 2 hours.
2) Preheat the air fryer at 390°F.
3) Place the grill pan accessory in the air fryer.
4) Grill the chicken for 40 minutes making sure to flip the chicken every 10 minutes to grill evenly on all sides.

Nutrition information:
Calories:467 ; Carbs: 38.9g; Protein:52.5g; Fat: 10.2g

Grilled Jerk Chicken

(Servings: 8, Cooking Time: 60 minutes)

Ingredients:

- 4 habanero chilies
- 5 cloves of garlic, minced
- ¾ malt vinegar
- ¾ soy sauce
- 2 tablespoons rum
- 2 tablespoon salt
- 2 ½ teaspoons ground allspice
- 1 ½ teaspoons ground nutmeg
- ¾ ground cloves
- 8 pieces chicken legs

Directions for Cooking:

1) Place all ingredients in a Ziploc bag and give a good shake. Allow to marinate in the fridge for at least 2 hours.
2) Preheat the air fryer at 390°F.
3) Place the grill pan accessory in the air fryer.
4) Grill the chicken for 60 minutes and flip the chicken every 10 minutes for even grilling.

Nutrition information:
Calories: 204; Carbs: 1.2g; Protein:28.7 g; Fat: 8.1g

Butterflied Chicken with Herbs

(Servings: 4, Cooking Time: 1 hour)

Ingredients:

- 2 pounds whole chicken, backbones removed and butterflied
- Salt and pepper to taste
- 6 cloves of garlic, minced
- ¼ cup Aleppo-style pepper
- 1.4 cup chopped rosemary
- ¼ cup fresh lemon juice
- ¼ cup oregano
- 1 cup green olives, pitted and cracked

Directions for Cooking:

1) Place the chicken breast side up and slice through the breasts. Using your palms, press against the breastbone to flatten the breasts or you may remove the bones altogether.
2) Once the bones have been removed, season the chicken with salt, pepper, garlic, pepper, rosemary, lemon juice, and oregano.
3) Allow to marinate in the fridge for at least 12 hours.
4) Preheat the air fryer at 390°F.
5) Place the grill pan accessory in the air fryer.
6) Place the chicken on the grill pan and place the olives around the chicken.
7) Grill for 1 hour and make sure to flip the chicken every 10 minutes for even grilling.

Nutrition information:
Calories: 492; Carbs:50.4 g; Protein:37.6 g; Fat: 16.6g

4-Ingredient Garlic Herb Chicken Wings

(Servings: 4, Cooking Time: 35 minutes)

Ingredients:
- 2 pounds chicken wings
- 6 medium garlic cloves , grated
- ¼ cup chopped rosemary
- Salt and pepper to taste

Directions for Cooking:
1) Season the chicken with garlic, rosemary, salt and pepper.
2) Preheat the air fryer at 390ºF.
3) Place the grill pan accessory in the air fryer.
4) Grill for 35 minutes and make sure to flip the chicken every 10 minutes.

Nutrition information:
Calories:299 ; Carbs: 2.9g; Protein: 50.4g; Fat: 8.2g

Pesto Grilled Chicken

(Servings: 8, Cooking Time: 30 minutes)

Ingredients:
- 1 ¾ cup commercial pesto
- 8 chicken thighs
- Salt and pepper to taste

Directions for Cooking:
1) Place all ingredients in the Ziploc bag and allow to marinate in the fridge for at least 2 hours.
2) Preheat the air fryer at 390ºF.
3) Place the grill pan accessory in the air fryer.
4) Grill the chicken for at least 30 minutes.
5) Make sure to flip the chicken every 10 minutes for even grilling.

Nutrition information:
Calories: 481; Carbs: 3.8g; Protein: 32.6g; Fat: 36.8g

Chili and Yogurt Marinated Chicken

(Servings: 3, Cooking Time: 40 minutes)

Ingredients:

- 7 dried chilies, seeds removed and broken into pieces
- 1-inch ginger, peeled and chopped
- 4 cloves of garlic, minced
- ½ cup whole milk yogurt
- 3 tablespoons fresh lime juice
- 2 tablespoons prepared mustard
- 1 tablespoon ground coriander
- 1 tablespoon smoked paprika
- 1 ½ teaspoon garam masala
- ½ teaspoon ground cumin
- 1 ½ pounds skinless chicken thighs
- Salt and pepper to taste

Directions for Cooking:

1) Place all ingredients in a Ziploc bag and give a good shake to combine everything.
2) Allow to marinate for at least 2 hours in the fridge.
3) Preheat the air fryer at 3900F.
4) Place the grill pan accessory in the air fryer.
5) Grill for at least 40 minutes.
6) Make sure to flip the chicken every 10 minutes.

Nutrition information:

Calories: 583; Carbs: 25.5g; Protein:54.6 g; Fat: 29.8g

Grilled Chicken with Board Dressing

(Servings: 8, Cooking Time: 40 minutes)

Ingredients:

- 1 dried Mexican chili, shredded
- ½ teaspoon crushed red pepper flakes
- ¾ cup fresh cilantro
- ¼ cup chopped oregano
- 1 teaspoon lime zest
- Salt and pepper to taste
- 4 pounds chicken breasts

Directions for Cooking:

1) Place all ingredients in a Ziploc bag and give a good shake.
2) Allow to marinate in the fridge for at least 2 hours.
3) Preheat the air fryer at 390ºF.
4) Place the grill pan accessory in the air fryer.
5) Grill for at least 40 minutes making sure to flip the chicken every 10 minutes for even grilling.

Nutrition information:

Calories: 394; Carbs:0.9 g; Protein: 47.4g; Fat: 21g

Indian Spiced Chicken Eggplant and Tomato Skewers

(Servings: 4, Cooking Time: 25 minutes)

Ingredients:

- 4 cloves of garlic, minced
- 1-inch ginger, grated
- 1 can coconut milk
- 3 teaspoons lime zest
- 2 tablespoons fresh lime juice
- 2 tablespoons tomato paste
- Salt and pepper to taste
- 1 ½ teaspoon ground turmeric
- ¼ teaspoon cayenne pepper
- ¼ teaspoon ground cardamom
- 2 pounds boneless chicken breasts, cut into cubes
- 1 medium eggplant, cut into cubes
- 1 onion, cut into wedges
- 1 cup cherry tomatoes

Directions for Cooking:

1) Place in a bowl the garlic, ginger, coconut milk, lime zest, lime juice, tomato paste, salt, pepper, turmeric, cayenne pepper, cardamom, and chicken breasts. Allow to marinate in the fridge for at least for 2 hours.
2) Preheat the air fryer at 390°F.
3) Place the grill pan accessory in the air fryer.
4) Skewer the chicken cubes with eggplant, onion, and cherry tomatoes on bamboo skewers.
5) Place on the grill pan and cook for 25 minutes making sure to flip the chicken every 5 minutes for even cooking.

Nutrition information:
Calories: 479; Carbs:19.7 g; Protein: 55.2g; Fat: 20.6g

Easy Curry Grilled Chicken Wings

(Servings: 4, Cooking Time: 35 minutes)

Ingredients:

- 2 pounds chicken wings
- ½ cup plain yogurt
- 1 tablespoons curry powder
- Salt and pepper to taste

Directions for Cooking:

1) Season the chicken wings with yogurt, curry powder, salt and pepper. Toss to combine everything.
2) Allow to marinate in the fridge for at least 2 hours.
3) Preheat the air fryer at 390°F.
4) Place the grill pan accessory in the air fryer.
5) Grill the chicken for 35 minutes and make sure to flip the chicken halfway through the cooking time.

Nutrition information:
Calories:314 ; Carbs: 3.3g; Protein: 51.3g; Fat: 9.2g

Spicy Chicken with Lemon and Parsley in A Packet

(Servings: 4, Cooking Time: 45 minutes)

Ingredients:
- 2 pounds chicken thighs
- ¼ cup smoked paprika
- ½ teaspoon liquid smoke seasoning
- Salt and pepper to taste
- 1 ½ tablespoon cayenne pepper
- 4 lemons, halved
- ½ cup parsley leaves

Directions for Cooking:
1) Preheat the air fryer at 390°F.
2) Place the grill pan accessory in the air fryer.
3) In a large foil, place the chicken and season with paprika, liquid smoke seasoning, salt, pepper, and cayenne pepper.
4) Top with lemon and parsley.
5) Directions for Cooking:
6) Place on the grill and cook for 45 minutes.

Nutrition information:
Calories: 546; Carbs: 10.4g; Protein: 39.2g; Fat: 39.1g

Korean Grilled Chicken

(Servings: 4, Cooking Time: 30 minutes)

Ingredients:
- 2 pounds chicken wings
- 1 teaspoon salt
- ½ teaspoon fresh ground black pepper
- ½ cup gochujang
- 1 scallion, sliced thinly

Directions for Cooking:
1) Place in a Ziploc bag the chicken wings, salt, pepper, and gochujang sauce.
2) Allow to marinate in the fridge for at least 2 hours.
3) Preheat the air fryer at 390°F.
4) Place the grill pan accessory in the air fryer.
5) Grill the chicken wings for 30 minutes making sure to flip the chicken every 10 minutes.
6) Top with scallions and serve with more gochujang.

Nutrition information:
Calories: 289; Carbs: 0.8g; Protein: 50.1g; Fat: 8.2g

Grilled Chicken with Shishito Peppers

(Servings: 6, Cooking Time: 30 minutes)

Ingredients:
- 3 pounds chicken wings
- Salt and pepper to taste
- 2 tablespoons sesame oil
- 1 ½ cups shishito peppers, pureed

Directions for Cooking:
1) Place all ingredients in a Ziploc bowl and allow to marinate for at least 2 hours in the fridge.
2) Preheat the air fryer at 390°F.
3) Place the grill pan accessory in the air fryer.
4) Grill for at least 30 minutes flipping the chicken every 5 minutes and basting with the remaining sauce.

Nutrition information:
Calories: 333; Carbs: 1.7g; Protein: 50.2g; Fat: 12.6g

Grilled Chicken with Scallions

(Servings: 4, Cooking Time: 1 hour)

Ingredients:
- 2 pounds whole chicken
- Salt and pepper to taste
- 4 sprigs rosemary
- 2 heads of garlic, peeled and crushed
- 2 bunches scallions

Directions for Cooking:
1) Season the whole chicken with salt and pepper.
2) Place inside the chicken cavity the rosemary, garlic, and scallions.
3) Preheat the air fryer at 390°F.
4) Place the grill pan accessory in the air fryer.
5) Grill the chicken for 1 hour.

Nutrition information:
Calories: 470; Carbs: 46.2g; Protein: 37.2g; Fat: 15.9g

Piri Piri Chicken

(Servings: 6, Cooking Time: 45 minutes)

Ingredients:

- 3 pounds chicken breasts
- ½ cup piri piri sauce
- ¼ cup fresh lemon juice
- Salt and pepper to taste
- 1-inch fresh ginger, peeled and sliced thinly
- 1 large shallots, quartered
- 3 cloves of garlic, minced

Directions for Cooking:

1) Preheat the air fryer at 390°F.
2) Place the grill pan accessory in the air fryer.
3) On a large foil, place the chicken top with the rest of the ingredients.
4) Fold the foil and crimp the edges.
5) Grill for 45 minutes.

Nutrition information:
Calories:404 ; Carbs: 3.4g; Protein: 47.9g; Fat: 21.1g

Grilled Turmeric and Lemongrass Chicken

(Servings: 6, Cooking Time: 40 minutes)

Ingredients:

- 3 shallots, chopped
- 3 cloves of garlic, minced
- 2 lemongrass stalks
- 1 teaspoon turmeric
- Salt and pepper to taste
- 2 tablespoons fish sauce
- 3 pounds whole chicken

Directions for Cooking:

1) Place all ingredients in a Ziploc bag and allow to marinate for at least 2 hours in the fridge.
2) Preheat the air fryer at 390°F.
3) Place the grill pan accessory in the air fryer.
4) Grill the chicken for 40 minutes making sure to flip every 10 minutes for even grilling.

Nutrition information:
Calories: 486; Carbs: 49.1g; Protein: 38.5g; Fat: 16.1g

Peruvian Grilled Chicken

(Servings: 4, Cooking Time: 40 minutes)

Ingredients:
- 1/3 cup soy sauce
- 2 tablespoons fresh lime juice
- 5 cloves of garlic, minced
- 2 teaspoons ground cumin
- 1 teaspoon paprika
- ½ teaspoon dried oregano
- 2 ½ pounds chicken, quartered

Directions for Cooking:
1) Place all ingredients in a Ziploc bag and shake to mix everything.
2) Allow to marinate for at least 2 hours in the fridge.
3) Preheat the air fryer at 390°F.
4) Place the grill pan accessory in the air fryer.
5) Grill the chicken for 40 minutes making sure to flip the chicken every 10 minutes for even grilling.

Nutrition information:
Calories:389 ; Carbs: 7.9g; Protein: 59.7g; Fat: 11.8g

Air Fryer Grilled Moroccan Chicken

(Servings: 4, Cooking Time: 40 minutes)

Ingredients:
- 2 pounds of boneless chicken thighs
- 4 cloves of garlic, chopped
- Salt and pepper to taste
- 2 teaspoons paprika
- ¼ teaspoons crushed red pepper flakes
- 2 teaspoons ground cumin

Directions for Cooking:
1) On a dish, season the chicken with garlic, salt, pepper, paprika, crushed red pepper flakes, and ground cumin.
2) Preheat the air fryer at 390°F.
3) Place the grill pan accessory in the air fryer.
4) Grill the chicken for 40 minutes.
5) Flip the chicken every 10 minutes to cook evenly.

Nutrition information:
Calories:755; Carbs: 35.6g; Protein: 43.1g; Fat: 51.3g

Rotisserie Chicken with Herbes De Provence

(Servings: 6, Cooking Time: 1 hour)

Ingredients:

- 3 pounds chicken, whole
- 2 tablespoons dried herbes de Provence
- 1 tablespoon salt

Directions for Cooking:

1) Season the whole chicken with dried herbes de Provence and salt. Rub all the seasoning on the chicken including the cavity.
2) Preheat the air fryer at 390°F.
3) Place the grill pan accessory in the air fryer.
4) Place the chicken and grill for 1 hour.

Nutrition information:
Calories: 256; Carbs:1.1 g; Protein: 46.2g; Fat: 6.2g

Grilled Oregano Chicken

(Servings: 6, Cooking Time: 40 minutes)

Ingredients:

- 3 pounds chicken breasts
- 2 tablespoons oregano, chopped
- 4 cloves of garlic, minced
- 1 tablespoon grated lemon zest
- 2 tablespoons fresh lemon juice
- Salt and pepper to taste

Directions for Cooking:

1) Preheat the air fryer at 390°F.
2) Place the grill pan accessory in the air fryer.
3) Season the chicken with oregano, garlic, lemon zest, lemon juice, salt and pepper.
4) Grill for 40 minutes and flip every 10 minutes to cook evenly.

Nutrition information:
Calories: 398; Carbs: 1.9g; Protein: 47.5g; Fat: 21.2g

Honey Sriracha Chicken

(Servings: 4, Cooking Time: 40 minutes)

Ingredients:
- 3 tablespoons rice vinegar
- 2 tablespoons sriracha
- 1 tablespoon honey
- 1 teaspoon Dijon mustard
- 4 chicken breasts
- ½ teaspoon paprika
- ½ teaspoon garlic powder
- Salt and pepper to taste

Directions for Cooking:

1) Place all ingredients in a Ziploc bag and allow to marinate for at least 2 hours in the fridge.
2) Preheat the air fryer at 390ºF.
3) Place the grill pan accessory in the air fryer.
4) Grill the chicken for at least 40 minutes and flip the chicken every 10 minutes for even cooking.

Nutrition information:
Calories: 525; Carbs: 6.1g; Protein: 60.8g; Fat: 26.9g

Tequila Glazed Chicken

(Servings: 6, Cooking Time: 40 minutes)

Ingredients:
- 2 tablespoons whole coriander seeds
- Salt and pepper to taste
- 3 pounds chicken breasts
- 1/3 cup orange juice
- ¼ cup tequila
- 2 tablespoons brown sugar
- 2 tablespoons honey
- 3 cloves of garlic, minced
- 1 shallot, minced

Directions for Cooking:
1) Place all ingredients in a Ziploc bag and allow to marinate for at least 2 hours in the fridge.
2) Preheat the air fryer at 390ºF.
3) Place the grill pan accessory in the air fryer.
4) Grill the chicken for at least 40 minutes
5) Flip the chicken every 10 minutes for even cooking.
6) Meanwhile, pour the marinade in a saucepan and simmer until the sauce thickens.
7) Brush the chicken with the glaze before serving.

Nutrition information:
Calories: 449; Carbs: 11.2g; Protein: 48.1g; Fat: 22.5g

Grilled Sambal Chicken

(Servings: 3, Cooking Time: 25 minutes)

Ingredients:

- ½ cup light brown sugar
- ½ cup rice vinegar
- 1/3 cup hot chili paste
- ¼ cup fish sauce
- ¼ cup sriracha
- 2 teaspoons grated and peeled ginger
- 1 ½ pounds chicken breasts, pounded

Directions for Cooking:

1) Place all ingredients in a Ziploc bag and allow to marinate for at least 2 hours in the fridge.
2) Preheat the air fryer at 390°F.
3) Place the grill pan accessory in the air fryer.
4) Grill the chicken for 25 minutes.
5) Flip the chicken every 10 minutes for even grilling.
6) Meanwhile, pour the marinade in a saucepan and heat over medium flame until the sauce thickens.
7) Before serving the chicken, brush with the sriracha glaze.

Nutrition information:

Calories: 434; Carbs: 5.4g; Protein: 49.3g; Fat: 21.8g

Smoked Chicken Wings

(Servings: 8, Cooking Time: 30 minutes)

Ingredients:

- 3 tablespoons paprika
- 4 teaspoons salt
- 1 tablespoon chili powder
- 1 tablespoon garlic powder
- 1 teaspoon chipotle chili powder
- 1 teaspoon mustard powder
- 4 pounds chicken wings
- ½ cup barbecue sauce
- 1 tablespoon liquid smoke seasoning

Directions for Cooking:

1) Place all ingredients in a Ziploc bag
2) Allow to marinate for at least 2 hours in the fridge.
3) Preheat the air fryer at 390°F.
4) Place the grill pan accessory in the air fryer.
5) Grill the chicken for 30 minutes.
6) Flip the chicken every 10 minutes for even grilling.
7) Meanwhile, pour the marinade in a saucepan and heat over medium flame until the sauce thickens.
8) Before serving the chicken, brush with the glaze.

Nutrition information:

Calories: 353; Carbs: 10.8g; Protein: 50.7g; Fat: 8.6g

Sweet and Sour Grilled Chicken

(Servings: 6, Cooking Time: 40 minutes)

Ingredients:
- 6 chicken drumsticks
- 1 cup water
- ¼ cup tomato paste
- 1 cup soy sauce
- 1 cup white vinegar
- ¾ cup sugar
- ¾ cup minced onion
- ¼ cup minced garlic
- Salt and pepper to taste

Directions for Cooking:
1) Place all ingredients in a Ziploc bag
2) Allow to marinate for at least 2 hours in the fridge.
3) Preheat the air fryer at 390°F.
4) Place the grill pan accessory in the air fryer.
5) Grill the chicken for 40 minutes.
6) Flip the chicken every 10 minutes for even grilling.
7) Meanwhile, pour the marinade in a saucepan and heat over medium flame until the sauce thickens.
8) Before serving the chicken, brush with the glaze.

Nutrition information:
Calories: 416; Carbs:29.6 g; Protein: 27.8g; Fat: 19.7g

Lemon Grilled Chicken Breasts

(Servings: 6, Cooking Time: 40 minutes)

Ingredients:
- 3 tablespoons fresh lemon juice
- 2 tablespoons olive oil
- 2 cloves of garlic, minced
- 6 boneless chicken breasts, halved
- Salt and pepper to taste

Directions for Cooking:
1) Place all ingredients in a Ziploc bag
2) Allow to marinate for at least 2 hours in the fridge.
3) Preheat the air fryer at 390°F.
4) Place the grill pan accessory in the air fryer.
5) Grill for 40 minutes and make sure to flip the chicken every 10 minutes for even cooking.

Nutrition information:
Calories: 372; Carbs: 1.5g; Protein: 61.5g; Fat: 11.7g

Spicy Peach Glazed Grilled Chicken

(Servings: 4, Cooking Time: 40 minutes)

Ingredients:

- 2 cups peach preserves
- 2 pounds chicken thighs
- 3 tablespoons olive oil
- 2 tablespoons soy sauce
- 1 tablespoons Dijon mustard
- 1 tablespoon chili powder
- 1 tablespoon minced garlic
- 1 jalapeno chopped
- Salt and pepper to taste

Directions for Cooking:

1) Place all ingredients in a Ziploc bag and allow to rest in the fridge for at least 2 hours.
2) Preheat the air fryer at 390°F.
3) Place the grill pan accessory in the air fryer.
4) Grill for 40 minutes while flipping the chicken every 10 minutes.
5) Meanwhile, pour the marinade in a saucepan and allow to simmer for 5 minutes until the sauce thickens.
6) Brush the chicken with the glaze before serving.

Nutrition information:
Calories: 726; Carbs: 31.7g; Protein: 39.4g; Fat: 49.5g

Chinese Style Chicken

(Servings: 4, Cooking Time: 40 minutes)

Ingredients:

- 2 teaspoons brown sugar
- 1 ½ teaspoon five spice powder
- Salt and pepper to taste
- 2 chicken breasts, halved
- 3 ½ teaspoon grated ginger
- ¼ cup hoisin sauce
- 2 tablespoons rice vinegar
- 3 ½ teaspoons honey
- 1 ¼ teaspoons sesame oil
- 3 cucumbers, sliced

Directions for Cooking:

1) Place all ingredients except for the cucumber in a Ziploc bag.
2) Allow to rest in the fridge for at least 2 hours.
3) Preheat the air fryer at 390°F.
4) Place the grill pan accessory in the air fryer.
5) Grill for 40 minutes and make sure to flip the chicken often for even cooking.
6) Serve chicken with cucumber once cooked.

Nutrition information:
Calories:336 ; Carbs:16.7 g; Protein: 31.2g; Fat: 15.4g

Seafood Recipe

Grilled Garlic and Black Pepper Shrimp

(Servings: 2, Cooking Time: 6 minutes)

Ingredients:

- 1 red chili, seeds removed
- 3 cloves of garlic, grated
- 1 tablespoon ground pepper
- 1 tablespoon fresh lime juice
- 1-pound large shrimp, peeled and deveined
- Salt to taste

Directions for Cooking:

1) Place all ingredients in a Ziploc bag and give a good shake.
2) Preheat the air fryer at 375°F.
3) Pour the mixture into the Air Fryer grill pan, then place the grill pan accessory in the air fryer.
4) Grill the shrimp for 6 minutes. Serve once cooked

Nutrition information:
Calories:179; Carbs: 6.3g; Protein: 31.6g; Fat: 2.3g

Grilled Salmon with Cucumbers

(Servings: 4, Cooking Time: 10 minutes)

Ingredients:

- 4 6-ounces salmon fillets
- 1 teaspoon lemon zest
- Juice from 1 lemon, freshly squeezed
- 1 tablespoon fresh dill
- Salt and pepper to taste
- ½ cup mayonnaise
- ½ cup sour cream
- 2 cucumbers peeled and sliced

Directions for Cooking:

1) Preheat the air fryer at 375°F.
2) Place the grill pan accessory in the air fryer.
3) Season the salmon fillets with lemon zest, lemon juice, dill, salt, and pepper.
4) Grill the salmon for 10 minutes making sure to flip halfway through the cooking time.
5) Meanwhile, prepare the cucumber salad by mixing in a bowl the mayonnaise, sour cream, and cucumber slices. Season with salt and pepper.
6) Serve the salmon with the cucumber salad.

Nutrition information:
Calories: 409; Carbs: 5.9g; Protein: 38.4g; Fat: 25.1g

Grilled Shrimp, Zucchini, And Tomatoes

(Servings: 2, Cooking Time: 15 minutes)

Ingredients:
- 10 jumbo shrimp, peeled and deveined
- Salt and pepper to taste
- 1 clove of garlic, minced
- 1 medium zucchini, sliced
- 1-pint cherry tomatoes
- ¼ cup feta cheese

Directions for Cooking:
1) Preheat the air fryer at 375°F.
2) Place the grill pan accessory in the air fryer.
3) In a mixing bowl, season the shrimp with salt and pepper. Stir in the garlic, zucchini, and tomatoes.
4) Place on the grill pan and cook for 15 minutes.
5) Once cooked, transfer to a bowl and sprinkle with feta cheese.

Nutrition information:
Calories: 257; Carbs:4.2 g; Protein: 48.9g; Fat: 5.3g

Grilled Halibut with Tomatoes and Hearts of Palm

(Servings: 4, Cooking Time: 15 minutes)

Ingredients:
- 4 halibut fillets
- Juice from 1 lemon
- Salt and pepper to taste
- 2 tablespoons oil
- ½ cup hearts of palm, drained and rinsed
- 1 cup cherry tomatoes

Directions for Cooking:
1) Preheat the air fryer at 375°F.
2) Place the grill pan accessory in the air fryer.
3) Season the halibut fillets with lemon juice, salt and pepper. Brush with oil.
4) Place the fish on the grill pan.
5) Arrange the hearts of palms and cherry tomatoes on the side and sprinkle with more salt and pepper.
6) Cook for 15 minutes.

Nutrition information:
Calories: 208; Carbs: 7g; Protein: 21 g; Fat: 11g

Grilled Spiced Snapper

(Servings: 5, Cooking Time: 25 minutes)

Ingredients:
- 2 ½ pounds whole fish
- Salt to taste
- 1/3 cup chat masala
- 3 tablespoons fresh lime juice
- 5 tablespoons olive oil

Directions for Cooking:
1) Preheat the air fryer at 375°F.
2) Place the grill pan accessory in the air fryer.
3) Season the fish with salt, chat masala, and lime juice.
4) Brush with oil
5) Place the fish on a foil basket and place inside the grill.
6) Cook for 25 minutes.

Nutrition information:
Calories:308; Carbs: 0.7g; Protein: 35.2g; Fat: 17.4g

One-Pan Shrimp and Chorizo Mixed Grill

(Servings: 4, Cooking Time: 15 minutes)

Ingredients:
- 1 ½ pounds large shrimp, peeled and deveined
- Salt and pepper to taste
- 6 links fresh chorizo sausage
- 2 bunches asparagus spears, trimmed
- Lime wedges

Directions for Cooking:
1) Preheat the air fryer at 375°F.
2) Place the grill pan accessory in the air fryer.
3) Season the shrimp with salt and pepper to taste. Set aside.
4) Place the chorizo and shrimp on the grill pan.
5) Place the asparagus on top.
6) Grill for 15 minutes.
7) Serve with lime wedges.

Nutrition information:
Calories:124; Carbs: 9.4g; Protein: 8.2g; Fat: 7.1g

Grilled Scallops

(Servings: 2, Cooking Time: 10 minutes)

Ingredients:
- 1-pound sea scallops, cleaned and patted dry
- Salt and pepper to taste
- 3 dried chilies
- 2 tablespoon dried thyme
- 1 tablespoon dried oregano
- 1 tablespoon ground coriander
- 1 tablespoon ground fennel
- 2 teaspoons chipotle pepper

Directions for Cooking:
1) Preheat the air fryer at 375°F.
2) Place the grill pan accessory in the air fryer.
3) Mix all ingredients in a bowl.
4) Dump the scallops on the grill pan and cook for 10 minutes.

Nutrition information:
Calories:291; Carbs: 20.7g; Protein: 48.6g; Fat: 2.5g

Grilled Clam with Lemons

(Servings: 6, Cooking Time: 6 minutes)

Ingredients:
- 4 pounds littleneck clams
- Salt and pepper to taste
- 1 clove of garlic, minced
- ½ cup parsley, chopped
- 1 teaspoon crushed red pepper flakes
- 5 tablespoons olive oil
- 1 loaf crusty bread, halved
- ½ cup parmesan cheese, grated

Directions for Cooking:
1) Preheat the air fryer at 375°F.
2) Place the grill pan accessory in the air fryer.
3) Place the clams on the grill pan and cook for 6 minutes.
4) Once the clams have opened, take them out and extract the meat.
5) Transfer the meat into a bowl and season with salt and pepper.
6) Stir in the garlic, parsley, red pepper flakes, and olive oil.
7) Serve on top of bread and sprinkle with parmesan cheese.

Nutrition information:
Calories: 341; Carbs: 26g; Protein:48.3g; Fat: 17.2g

Fish Taco Wraps with Mango Salsa

(Servings: 4, Cooking Time: 10 minutes)

Ingredients:

- 4 pieces fish fillets
- Juice from ½ lemon
- Salt and pepper to taste
- 4 large burrito-size tortillas
- 1 yellow onion, peeled and diced
- 1 red bell pepper, seeded and diced
- 1 cup corn kernels
- 1 cup mixed greens
- ½ cup mango salsa of your choice

Directions for Cooking:

1) Preheat the air fryer at 330°F.
2) Season the fish with lemon juice, salt and pepper.
3) Place seasoned fish on the double layer rack.
4) Cook for 10 minutes.
5) Assemble the taco wraps by laying the tortillas on a flat surface and add fish fillet together with the onions, pepper, corn kernels, and mixed greens.
6) This makes 4 tortilla wraps
7) Serve with mango salsa.

Nutrition information:
Calories: 378; Carbs: 36g; Protein: 26.8g; Fat: 14g

Easy Air Fryer Salmon

(Servings: 2, Cooking Time: 10 minutes)

Ingredients:

- 2 wild caught salmon fillets
- 2 teaspoons avocado oil
- 2 teaspoons paprika
- Salt and pepper to taste
- ½ of lemon

Directions for Cooking:

1) Preheat the air fryer at 390°F.
2) Season the salmon fillets with avocado oil, paprika, salt, and pepper. Drizzle with lemon juice on both sides.
3) Place the grill pan accessory in the air fryer.
4) Place the salmon fillets and cook for 10 minutes.
5) Be sure to flip the fillets halfway through the cooking time.

Nutrition information:
Calories: 382; Carbs: 2.2g; Protein: 66.1g; Fat: 12g

Roasted Salmon with Fennel Salad

(Servings: 4, Cooking Time: 10 minutes)

Ingredients:

- 4 pieces salmon fillets
- 2 teaspoons chopped parsley
- 1 teaspoon fresh thyme, chopped
- 1 teaspoon salt
- 2 tablespoons olive oil
- 4 cups sliced fennel
- 2/3 cup Greek yogurt
- 1 clove of garlic, grated
- 2 tablespoons orange juice
- 2 tablespoons chopped dill

Directions for Cooking:

1) Preheat the air fryer at 390°F.
2) Season the salmon fillets with parsley, thyme, salt, and olive oil. Rub the spices on the salon.
3) Place the grill pan accessory in the air fryer.
4) Place the fish and cook for 10 minutes.
5) Flip the fish halfway through the cooking time to brown all sides evenly.
6) While the fish is cooking, prepare the salad by combining the rest of the rest of the ingredients in a bowl.
7) Serve the fish with the salad.

Nutrition information:

Calories: 458; Carbs: 9g; Protein: 38g; Fat: 30g

Crispy Battered Air Fryer Fish

(Servings: 6, Cooking Time: 15 minutes)

Ingredients:

- ¾ cup fine cornmeal
- ¼ cup flour
- 2 teaspoons old bay seasoning
- Salt and pepper to taste
- 1 teaspoon paprika
- ½ teaspoon garlic powder
- 6 fish fillets cut in half

Directions for Cooking:

1) Preheat the air fryer at 330°F.
2) Place the cornmeal, flour, and seasonings in a Ziploc bag.
3) Add the fish fillets and shake until the fish is covered in flour.
4) Place on the double layer rack and cook for 15 minutes.

Nutrition information:

Calories: 239; Carbs: 10.1g; Protein:22.9g; Fat: 11.8g

Healthily Crispy Coconut Shrimps

(Servings: 3, Cooking Time: 6 minutes)

Ingredients:
- ½ cup all-purpose flour
- 1 ½ teaspoon black pepper
- 2 large eggs beaten
- 2/3 cup unsweetened coconut flakes
- 1/3 cup panko
- Salt and pepper to taste
- 12 ounces raw shrimp, peeled and deveined
- ¼ cup honey
- ¼ cup lime juice
- 2 teaspoons chopped fresh cilantro

Directions for Cooking:
1) Preheat the air fryer at 390°F.
2) In a bowl, mix together the flour and black pepper. Set aside.
3) Place the beaten egg in another bowl.
4) In the third bowl, stir the coconut flakes, salt and pepper.
5) Dredge the shrimps in the flour before dipping them in the panko mixture.
6) Place on the double layer rack and cook for 6 minutes.
7) Meanwhile, mix the honey and lime juice. Season with salt and pepper.
8) Serve the shrimps with the honey dressing and garnish with cilantro.

Nutrition information:
Calories: 201; Carbs: 15g; Protein: 15g; Fat: 9g

Air Fryer Bang Bag Fried Shrimps

(Servings: 1, Cooking Time: 6 minutes)

Ingredients:
- ½ pound raw shrimps, peeled and deveined
- 1 egg, beaten
- Salt and pepper to taste
- 1 teaspoon chili powder
- ½ cup flour
- ½ cup sweet chili sauce

Directions for Cooking:
1) Mix together the shrimps and eggs in a bowl. Season with salt and pepper to taste.
2) In another bowl, mix the chili powder and flour.
3) Dredge the shrimps in the flour mixture.
4) Preheat the air fryer at 330°F.
5) Place the shrimps on the double layer rack.
6) Cook for 6 minutes.
7) Serve with chili sauce.

Nutrition information:
Calories: 719; Carbs: 81.3g; Protein: 66.4g; Fat: 14.2g

Air Fried Fish and Chips

(Servings: 4, Cooking Time: 25 minutes)

Ingredients:

- 2 russet potatoes, scrubbed and sliced
- Cooking spray
- 1 ¼ teaspoon salt
- 1 cup all-purpose flour
- 2 large eggs
- 4 pieces tilapia fillets
- ½ cup malt vinegar

Directions for Cooking:

1) Preheat the air fryer at 390°F.
2) Toss the potatoes in the air fryer basket and spray with cooking oil. Sprinkle with salt.
3) Cook for 10 minutes.
4) Meanwhile, stir the flour and eggs together to form batter. Season with more salt. Set aside.
5) Once the potatoes are cooked, set aside.
6) Place the double layer rack in the air fryer.
7) Dip the tilapia filets in the batter and place on the double layer rack.
8) Cook for 15 minutes.
9) Serve with malt vinegar

Nutrition information:
Calories: 423; Carbs: 46g; Protein: 44g; Fat: 7g

Air Fried Tortilla-Crusted Fishes

(Servings: 4, Cooking Time: 15 minutes)

Ingredients:

- 4 fillets of white fish fillet
- Salt and pepper to taste
- 1 tablespoon lemon juice
- 1 egg, beaten
- 1 cup tortilla chips, pulverized

Directions for Cooking:

1) Preheat the air fryer at 390°F.
2) Place a grill pan in the air fryer.
3) Season the fish fillet with salt, pepper, and lemon juice.
4) Soak in beaten eggs and dredge in tortilla chips.
5) Place on the grill pan.
6) Cook for 15 minutes.
7) Make sure to flip the fish halfway through the cooking time.

Nutrition information:
Calories: 300; Carbs: 8.4g; Protein: 24.8g; Fat:18.6 g

Shrimp Spring Rolls with Sweet and Chili Sauce

(Servings: 8, Cooking Time: 9 minutes)

Ingredients:
- 2 ½ tablespoons sesame oil, divided
- 2 cups cabbage, shredded
- 1 cup carrots, julienned
- 1 cup red bell pepper, seeded and julienned
- 4 ounces raw shrimps, deveined and chopped
- ¾ cup snow peas, julienned
- 2 teaspoons fish sauce
- ¼ teaspoon crushed red pepper
- 8 spring roll wrappers
- ½ cup sweet chili sauce

Directions for Cooking:
1) Heat sesame oil in a skillet over medium flame and stir in the cabbage, carrots, and bell pepper for 2 minutes. Set aside and allow to cool.
2) Once cooled, Add shrimps and snow peas. Season with fish sauce and red pepper.
3) Lay spring roll wrapper on a flat surface and place a tablespoon or two of the vegetable mixtures in the middle of the spring roll wrapper. Fold the wrapper and seal the edges with water.
4) Preheat the air fryer at 390°F.
5) Place the spring rolls in the double layer rack accessory. Spray with cooking oil.
6) Cook for 7 minutes.
7) Serve with chili sauce.

Nutrition information:
Calories: 185; Carbs: 19g; Protein: 7g; Fat: 9g

Fried Cocktail Prawns

(Servings: 1, Cooking Time: 8 minutes)

Ingredients:
- 12 prawns, shelled and deveined
- 1 tablespoon white wine vinegar
- 1 tablespoon ketchup
- 1 teaspoon chili powder
- 1 teaspoon chili flakes
- ½ teaspoon black pepper
- ½ teaspoon sea salt

Directions for Cooking:
1) Preheat the air fryer at 390°F.
2) Place the shrimps in a bowl.
3) Stir in the rest of the Ingredients: until the shrimps are coated with the sauce.
4) Place the shrimps on the double layer rack and cook for 8 minutes.
5) Serve with mayonnaise if desired.

Nutrition information:
Calories: 148; Carbs: 9.8g; Protein: 21.9g; Fat: 2.3g

Turmeric Salmon Skewers

(Servings: 4, Cooking Time: 12 minutes)

Ingredients:

- 1 slab of salmon fillets, sliced into cubes
- ½ tablespoon turmeric powder
- ½ tablespoon sugar
- 1 tablespoon soy sauce
- A dash of black pepper
- 1 cup cherry tomatoes
- Chopped coriander for garnish

Directions for Cooking:

1) Season the salmon fillets with turmeric powder, sugar, soy sauce, and black pepper. Allow to marinate for 30 minutes in the fridge.
2) Preheat the air fryer at 330°F.
3) Skewer the salmon cubes alternating with tomatoes
4) Place on the double layer rack.
5) Cook for 10 to 12 minutes.

Nutrition information:

Calories: 302.3; Carbs: 4.2g; Protein: 47.3g; Fat: 10.7g

Crisped Fried Crumbed Fish

(Servings: 4, Cooking Time: 15 minutes)

Ingredients:

- 4 pieces of flounder fillets
- 5 tablespoons vegetable oil
- 1 cup dry bread crumbs
- 1 egg beaten
- 1 lemon, sliced

Directions for Cooking:

1) Brush flounder fillets with vegetable oil before dredging in bread crumbs.
2) Preheat the air fryer at 390°F.
3) Place the fillets on the double layer rack.
4) Cook for 15 minutes.

Nutrition information:

Calories: 277; Carbs: 22.5g; Protein: 26.9g; Fat: 17.7g

Air Fryer Coconut Shrimps

(Servings: 4, Cooking Time: 20 minutes)

Ingredients:

- 1-pound salmon fillets, cut into small cubes
- ½ tablespoon lemon juice
- Salt and pepper to taste
- ½ cup flour
- ½ stick cold butter, cut into cubes
- 3 tablespoons whipping cream
- 4 eggs, beaten
- 1 egg yolk, beaten
- 1 green onion, chopped

Directions for Cooking:

1) Preheat the air fryer at 390°F.
2) Season salmon fillets with lemon juice, salt and pepper.
3) In another bowl, combine the flour and butter. Add cold water gradually to form a dough. Knead the dough on a flat surface to form a sheet.
4) Place the dough on the baking dish and press firmly on the dish.
5) Beat the eggs and egg yolk and season with salt and pepper to taste.
6) Place the salmon cubes on the pan lined with dough and pour the egg over.
7) Cook for 15 to 20 minutes.
8) Garnish with green onions once cooked.

Nutrition information:
Calories: 483; Carbs: 5.2g; Protein: 45.2g; Fat: 31.2g

Buttered Lobster Tail Roast

(Servings: 4, Cooking Time: 6 minutes)

Ingredients:

- 4 lobster tails
- 2 tablespoons melted butter
- Salt and pepper to taste

Directions for Cooking:

1) Preheat the air fryer at 390°F.
2) Place the grill pan accessory.
3) Cut the lobster through the tail section using a pair of kitchen scissors.
4) Brush the lobster tails with melted butter and season with salt and pepper to taste.
5) Place on the grill pan and cook for 6 minutes.

Nutrition information:
Calories: 170; Carbs: 1.1g; Protein: 25.7g; Fat: 6.9g

Crispy Air Fryer Tuna Patties

(Servings: 4, Cooking Time: 10 minutes)

Ingredients:

- 2 cans of tuna in brine
- 2 teaspoons Dijon mustard
- ½ cup panko bread crumbs
- 1 tablespoon lemon juice
- 2 tablespoons chopped parsley
- 1 egg, beaten
- A drizzle Tabasco sauce
- 3 tablespoons olive oil

Directions for Cooking:

1) Drain the liquid from the canned tuna and put in a bowl.
2) Mix the tuna and season with mustard, bread crumbs, lemon juice, and parsley.
3) Add the egg and Tabasco sauce. Mix until well combined.
4) Form patties using your hands and place in the fried to set for at least 2 hours.
5) Preheat the air fryer at 390°F.
6) Place the grill pan accessory.
7) Brush the patties with olive oil and place on the grill pan.
8) Cook for 10 minutes.
9) Make sure to flip the patties halfway through the cooking time for even browning.

Nutrition information:
Calories: 209; Carbs: 2.9g; Protein: 18.8g; Fat: 13.5g

Lip Smacking Good Clams Oreganata

(Servings: 4, Cooking Time: 5 minutes)

Ingredients:

- 1 cup breadcrumbs
- ¼ cup parmesan cheese, grated
- ¼ cup parsley, chopped
- 1 teaspoon dried oregano
- 3 cloves of garlic, minced
- 4 tablespoons butter, melted
- 2 dozen clams, shucked

Directions for Cooking:

1) In a medium bowl, mix together the breadcrumbs, parmesan cheese, parsley, oregano, and garlic. Stir in the melted butter.
2) Preheat the air fryer at 390°F.
3) Place the baking dish accessory in the air fryer and place the clams.
4) Sprinkle the crumb mixture over the clams.
5) Cook for 5 minutes.

Nutrition information:
Calories: 160; Carbs: 6.3g; Protein: 2.9g; Fat: 13.6g

Easy Crisped 'n Breaded Shrimps

(Servings: 2, Cooking Time: 10 minutes)

Ingredients:

- 1-pound shrimps, peeled and deveined
- 2 eggs, beaten
- ½ cup panko bread crumbs
- ½ cup of onion, peeled and diced
- 1 teaspoon ginger
- 1 teaspoon garlic powder
- Salt to taste
- 1 teaspoon black pepper

Directions for Cooking:

1) Preheat the air fryer at 330°F.
2) In a bowl, beat the eggs and set aside.
3) In another bowl, mix the panko, onion, ginger, garlic powder, salt and pepper.
4) Dip the shrimps in the eggs and dredge in the panko mixture.
5) Place on the double layer rack and air fry for 10 minutes.

Nutrition information:

Calories: 386; Carbs: 10.2g; Protein: 56.8g; Fat:13.1g

Shrimps with Lemon and Chile Flavor

(Servings: 2, Cooking Time: 6 minutes)

Ingredients:

- 1-pound large shrimps, peeled and deveined
- 1 lemon, thinly sliced
- 1 tablespoon extra-virgin olive oil
- ½ teaspoon garlic powder
- Salt and pepper to taste
- 1 red chili, thinly sliced

Directions for Cooking:

1) Preheat the air fryer at 330°F.
2) Place the baking dish accessory in the air fryer.
3) In a mixing bowl, combine all ingredients.
4) Place the shrimps and cook for 6 minutes.

Nutrition information:

Calories: 244; Carbs: 4.3g; Protein: 46.8g; Fat: 4.3g

Southern Fried Catfish

(Servings: 4, Cooking Time: 15 minutes)

Ingredients:
- 2 pounds catfish fillets
- 1 cup milk
- 1 lemon, juice squeezed
- ½ cup yellow mustard
- ½ cup cornmeal
- ¼ cup all-purpose flour
- 2 tablespoons dried parsley flakes
- Salt and pepper to taste
- ¼ teaspoon chili powder
- ¼ teaspoon garlic powder
- ¼ teaspoon onion powder
- ¼ teaspoon cayenne pepper

Directions for Cooking:

1) Place the catfish in a bowl and Add milk and lemon juice.
2) Allow to marinate in the fridge for at least 30 minutes.
3) Meanwhile, mix in a bowl the mustard, cornmeal, flour, and the rest of the Ingredients.
4) Preheat the air fryer at 330°F.
5) Dredge the marinated fish in the flour mixture and place on the double layer rack accessory.
6) Cook for 15 minutes.

Nutrition information:
Calories: 375; Carbs: 28.6g; Protein: 42.8g; Fat: 9.9g

Easy Cajun Shrimps

(Servings: 2, Cooking Time: 6 minutes)

Ingredients:
- 1-pound shrimps, peeled and deveined
- 1 tablespoon olive oil
- 1 teaspoon old bay seasoning
- ½ teaspoon sweet paprika
- A pinch of cayenne pepper
- Salt and pepper to taste

Directions for Cooking:
1) Preheat the air fryer at 330°F.
2) Place the grill pan accessory in the air fryer.
3) In a bowl, season the shrimps with the rest of the Ingredients. Mix until well combined.
4) Place shrimps on the grill pan.
5) Cook for 6 minutes

Nutrition information:
Calories: 132; Carbs: 1.7g; Protein: 20.2g; Fat: 4.9g

Lemon Garlic Shrimps

(Servings: 2, Cooking Time: 3 minutes)

Ingredients:
- 1-pound small shrimps, peeled and deveined
- 1 tablespoon olive oil
- 4 cloves of garlic, minced
- 1 lemon, juiced and zested
- A pinch of red pepper flakes
- ¼ cup chopped parsley
- Salt and pepper to taste

Directions for Cooking:
1) Preheat the air fryer at 390ºF.
2) Place the grill pan accessory in the air fryer.
3) In a bowl, mix all Ingredients.
4) Place shrimps on the grill pan.
5) Cook for 3 minutes.

Nutrition information:
Calories: 226; Carbs: 3.4g; Protein: 32g; Fat: 9.3g

Shrimps and Veggies in Air Fryer

(Servings: 2, Cooking Time: 8 minutes)

Ingredients:
- ½ pound shrimps, peeled and deveined
- 1 bag frozen mix vegetables
- 1 tablespoon Cajun seasoning
- 1 tablespoon olive oil

Directions for Cooking:
1) Preheat the air fryer at 390ºF.
2) Place the baking dish accessory in the air fryer.
3) In a bowl, mix all Ingredients: and toss to combine.
4) Place in the shrimps and the vegetables in the baking dish.
5) Cook for 4 minutes.
6) Open and air fryer and give the shrimps a good shake.
7) Cook for another 4 minutes.

Nutrition information:
Calories: 243; Carbs: 20.9g; Protein: 27.8g; Fat: 5.3g

Garlic Lime Shrimps Skewers

(Servings: 1, Cooking Time: 6 minutes)

Ingredients:
- 1 cup raw shrimps
- 1 clove of garlic, minced
- 1 lime, juiced and zested
- Salt and pepper to taste

Directions for Cooking:
1) In a mixing bowl, combine all Ingredients: and give a good stir.
2) Preheat the air fryer at 390°F.
3) Skewer the shrimps onto the metal skewers that come with the double layer rack accessory.
4) Place on the rack and cook for 6 minutes.

Nutrition information:
Calories: 280; Carbs: 8g; Protein: 26g; Fat: 16g

Crispylicious Crab Cakes

(Servings: 2, Cooking Time: 10 minutes)

Ingredients:
- 2 large eggs
- 1 teaspoon Dijon mustard
- 1 teaspoon Worcestershire sauce
- 1 ½ teaspoon old bay seasoning
- Salt and pepper to taste
- ¼ cup chopped green onion
- 1-pound lump crab meat
- ½ cup panko

Directions for Cooking:
1) Preheat the air fryer at 390°F.
2) Place the grill pan accessory in the air fryer.
3) In a mixing bowl, combine all Ingredients: until everything is well-incorporated.
4) Use your hands to form small patties of crab cakes.
5) Place on the grill pan and cook for 10 minutes.
6) Flip the crab cakes halfway through the cooking time for even browning.

Nutrition information:
Calories: 129; Carbs: 4.3g; Protein: 16.2g; Fat: 5.1g

Coconut Shrimps with Pina Colada Dip

(Servings: 4, Cooking Time: 6 minutes)

Ingredients:

- 1 ½ pounds jumbo shrimps, peeled and deveined
- ½ cup cornstarch
- 2/3 cup coconut milk
- 2 tablespoons honey
- 1 cup shredded coconut flakes
- ¾ cups panko bread crumbs
- 1/3 cup light coconut milk
- 1/3 cup non-fat Greek yogurt
- ¼ cup pineapple chunks, drained
- Salt and pepper to taste
- Toasted coconut meat for garnish

Directions for Cooking:

1) Preheat the air fryer at 390°F.
2) Place the shrimps and cornstarch in a Ziploc bag and give a good shake.
3) In a bowl, stir in coconut milk and honey. Set aside.
4) In another bowl, mix the coconut flakes and bread crumbs. Set aside.
5) Dip the shrimps in the milk mixture then dredge in the bread crumbs.
6) Place in the double layer rack and cook for 6 minutes.
7) Meanwhile, combine the rest of the Ingredients: to create the dipping sauce.

Nutrition information:
Calories: 493; Carbs: 21.4g; Protein: 38.9g; Fat: 27.9g

Beer Battered Air Fried Fish

(Servings: 2, Cooking Time: 15 minutes)

Ingredients:

- 2 cod fillets
- 2 eggs, beaten
- 1 ¼ cup lager beer
- ½ cup all-purpose flour
- ¾ teaspoon baking powder
- Salt and pepper to taste

Directions for Cooking:

1) Preheat the air fryer at 390°F.
2) Pat the fish fillets dry then set aside.
3) In a bowl, combine the rest of the Ingredients: to create a batter.
4) Dip the fillets on the batter and place on the double layer rack.
5) Cook for 15 minutes.

Nutrition information:
Calories: 229; Carbs: 33.2g; Protein: 31.1g; Fat: 10.2g

Alaskan Cod Fish with Apple Slaw

(Servings: 3, Cooking Time: 15 minutes)

Ingredients:

- 1 ½ pounds frozen Alaskan cod
- 1 tablespoon vegetable oil
- 1 box whole wheat panko bread crumbs
- 1 granny smith apple, julienned
- 2 cups Napa cabbage, shredded
- ½ red onion, diced
- ¼ cup mayonnaise
- 1 teaspoon paprika
- Salt and pepper to taste

Directions for Cooking:

1) Preheat the air fryer at 390°F.
2) Place the grill pan accessory in the air fryer.
3) Brush the fish with oil and dredge in the breadcrumbs.
4) Place the fish on the grill pan and cook for 15 minutes. Make sure to flip the fish halfway through the cooking time.
5) Meanwhile, prepare the slaw by mixing the remaining Ingredients: in a bowl.
6) Serve the fish with the slaw.

Nutrition information:
Calories: 316; Carbs: 13.5g; Protein: 37.8g; Fat: 12.2g

Blackened Shrimps in Air Fryer

(Servings: 4, Cooking Time: 6 minutes)

Ingredients:
- 20 jumbo shrimps, peeled and deveined
- 2 tablespoons coconut oil
- 2 teaspoons cilantro
- 2 teaspoons smoked paprika
- 2 teaspoons onion powder
- 1 teaspoon cumin
- 1 teaspoon salt
- 1 teaspoon thyme
- 1 teaspoon oregano
- ¼ teaspoon cayenne pepper
- ¼ teaspoon red chili flakes

Directions for Cooking:
1) Preheat the air fryer at 390°F.
2) Season the shrimps with all the Ingredients.
3) Place the seasoned shrimps in the double layer rack.
4) Cook for 6 minutes.

Nutrition information:
Calories: 220; Carbs: 2.5g; Protein: 34.2g; Fat: 8.1g

Herb and Garlic Fish Fingers

(Servings: 1, Cooking Time: 10 minutes)

Ingredients:

- ½ pound fish, cut into fingers
- ½ teaspoon salt
- 2 tablespoons lemon juice
- ½ teaspoon turmeric powder
- ½ teaspoon red chili flakes
- 2 teaspoons garlic powder
- ½ teaspoon crushed black pepper
- 1 teaspoon ginger garlic paste
- 2 teaspoons corn flour
- 2 eggs, beaten
- ¼ teaspoon baking soda
- 1 cup bread crumbs
- Oil for brushing

Directions for Cooking:

1) Preheat the air fryer at 390°F.
2) Season the fish fingers with salt, lemon juice, turmeric powder, chili flakes, garlic powder, black pepper, and garlic paste. Add the corn flour, eggs, and baking soda.
3) Dredge the seasoned fish in breadcrumbs and brush with cooking oil.
4) Place on the double layer rack.
5) Cook for 10 minutes.

Nutrition information:

Calories: 773; Carbs: 32.7g; Protein: 64.9g; Fat: 42.5g

Garlic and Black Pepper Shrimp Grill

(Servings: 2, Cooking Time: 6 minutes)

Ingredients:

- 1 red chili, seeds removed
- 3 cloves of garlic, grated
- 1 tablespoon ground pepper
- 1 tablespoon fresh lime juice
- 1-pound large shrimps, peeled and deveined
- Salt to taste

Directions for Cooking:

1) Preheat the air fryer at 390°F.
2) Place the grill pan accessory in the air fryer.
3) Grill the shrimps for 6 minutes.

Nutrition information:

Calories:179 ; Carbs: 6.3g; Protein: 31.6g; Fat: 2.3g

Crispy Cod Nuggets with Tartar Sauce

(Servings: 3, Cooking Time: 10 minutes)

Ingredients:

- 1 ½ pounds cod fillet
- Salt and pepper to taste
- ½ cup flour
- 1 egg, beaten
- 1 cup cracker crumbs
- 1 tablespoon vegetable oil
- ½ cup non-fat mayonnaise
- 1 teaspoon honey
- Zest from half of a lemon
- Juice from half a lemon
- ½ teaspoon Worcestershire sauce
- 1 tablespoon sweet pickle relish
- Salt and pepper to taste

Directions for Cooking:

1) Preheat the air fryer at 390°F.
2) Season the cods with salt and pepper.
3) Dredge the fish on flour and dip in the beaten egg before dredging on the cracker crumbs. Brush with oil.
4) Place the fish on the double layer rack and cook for 10 minutes.
5) Meanwhile, prepare the sauce by mixing all ingredients in a bowl.
6) Serve the fish with the sauce.

Nutrition information:
Calories: 470; Carbs: 25.4g; Protein: 42.9g; Fat: 21.8g

Grilled Salmon with Cucumbers

(Servings: 4, Cooking Time: 10 minutes)

Ingredients:

- 4 6-ounces salmon fillets
- 1 teaspoon lemon zest
- Juice from 1 lemon, freshly squeezed
- 1 tablespoon fresh dill
- Salt and pepper to taste
- ½ cup mayonnaise
- ½ cup sour cream
- 2 cucumbers peeled and sliced

Directions for Cooking:

1) Preheat the air fryer at 390°F.
2) Place the grill pan accessory in the air fryer.
3) Season the salmon fillets with lemon zest, lemon juice, dill, salt and pepper.
4) Grill the salmon for 10 minutes making sure to flip halfway through the cooking time.
5) Meanwhile, prepare the cucumber salad by mixing in a bowl the mayonnaise, sour cream and cucumber slices. Season with salt and pepper.
6) Serve the salmon with the cucumber salad.

Nutrition information:
Calories: 409; Carbs: 5.9g; Protein: 38.4g; Fat: 25.1g

Shrimps, Zucchini, And Tomatoes on the Grill

(Servings: 2, Cooking Time: 15 minutes)

Ingredients:

- 10 jumbo shrimps, peeled and deveined
- Salt and pepper to taste
- 1 clove of garlic, minced
- 1 medium zucchini, sliced
- 1-pint cherry tomatoes
- ¼ cup feta cheese

Directions for Cooking:

1) Preheat the air fryer at 390°F.
2) Place the grill pan accessory in the air fryer.
3) In a mixing bowl, season the shrimps with salt and pepper. Stir in the garlic, zucchini, and tomatoes.
4) Place on the grill pan and cook for 15 minutes.
5) Once cooked, transfer to a bowl and sprinkle with feta cheese.

Nutrition information:
Calories: 257; Carbs:4.2 g; Protein: 48.9g; Fat: 5.3g

Grilled Halibut with Tomatoes and Hearts of Palm

(Servings: 4, Cooking Time: 15 minutes)

Ingredients:

- 4 halibut fillets
- Juice from 1 lemon
- Salt and pepper to taste
- 2 tablespoons oil
- ½ cup hearts of palm, rinse and drained
- 1 cup cherry tomatoes

Directions for Cooking:

1) Preheat the air fryer at 390°F.
2) Place the grill pan accessory in the air fryer.
3) Season the halibut fillets with lemon juice, salt and pepper. Brush with oil.
4) Place the fish on the grill pan.
5) Arrange the hearts of palms and cherry tomatoes on the side and sprinkle with more salt and pepper.
6) Cook for 15 minutes.

Nutrition information:
Calories: 208; Carbs: 7g; Protein: 21 g; Fat: 11g

Chat Masala Grilled Snapper

(Servings: 5, Cooking Time: 25 minutes)

Ingredients:
- 2 ½ pounds whole fish
- Salt to taste
- 1/3 cup chat masala
- 3 tablespoons fresh lime juice
- 5 tablespoons olive oil

Directions for Cooking:
1) Preheat the air fryer at 390°F.
2) Place the grill pan accessory in the air fryer.
3) Season the fish with salt, chat masala and lime juice.
4) Brush with oil
5) Place the fish on a foil basket and place inside the grill.
6) Cook for 25 minutes.

Nutrition information:
Calories:308 ; Carbs: 0.7g; Protein: 35.2g; Fat: 17.4g

One-Pan Shrimp and Chorizo Mix Grill

(Servings: 4, Cooking Time: 15 minutes)

Ingredients:
- 1 ½ pounds large shrimps, peeled and deveined
- Salt and pepper to taste
- 6 links fresh chorizo sausage
- 2 bunches asparagus spears, trimmed
- Lime wedges

Directions for Cooking:
1) Preheat the air fryer at 390°F.
2) Place the grill pan accessory in the air fryer.
3) Season the shrimps with salt and pepper to taste. Set aside.
4) Place the chorizo on the grill pan and the sausage.
5) Place the asparagus on top.
6) Grill for 15 minutes.
7) Serve with lime wedges.

Nutrition information:
Calories:124 ; Carbs: 9.4g; Protein: 8.2g; Fat: 7.1g

Grilled Tasty Scallops

(Servings: 2, Cooking Time: 10 minutes)

Ingredients:
- 1-pound sea scallops, cleaned and patted dry
- Salt and pepper to taste
- 3 dried chilies
- 2 tablespoon dried thyme
- 1 tablespoon dried oregano
- 1 tablespoon ground coriander
- 1 tablespoon ground fennel
- 2 teaspoons chipotle pepper

Directions for Cooking:
1) Preheat the air fryer at 390°F.
2) Place the grill pan accessory in the air fryer.
3) Mix all Ingredients: in a bowl.
4) Dump the scallops on the grill pan and cook for 10 minutes.

Nutrition information:
Calories:291 ; Carbs: 20.7g; Protein: 48.6g; Fat: 2.5g

Clam with Lemons on the Grill

(Servings: 6, Cooking Time: 6 minutes)

Ingredients:
- 4 pounds littleneck clams
- Salt and pepper to taste
- 1 clove of garlic, minced
- ½ cup parsley, chopped
- 1 teaspoon crushed red pepper flakes
- 5 tablespoons olive oil
- 1 loaf crusty bread, halved
- ½ cup parmesan cheese, grated

Directions for Cooking:
1) Preheat the air fryer at 390°F.
2) Place the grill pan accessory in the air fryer.
3) Place the clams on the grill pan and cook for 6 minutes.
4) Once the clams have opened, take them out and extract the meat.
5) Transfer the meat into a bowl and season with salt and pepper.
6) Stir in the garlic, parsley, red pepper flakes, and olive oil.
7) Serve on top of bread and sprinkle with parmesan cheese.

Nutrition information:
Calories: 341; Carbs: 26g; Protein:48.3g; Fat: 17.2g

Salmon Steak Grilled with Cilantro Garlic Sauce

(Servings: 2, Cooking Time: 15 minutes)

Ingredients:
- 2 salmon steaks
- Salt and pepper to taste
- 2 tablespoons vegetable oil
- 2 cloves of garlic, minced
- 1 cup cilantro leaves
- ½ cup Greek yogurt
- 1 teaspoon honey

Directions for Cooking:
1) Preheat the air fryer at 390ºF.
2) Place the grill pan accessory in the air fryer.
3) Season the salmon steaks with salt and pepper. Brush with oil.
4) Grill for 15 minutes and make sure to flip halfway through the cooking time.
5) In a food processor, mix the garlic, cilantro leaves, yogurt and honey. Season with salt and pepper to taste. Pulse until smooth.
6) Serve the salmon steaks with the cilantro sauce.

Nutrition information:
Calories: 485; Carbs: 6.3g; Protein: 47.6g; Fat: 29.9g

Tasty Grilled Red Mullet

(Servings: 8, Cooking Time: 15 minutes)

Ingredients:
- 8 whole red mullets, gutted and scales removed
- Salt and pepper to taste
- Juice from 1 lemon
- 1 tablespoon olive oil

Directions for Cooking:
1) Preheat the air fryer at 390ºF.
2) Place the grill pan accessory in the air fryer.
3) Season the red mullet with salt, pepper, and lemon juice.
4) Brush with olive oil.
5) Grill for 15 minutes.

Nutrition information:
Calories: 152; Carbs: 0.9g; Protein: 23.1g; Fat: 6.2g

Chargrilled Halibut Niçoise With Vegetables

(Servings: 6, Cooking Time: 15 minutes)

Ingredients:
- 1 ½ pounds halibut fillets
- Salt and pepper to taste
- 2 tablespoons olive oil
- 2 pounds mixed vegetables
- 4 cups torn lettuce leaves
- 1 cup cherry tomatoes, halved
- 4 large hard-boiled eggs, peeled and sliced

Directions for Cooking:
1) Preheat the air fryer at 390°F.
2) Place the grill pan accessory in the air fryer.
3) Rub the halibut with salt and pepper. Brush the fish with oil.
4) Place on the grill.
5) Surround the fish fillet with the mixed vegetables and cook for 15 minutes.
6) Assemble the salad by serving the fish fillet with grilled mixed vegetables, lettuce, cherry tomatoes, and hard-boiled eggs.

Nutrition information:
Calories: 312; Carbs:16.8 g; Protein: 19.8g; Fat: 18.3g

Spiced Salmon Kebabs

(Servings: 3, Cooking Time: 15 minutes)

Ingredients:
- 2 tablespoons chopped fresh oregano
- 2 teaspoons sesame seeds
- 1 teaspoon ground cumin
- Salt and pepper to taste
- 1 ½ pounds salmon fillets
- 2 tablespoons olive oil
- 2 lemons, sliced into rounds

Directions for Cooking:
1) Preheat the air fryer at 390°F.
2) Place the grill pan accessory in the air fryer.
3) Create the dry rub by combining the oregano, sesame seeds, cumin, salt and pepper.
4) Rub the salmon fillets with the dry rub and brush with oil.
5) Grill the salmon for 15 minutes.
6) Serve with lemon slices once cooked.

Nutrition information:
Calories per serving 447 ; Carbs: 4.1g; Protein:47.6 g; Fat:26.6 g

Roasted Tuna on Linguine

(Servings: 2, Cooking Time: 20 minutes)

Ingredients:

- 1-pound fresh tuna fillets
- Salt and pepper to taste
- 1 tablespoon olive oil
- 12 ounces linguine, cooked according to package Directions for Cooking:
- 2 cups parsley leaves, chopped
- 1 tablespoon capers, chopped
- Juice from 1 lemon

Directions for Cooking:

1) Preheat the air fryer at 390°F.
2) Place the grill pan accessory in the air fryer.
3) Season the tuna with salt and pepper. Brush with oil.
4) Grill for 20 minutes.
5) Once the tuna is cooked, shred using forks and place on top of cooked linguine. Add parsley and capers. Season with salt and pepper and add lemon juice.

Nutrition information:

Calories: 520; Carbs: 60.6g; Protein: 47.7g; Fat: 9.6g

Chili Lime Clams with Tomatoes

(Servings: 3, Cooking Time: 15 minutes)

Ingredients:

- 25 littleneck clams
- 1 tablespoon fresh lime juice
- Salt and pepper to taste
- 6 tablespoons unsalted butter
- 4 cloves of garlic, minced
- ½ cup tomatoes, chopped
- ½ cup basil leaves

Directions for Cooking:

1) Preheat the air fryer at 390°F.
2) Place the grill pan accessory in the air fryer.
3) On a large foil, place all ingredients. Fold over the foil and close by crimping the edges.
4) Place on the grill pan and cook for 15 minutes.
5) Serve with bread.

Nutrition information:

Calories: 163; Carbs: 4.1g; Protein: 1.7g; Fat: 15.5g

Air Fryer Garlicky-Grilled Turbot

(Servings: 2, Cooking Time: 20 minutes)

Ingredients:
- 2 whole turbot, scaled and head removed
- Salt and pepper to taste
- 1 clove of garlic, minced
- ½ cup chopped celery leaves
- 2 tablespoons olive oil

Directions for Cooking:
1) Preheat the air fryer at 390°F.
2) Place the grill pan accessory in the air fryer.
3) Season the turbot with salt, pepper, garlic, and celery leaves.
4) Brush with oil.
5) Place on the grill pan and cook for 20 minutes until the fish becomes flaky.

Nutrition information:
Calories: 269; Carbs: 3.3g; Protein: 66.2g; Fat: 25.6g

Broiled Spiced-Lemon Squid

(Servings: 4, Cooking Time: 15 minutes)

Ingredients:
- 2 pounds squid, gutted and cleaned
- Salt and pepper to taste
- 1 tablespoon fresh lemon juice
- 5 cloves of garlic
- ½ cup tomatoes, chopped
- ½ cup green onions, chopped
- 2 tablespoons olive oil

Directions for Cooking:
1) Preheat the air fryer at 390°F.
2) Place the grill pan accessory in the air fryer.
3) Season the squid with salt, pepper, and lemon juice.
4) Stuff the cavity with garlic, tomatoes, and onions.
5) Brush the squid with olive oil.
6) Place on the grill pan and cook for 15 minutes.
7) Halfway through the cooking time, flip the squid.

Nutrition information:
Calories: 277; Carbs: 10.7g; Protein: 36g; Fat: 10g

Tuna Grill with Ginger Sauce

(Servings: 3, Cooking Time: 20 minutes)

Ingredients:
- 1 ½ pounds tuna, thick slices
- 2 tablespoons rice vinegar
- 2 tablespoons grated fresh ginger
- 2 tablespoons peanut oil
- 2 tablespoons soy sauce
- 2 tablespoons honey
- 1 serrano chili, seeded and minced

Directions for Cooking:
1) Place all ingredients in a Ziploc bag.
2) Allow to marinate in the fridge for at least 2 hours.
3) Preheat the air fryer at 390°F.
4) Place the grill pan accessory in the air fryer.
5) Grill the fish for 15 to 20 minutes.
6) Flip the fish halfway through the cooking time.
7) Meanwhile, pour the marinade in a saucepan and allow to simmer for 10 minutes until the sauce thickens.
8) Brush the tuna with the sauce before serving.

Nutrition information:
Calories: 357; Carbs:14.8 g; Protein: 44.9g; Fat: 13.1g

Char-Grilled Spicy Halibut

(Servings: 6, Cooking Time: 20 minutes)

Ingredients:
- 3 pounds halibut fillet, skin removed
- Salt and pepper to taste
- 4 tablespoons dry white wine
- 4 tablespoons olive oil
- 2 cloves of garlic, minced
- 1 tablespoon chili powder

Directions for Cooking:
1) Place all ingredients in a Ziploc bag.
2) Allow to marinate in the fridge for at least 2 hours.
3) Preheat the air fryer at 390°F.
4) Place the grill pan accessory in the air fryer.
5) Grill the fish for 20 minutes making sure to flip every 5 minutes.

Nutrition information:
Calories: 385; Carbs: 1.7g; Protein: 33g; Fat: 40.6g

Roasted Swordfish with Charred Leeks

(Servings: 4, Cooking Time: 20 minutes)

Ingredients:
- 4 swordfish steaks
- Salt and pepper to taste
- 3 tablespoons lime juice
- 2 tablespoons olive oil
- 4 medium leeks, cut into an inch long

Directions for Cooking:
1) Preheat the air fryer at 390°F.
2) Place the grill pan accessory in the air fryer.
3) Season the swordfish with salt, pepper and lime juice.
4) Brush the fish with olive oil
5) Place fish fillets on grill pan and top with leeks.
6) Grill for 20 minutes.

Nutrition information:
Calories: 611; Carbs: 14.6g; Protein: 48g; Fat: 40g

Citrusy Branzini on the Grill

(Servings: 2, Cooking Time: 15 minutes)

Ingredients:
- 2 branzini fillets
- Salt and pepper to taste
- 3 lemons, juice freshly squeezed
- 2 oranges, juice freshly squeezed

Directions for Cooking:
1) Place all ingredients in a Ziploc bag. Allow to marinate in the fridge for 2 hours.
2) Preheat the air fryer at 390°F.
3) Place the grill pan accessory in the air fryer.
4) Place the fish on the grill pan and cook for 15 minutes until the fish is flaky.

Nutrition information:
Calories: 318; Carbs: 20.8g; Protein: 23.5g; Fat: 15.6g

Grilled Squid Rings with Kale and Tomatoes

(Servings: 3, Cooking Time: 15 minutes)

Ingredients:

- 1 2-pound squid, cleaned and sliced into rings
- Salt and pepper to taste
- 3 cloves of garlic, minced
- 1 sprig rosemary, chopped
- ¼ cup red wine vinegar
- 3 pounds kale, torn
- 3 tomatoes, chopped

Directions for Cooking:

1) Preheat the air fryer at 390°F.
2) Place the grill pan accessory in the air fryer.
3) Season the squid rings with salt, pepper, garlic, rosemary, and wine vinegar.
4) Grill for 15 minutes.
5) Serve octopus on a bed of kale leaves and garnish with tomatoes on top.

Nutrition information:
Calories: 575; Carbs: 56.2g; Protein: 68.1g; Fat: 8.6g

Butterflied Sriracha Prawns Grilled

(Servings: 2, Cooking Time: 15 minutes)

Ingredients:

- 1-pound large prawns, shells removed and cut lengthwise or butterflied
- 1 tablespoon sriracha
- 2 tablespoons melted butter
- 2 tablespoons minced garlic
- 1teaspoon fish sauce
- 1 tablespoon lime juice
- Salt and pepper to taste

Directions for Cooking:

1) Preheat the air fryer at 390°F.
2) Place the grill pan accessory in the air fryer.
3) Season the prawns with the rest of the ingredients.
4) Place on the grill pan and cook for 15 minutes. Make sure to flip the prawns halfway through the cooking time.

Nutrition information:
Calories: 443; Carbs:9.7 g; Protein: 62.8g; Fat: 16.9g

Grilled Shrimp with Butter

(Servings: 4, Cooking Time: 15 minutes)

Ingredients:

- 6 tablespoons unsalted butter
- ½ cup red onion, chopped
- 1 ½ teaspoon red pepper
- 1 teaspoon shrimp paste or fish sauce
- 1 ½ teaspoon lime juice
- Salt and pepper to taste
- 24 large shrimps, shelled and deveined

Directions for Cooking:

1) Preheat the air fryer at 390°F.
2) Place the grill pan accessory in the air fryer.
3) Place all ingredients in a Ziploc bag and give a good shake.
4) Skewer the shrimps through a bamboo skewer and place on the grill pan.
5) Cook for 15 minutes.
6) Flip the shrimps halfway through the cooking time.

Nutrition information:

Calories: 153; Carbs: 2.3g; Protein: 6.9g; Fat: 12.9g

Char-Grilled 'n Herbed Sea Scallops

(Servings: 3, Cooking Time: 10 minutes)

Ingredients:

- 1-pound sea scallops, meat only
- 3 tablespoons olive oil, divided
- 1 teaspoon dried sage
- Salt and pepper to taste
- 1 cup grape tomatoes, halved
- 1/3 cup basil leaves, shredded

Directions for Cooking:

1) Preheat the air fryer at 390°F.
2) Place the grill pan accessory in the air fryer.
3) Season the scallops with half of the olive oil, sage, salt and pepper.
4) Toss into the air fryer and grill for 10 minutes.
5) Once cooked, serve with tomatoes and basil leaves.
6) Drizzle the remaining olive oil and season with more salt and pepper to taste.

Nutrition information:

Calories: 336; Carbs: 18g; Protein: 32g; Fat: 15g

Japanese Citrus Soy Squid

(Servings: 4, Cooking Time: 10 minutes)

Ingredients:
- ½ cup mirin
- 1 cup soy sauce
- 1/3 cup yuzu or orange juice, freshly squeezed
- 2 cups water
- 2 pounds squid body, cut into rings

Directions for Cooking:
1) Place all ingredients in a Ziploc bag and allow the squid rings to marinate in the fridge for at least 2 hours.
2) Preheat the air fryer at 390°F.
3) Place the grill pan accessory in the air fryer.
4) Grill the squid rings for 10 minutes.
5) Meanwhile, pour the marinade over a sauce pan and allow to simmer for 10 minutes or until the sauce has reduced.
6) Baste the squid rings with the sauce before serving.

Nutrition information:
Calories: 412; Carbs: 4.1g; Protein: 44.2g; Fat: 24.3g

Greek-Style Grilled Scallops

(Servings: 3, Cooking Time: 15 minutes)

Ingredients:
- ¼ cup Greek yogurt
- A pinch of saffron threads
- 1 ½ teaspoons rice vinegar
- Salt and pepper to taste
- 12 large sea scallops
- 2 tablespoons olive oil

Directions for Cooking:
1) Place all ingredients in a Ziploc bag and allow the scallops to marinate in the fridge for at least 2 hours.
2) Preheat the air fryer at 390°F.
3) Place the grill pan accessory in the air fryer.
4) Grill the scallops for 15 minutes.
5) Serve on bread and drizzle with more olive oil if desired.

Nutrition information:
Calories: 178; Carbs: 6g; Protein: 16g; Fat: 10g

Easy Grilled Pesto Scallops

(Servings: 3, Cooking Time: 15 minutes)

Ingredients:

- 12 large scallops, side muscles removed
- Salt and pepper to taste
- ½ cup prepared commercial pesto

Directions for Cooking:

1) Place all ingredients in a Ziploc bag and allow the scallops to marinate in the fridge for at least 2 hours.
2) Preheat the air fryer at 390°F.
3) Place the grill pan accessory in the air fryer.
4) Grill the scallops for 15 minutes.
5) Serve on pasta or bread if desired.

Nutrition information:
Calories: 137; Carbs: 7.7g; Protein:15.3 g; Fat: 5g

Clams with Herbed Butter in Packets

(Servings: 2, Cooking Time: 20 minutes)

Ingredients:

- 24 littleneck clams, scrubbed clean
- ½ cup unsalted butter, diced
- Salt and pepper to taste
- 1 tablespoon fresh lemon juice
- 1 tablespoon parsley, chopped
- 1 tablespoon dill, chopped
- Lemon wedges

Directions for Cooking:

1) Preheat the air fryer at 390°F.
2) Place the grill pan accessory in the air fryer.
3) On a large foil, place the clams and the rest of the ingredients.
4) Fold the foil and crimp the edges.
5) Place on the grill pan and cook for 15 to 20 minutes or until all clams have opened.

Nutrition information:
Calories: 384; Carbs: 6g; Protein: 18g; Fat: 32g

Simple Sesame Squid on the Grill

(Servings: 3, Cooking Time: 10 minutes)

Ingredients:
- 1 ½ pounds squid, cleaned
- 2 tablespoon toasted sesame oil
- Salt and pepper to taste

Directions for Cooking:
1) Preheat the air fryer at 390°F.
2) Place the grill pan accessory in the air fryer.
3) Season the squid with sesame oil, salt and pepper.
4) Grill the squid for 10 minutes.

Nutrition information:
Calories: 220; Carbs: 0.9g; Protein: 27g; Fat: 12g

Grilled Shellfish with Vegetables

(Servings: 8, Cooking Time: 30 minutes)

Ingredients:
- 1 bunch broccolini
- 8 asparagus spears
- 8 small carrots, peeled and sliced
- 4 tomatoes, halved
- 1 red onion, wedged
- 2 tablespoons olive oil
- Salt and pepper to taste
- 16 small oysters, scrubbed
- 16 littleneck clams, scrubbed
- 24 large mussels, scrubbed
- 2 tablespoons lemon juice
- 4 basil sprigs

Directions for Cooking:
1) Preheat the air fryer at 390°F.
2) Place the grill pan accessory in the air fryer.
3) Place all vegetables in a bowl and drizzle with oil. Season with salt and pepper then toss to coat the vegetables with the seasoning.
4) Place on the grill pan and grill for 15 minutes or until the edges of the vegetables are charred. Set aside
5) On a large foil, place all the shellfish and season with salt, lemon juice, and basil. Fold the foil and crimp the edges.
6) Place the foil packet on the grill pan and cook for another 15 minutes or until the shellfish have opened.
7) Serve the shellfish with the charred vegetables.

Nutrition information:
Calories: 282; Carbs: 20g; Protein: 26.7g; Fat: 10.5g

Grilled Meat Recipes

Tri-Tip in Chimichurri Marinade

(Servings: 4, Cooking Time: 40 minutes)

Ingredients:
- 2 pounds tri-tip steak, pounded
- 1 tablespoon smoked paprika
- 2 tablespoons olive oil
- Salt and pepper to taste
- 2 cloves of garlic, minced
- 2 cups chopped parsley
- ¼ cup red wine
- 1 tablespoon agave nectar

Directions for Cooking:

1) Place all ingredients in a Ziploc bag and allow to marinate for at least an hour.
2) Preheat the air fryer at 390°F.
3) Place the grill pan accessory in the air fryer.
4) Grill the meat for 40 minutes making sure to flip the meat every 10 minutes for even cooking.

Nutrition information:
Calories: 667; Carbs: 4.4g; Protein: 69.3g; Fat: 41.3g

Simply Grilled Flatiron Steak

(Servings: 4, Cooking Time: 40 minutes)

Ingredients:
- 1 ½ pound flatiron steak, cut into 4 pieces
- Salt and pepper to taste
- 1 tablespoon oil
- Serve with chopped tomatoes

Directions for Cooking:
1) Preheat the air fryer at 390°F.
2) Place the grill pan accessory in the air fryer.
3) Season the steak with salt and pepper. Brush with oil.
4) Place on the grill pan and cook for 40 minutes making sure to flip the steak every 10 minutes for even grilling.

Nutrition information:
Calories: 381; Carbs: 1.2g; Protein: 47.6g; Fat: 20.6g

Grilled Saffron Rack of Lamb

(Servings: 4, Cooking Time: 1 hour and 10 minutes)

Ingredients:
- 2 racks of lamb, rib bones frenched
- Salt and pepper to taste
- 2 cloves of garlic, minced
- 1 cup plain Greek yogurt
- 2 tablespoons olive oil
- 1 teaspoon lemon zest
- ½ teaspoon crumbled saffron threads

Directions for Cooking:
1) Preheat the air fryer at 390°F.
2) Place the grill pan accessory in the air fryer.
3) Season the lamb meat with salt and pepper to taste. Set aside.
4) In a bowl, combine the rest of ingredients.
5) Brush the mixture onto the lamb.
6) Place on the grill pan and cook for 1 hour and 10 minutes.

Nutrition information:
Calories: 1260; Carbs: 2g; Protein: 70g; Fat: 108g

Steak on the Grill with Tapenade

(Servings: 4, Cooking Time: 45 minutes)

Ingredients:
- 2 pounds flank steak, pounded
- Salt and pepper to taste
- 2 tablespoons fresh oregano
- 2 tablespoons smoked paprika
- 2 tablespoons onion powder
- 2 tablespoons garlic powder
- 1/3 cup olive oil
- 1 cup pitted olives
- 1 tablespoon capers, minced
- 1 clove of garlic, minced
- 1 anchovy fillet, minced

Directions for Cooking:
1) Preheat the air fryer at 390°F.
2) Place the grill pan accessory in the air fryer.
3) Season the steak with salt and pepper. Rub the oregano, paprika, onion powder, and garlic powder all over the steak.
4) Place on the grill pan and cook for 45 minutes. Make sure to flip the meat every 10 minutes for even cooking.
5) Meanwhile, mix together the olive oil, olives, capers, garlic, and anchovy fillets.
6) Serve the steak with the tapenade.

Nutrition information:
Calories: 553; Carbs: 11.6g; Protein: 51.5g; Fat: 33.4g

Traditionally Grilled Pork Rib Chops

(Servings: 6, Cooking Time: 50 minutes)

Ingredients:
- 8 cups water
- 1 cup salt
- 1 cup sugar
- 6 pork chops

Directions for Cooking:
1) Place all ingredients in a deep bowl and allow to soak the pork chops in the brine solution for at least 2 days in the fridge.
2) Preheat the air fryer at 390°F.
3) Place the grill pan accessory in the air fryer.
4) Place the meat on the grill pan and cook for 50 minutes making sure to flip every 10 minutes for even grilling.

Nutrition information:
Calories: 384; Carbs:16.6 g; Protein: 40.2g; Fat: 17.4g

Flank Steak with Bloody Mary Tomato Salad

(Servings: 5, Cooking Time: 50 minutes)

Ingredients:
- 2 ½ pound flank
- Salt and pepper to taste
- 1 teaspoon paprika
- ¼ teaspoon cayenne pepper
- 1 tablespoon oil
- 1 cup red onion, chopped
- 2 tablespoons Sherry vinegar
- 2 pounds cherry tomatoes, halved
- ½ cup green olives, pitted and sliced
- ¼ cup extra virgin olive oil

Directions for Cooking:
1) Preheat the air fryer at 390°F.
2) Place the grill pan accessory in the air fryer.
3) Season the steak with salt, pepper, paprika, and cayenne pepper. Brush with oil
4) Place on the grill pan and cook for 45 to 50 minutes.
5) Meanwhile, prepare the salad by mixing the remaining ingredients.
6) Serve the beef with salad.

Nutrition information:
Calories: 351; Carbs: 8g; Protein: 30g; Fat: 22g

Char-Grilled Herbed Skirt Steak

(Servings: 3, Cooking Time: 30 minutes)

Ingredients:
- 1 ½ pounds skirt steak, trimmed
- Salt and pepper to taste
- 1 tablespoon lemon zest
- 2 cups fresh herbs like tarragon, sage, and mint, chopped
- 4 cloves of garlic, minced
- 1 tablespoon olive oil

Directions for Cooking:
1) Preheat the air fryer at 390°F.
2) Place the grill pan accessory in the air fryer.
3) Season the steak with salt, pepper, lemon zest, herbs, and garlic.
4) Brush with oil.
5) Grill for 15 minutes and if needed cook in batches.

Nutrition information:
Calories: 478; Carbs: 18g; Protein: 25g; Fat: 34g

Roasted 'n Peppery Spareribs

(Servings: 4, Cooking Time: 1 hour)

Ingredients:
- ¼ cup brown sugar
- 2 tablespoons onion powder
- 1 tablespoon salt
- 1 tablespoon paprika
- 2 teaspoon Cajun seasoning
- 1 teaspoon coriander seed powder
- ½ teaspoon lemon
- 2 slabs spareribs

Directions for Cooking:
1) Preheat the air fryer at 390°F.
2) Place the grill pan accessory in the air fryer.
3) In a small bowl, combine the spaces.
4) Rub the spice mixture on to the spareribs.
5) Place the spareribs on the grill pan and cook for 20 minutes per batch.
6) Serve with your favorite barbecue sauce.

Nutrition information:
Calories: 490; Carbs: 18.2g; Protein: 24.4g; Fat: 35.5g

Marinated Sirloin Flap Steaks

(Servings: 4, Cooking Time: 45 minutes)

Ingredients:
- 2 pounds sirloin flap steaks, pounded
- 3 tablespoons soy sauce
- 3 tablespoons balsamic vinegar
- 3 tablespoons maple syrup
- 4 cloves of garlic, minced

Directions for Cooking:
1) Preheat the air fryer at 390°F.
2) Place the grill pan accessory in the air fryer.
3) On a deep dish, place the flap steaks and season with soy sauce, balsamic vinegar, and maple syrup, and garlic.
4) Place on the grill pan and cook for 15 minutes in batches.

Nutrition information:
Calories: 331; Carbs: 9g; Protein: 31g; Fat: 19g

Pork Chops on the Grill with Balsamic Glaze

(Servings: 4, Cooking Time: 50 minutes)

Ingredients:
- 3 tablespoons salt
- 1 ½ tablespoons sugar
- 4 pork rib chops
- 3 tablespoons olive oil
- ¾ cup balsamic vinegar
- 1 tablespoon butter

Directions for Cooking:
1) Place all ingredients in bowl and allow the meat to marinate in the fridge for at least 2 hours.
2) Preheat the air fryer at 390°F.
3) Place the grill pan accessory in the air fryer.
4) Grill the pork chops for 20 minutes making sure to flip the meat every 10 minutes for even grilling.
5) Meanwhile, pour the balsamic vinegar on a saucepan and allow to simmer for at least 10 minutes until the sauce thickens.
6) Brush the meat with the glaze before serving.

Nutrition information:
Calories: 274; Carbs: 11g; Protein: 17g; Fat: 18g

Grilled Lamb Steak with Chili Marmalade

(Servings: 4, Cooking Time: 1 hour and 30 minutes)

Ingredients:

- ½ cup dry white wine
- ¼ cup extra virgin olive oil
- 8 cloves of garlic, minced
- 3 tablespoons ancho chili powder
- 2 tablespoons lemon juice
- 1 tablespoon brown sugar
- Salt and pepper to taste
- 2 pounds lamb steak, pounded

Directions for Cooking:

1) Place all ingredients in bowl and allow the meat to marinate in the fridge for at least 2 hours.
2) Preheat the air fryer at 390°F.
3) Place the grill pan accessory in the air fryer.
4) Grill the meat for 20 minutes per batch.
5) Meanwhile, pour the marinade in a saucepan and allow to simmer for 10 minutes until the sauce thickens.

Nutrition information:
Calories: 500; Carbs: 8g; Protein: 38g; Fat: 35g

Oriental Curried Pork Roast

(Servings: 6, Cooking Time: 60 minutes)

Ingredients:

- 1 can unsweetened coconut milk
- 2 tablespoons fish sauce
- 2 tablespoons soy sauce
- 1 tablespoons sugar
- Salt and pepper to taste
- ½ teaspoon curry powder
- ½ teaspoon ground turmeric powder
- 3 pounds pork shoulder

Directions for Cooking:

1) Place all ingredients in bowl and allow the meat to marinate in the fridge for at least 2 hours.
2) Preheat the air fryer at 390°F.
3) Place the grill pan accessory in the air fryer.
4) Grill the meat for 20 minutes making sure to flip the pork every 10 minutes for even grilling and cook in batches.
5) Meanwhile, pour the marinade in a saucepan and allow to simmer for 10 minutes until the sauce thickens.
6) Baste the pork with the sauce before serving.

Nutrition information:
Calories: 688; Carbs: 38g; Protein: 17g; Fat: 52g

Cumin Chili Lamb Kebabs

(Servings: 3, Cooking Time: 1 hour)

Ingredients:

- 1 ½ pounds lamb shoulder, bones removed and cut into pieces
- 2 tablespoons cumin seeds, toasted
- 1 tablespoon Sichuan peppercorns
- 2 teaspoons caraway seeds, toasted
- 2 teaspoons crushed red pepper flakes
- 1 teaspoon sugar
- Salt and pepper to taste

Directions for Cooking:

1) Place all ingredients in bowl and allow the meat to marinate in the fridge for at least 2 hours.
2) Preheat the air fryer at 390°F.
3) Place the grill pan accessory in the air fryer.
4) Grill the meat for 15 minutes per batch.
5) Flip the meat every 8 minutes for even grilling.

Nutrition information:
Calories: 465; Carbs:7.7g; Protein: 22.8g; Fat: 46.9g

Spiced and Grilled Steaks

(Servings: 2, Cooking Time: 60 minutes)

Ingredients:

- 2 tablespoons coriander seeds
- 2 tablespoons ground coffee
- 2 tablespoons salt
- 4 teaspoons brown sugar
- 4 teaspoons unsweetened cocoa powder
- 1 tablespoon ground black pepper
- 2 hanger steaks
- 2 tablespoons olive oil

Directions for Cooking:

1) Preheat the air fryer at 390°F.
2) Place the grill pan accessory in the air fryer.
3) In a bowl, make the spice rub by combining the coriander seeds, ground coffee, salt, brown sugar, cocoa powder, and black pepper.
4) Rub the spice mixture on the steaks and brush with oil.
5) Grill for 30 minutes and make sure to flip the meat every 10 minutes for even grilling and cook in batches.

Nutrition information:
Calories: 680; Carbs: 16g; Protein:48 g; Fat: 47g

Hawaiian Rib Eye Steak

(Servings: 6, Cooking Time: 45 minutes)

Ingredients:
- 3 pounds rib eye steaks
- 2 cups pineapple juice
- ½ cup soy sauce
- ½ cup sugar
- 5 tablespoon apple cider vinegar
- 2 teaspoons sesame oil
- 1-inch ginger, grated

Directions for Cooking:
1) Combine all ingredients in a Ziploc bag and allow to marinate in the fridge for at least 2 hours.
2) Preheat the air fryer at 390°F.
3) Place the grill pan accessory in the air fryer.
4) Grill the meat for 15 minutes while flipping the meat every 8 minutes and cook in batches.
5) Meanwhile, pour the marinade in a saucepan and allow to simmer until the sauce thickens.
6) Brush the grilled meat with the glaze before serving.

Nutrition information:
Calories: 612; Carbs: 28g; Protein: 44g; Fat: 36g

Grilled Lamb with Herbed Salt

(Servings: 8, Cooking Time: 1 hour 20 minutes)

Ingredients:
- 4 pounds boneless leg of lamb, cut into 2-inch chunks
- 2 ½ tablespoons herb salt
- 2 tablespoons olive oil

Directions for Cooking:
1) Preheat the air fryer at 390°F.
2) Place the grill pan accessory in the air fryer.
3) Season the meat with the herb salt and brush with olive oil.
4) Grill the meat for 20 minutes per batch.
5) Make sure to flip the meat every 10 minutes for even cooking.

Nutrition information:
Calories: 347; Carbs: 0g; Protein: 46.6g; Fat: 17.8g

Delicious Dry Rubbed Flank Steak

(Servings: 3, Cooking Time: 45 minutes)

Ingredients:
- 2 tablespoons sugar
- 1 tablespoon chili powder
- 1 tablespoon paprika
- 2 teaspoons salt
- 2 teaspoons black pepper
- 1 teaspoon garlic powder
- 1 teaspoon mustard powder
- ½ teaspoon coriander
- ½ teaspoon ground cumin
- 1 ½ pounds flank steak

Directions for Cooking:

1) Preheat the air fryer at 390ºF.
2) Place the grill pan accessory in the air fryer.
3) In a small bowl, combine all the spices and rub all over the flank steak.
4) Place on the grill and cook for 15 minutes per batch.
5) Make sure to flip the meat every 8 minutes for even grilling.

Nutrition information:
Calories: 330; Carbs: 10.2g; Protein:50 g; Fat:12.1 g

Grilled Leg of Lamb with Mint Yogurt

(Servings: 6, Cooking Time: 1 hour)

Ingredients:
- 1 cup rosemary leaves
- ¾ cup peeled garlic cloves, crushed
- 2 tablespoons olive oil
- 3 pounds lamb shanks, boned removed and sliced into 2-inch chunks
- 1 tablespoon lemon zest
- Salt and pepper to taste
- 2 cups Greek yogurt
- 1 cup fresh mint, chopped
- 1 tablespoon lemon juice

Directions for Cooking:
1) Place in the Ziploc bag the rosemary leaves, garlic cloves, olive oil, lamb shanks, and lemon zest. Season with salt and pepper to taste.

2) Allow to marinate for 30 minutes in the fridge.
3) Preheat the air fryer at 390ºF.
4) Place the grill pan accessory in the air fryer.
5) Place the lamb shanks and garlic on the grill pan and cook for 20 minutes per batch.
6) Flip the meat every 10 minutes.
7) Meanwhile, mix together the Greek yogurt, fresh mint, and lemon juice. Season with salt and pepper to taste.
8) Serve the lamb shanks with the mint yogurt

Nutrition information:
Calories: 443; Carbs: 9.6g; Protein: 63.9g; Fat: 16.5g

Grilled Steak with Beet Salad

(Servings: 6, Cooking Time: 45 minutes)

Ingredients:
- 1-pound tri-tip, sliced
- 2 tablespoons olive oil
- Salt and pepper to taste
- 1 bunch scallions, chopped
- 1 bunch arugula, torn
- 3 beets, peeled and sliced thinly
- 3 tablespoons balsamic vinegar

Directions for Cooking:
1) Preheat the air fryer at 390°F.
2) Place the grill pan accessory in the air fryer.
3) Season the tri-tip with salt and pepper. Drizzle with oil.
4) Grill for 15 minutes per batch.
5) Meanwhile, prepare the salad by tossing the rest of the ingredients in a salad bowl.
6) Toss in the grilled tri-trip and drizzle with more balsamic vinegar.

Nutrition information:
Calories: 221; Carbs: 20.7g; Protein: 17.2g; Fat: 7.7g

Grilled Sweet and Sour Soy Pork Belly

(Servings: 4, Cooking Time: 60 minutes)

Ingredients:
- 2 pounds pork belly
- ¼ cup lemon juice
- ½ cup soy sauce
- 3 tablespoons brown sugar
- 2 tablespoons hoisin sauce
- Salt and pepper to taste
- 3-star anise
- 1 bay leaf

Directions for Cooking:
1) Place all ingredients in a Ziploc bag and allow to marinate in the fridge for at least 2 hours.
2) Preheat the air fryer at 390°F.
3) Place the grill pan accessory in the air fryer.
4) Grill the pork for at least 20 minutes per batch.
5) Make sure to flip the pork every 10 minutes.
6) Chop the pork before serving and garnish with green onions.

Nutrition information:
Calories: 1301; Carbs: 15.5g; Protein:24 g; Fat: 126.4g

Texas Rodeo-Style Beef

(Servings: 6, Cooking Time: 1 hour)

Ingredients:
- 3 pounds beef steak sliced
- Salt and pepper to taste
- 2 onion, chopped
- ½ cup honey
- ½ cup ketchup
- 1 clove of garlic, minced
- 1 tablespoon chili powder
- ½ teaspoon dry mustard

Directions for Cooking:
1) Place all ingredients in a Ziploc bag and allow to marinate in the fridge for at least 2 hours.
2) Preheat the air fryer at 390°F.
3) Place the grill pan accessory in the air fryer.
4) Grill the beef for 15 minutes per batch making sure that you flip it every 8 minutes for even grilling.
5) Meanwhile, pour the marinade on a saucepan and allow to simmer over medium heat until the sauce thickens.
6) Baste the beef with the sauce before serving.

Nutrition information:
Calories: 542; Carbs: 49g; Protein: 37g; Fat: 22g

Mustard-Marinated Flank Steak

(Servings: 3, Cooking Time: 45 minutes)

Ingredients:
- 1 ¼ pounds beef flank steak
- ½ teaspoon black pepper
- 1 cup Italian salad dressing
- ½ cup yellow mustard
- Salt to taste

Directions for Cooking:
1) Place all ingredients in a Ziploc bag and allow to marinate in the fridge for at least 2 hours.
2) Preheat the air fryer at 390°F.
3) Place the grill pan accessory in the air fryer.
4) Grill for 15 minutes per batch making sure to flip the meat halfway through the cooking time.

Nutrition information:
Calories: 576; Carbs: 3.1g; Protein:35 g; Fat: 47g

Grilled Rum Beef Ribeye Steak

(Servings: 4, Cooking Time: 50 minutes)

Ingredients:
- 2 pounds bone-in ribeye steak
- 2 tablespoons extra virgin olive oil
- Salt and black pepper to taste
- ½ cup rum

Directions for Cooking:
1) Place all ingredients in a Ziploc bag and allow to marinate in the fridge for at least 2 hours.
2) Preheat the air fryer at 390°F.
3) Place the grill pan accessory in the air fryer.
4) Grill for 25 minutes per piece.
5) Halfway through the cooking time, flip the meat for even grilling.

Nutrition information:
Calories: 394; Carbs: 0.1g; Protein: 48.9g; Fat: 21.5g

Oriental Grilled Family Steak

(Servings: 3, Cooking Time: 50 minutes)

Ingredients:
- 1/3 cup soy sauce
- 1/3 cup dry sherry
- 1 tablespoon brown sugar
- ½ teaspoon dry mustard
- 1 clove of garlic, minced
- 1 ½ pounds beef top round steak
- 2 green onions, chopped

Directions for Cooking:
1) Place all ingredients except for the green onions in a Ziploc bag and allow to marinate in the fridge for at least 2 hours.
2) Preheat the air fryer at 390°F.
3) Place the grill pan accessory in the air fryer. Add meat and cover top with foil.
4) Grill for 50 minutes.
5) Halfway through the cooking time, flip the meat for even grilling.
6) Meanwhile, pour the marinade into a saucepan and simmer for 10 minutes until the sauce thickens.
7) Baste the meat with the sauce and garnish with green onions before serving.

Nutrition information:
Calories: 170; Carbs: 3g; Protein: 28g; Fat: 5g

Tandoori Spiced Sirloin

(Servings: 3, Cooking Time: 25 minutes)

Ingredients:
- 1 ½ pounds boneless beef top loin steak
- ½ cup low-fat yogurt
- ¼ cup mint, chopped
- 3 tablespoons lemon juice
- 6 cloves of garlic, minced
- 2 teaspoons curry powder
- 2 teaspoons paprika
- Salt and pepper to taste

Directions for Cooking:

1) Place all ingredients except for the green onions in a Ziploc bag and allow to marinate in the fridge for at least 2 hours.
2) Preheat the air fryer at 390°F.
3) Place the grill pan accessory in the air fryer.
4) Grill for 25 to 30 minutes.
5) Flip the steaks halfway through the cooking time for even grilling.

Nutrition information:
Calories: 596; Carbs: 8.9g; Protein: 70.5g; Fat: 30.9g

Ribeye Steak with Peaches

(Servings: 2, Cooking Time: 45 minutes)

Ingredients:
- 1-pound T-bone steak
- 1 tablespoon paprika
- 2 teaspoons lemon pepper seasoning
- ¼ cup balsamic vinegar
- 1 cup peach puree
- Salt and pepper to taste
- 1 teaspoon thyme

Directions for Cooking:

1) Place all ingredients in a Ziploc bag and allow to marinate in the fridge for at least 2 hours.
2) Preheat the air fryer at 390°F.
3) Place the grill pan accessory in the air fryer.
4) Grill for 20 minutes and flip the meat halfway through the cooking time.

Nutrition information:
Calories: 570; Carbs: 35.7g; Protein: 47g; Fat: 26.5g

Kansas City Ribs

(Servings: 2, Cooking Time: 50 minutes)

Ingredients:

- 1-pound pork ribs, small
- 1 tablespoon brown sugar
- 1 teaspoon dry mustard
- ¼ teaspoon cayenne pepper
- 2 cloves of garlic
- 1 cup ketchup
- ¼ cup molasses
- ¼ cup apple cider vinegar
- 1 tablespoon Worcestershire sauce
- 1 tablespoon liquid smoke seasoning, hickory
- Salt and pepper to taste

Directions for Cooking:

1) Place all ingredients in a Ziploc bag and allow to marinate in the fridge for at least 2 hours.
2) Preheat the air fryer at 390°F.
3) Place the grill pan accessory in the air fryer.
4) Grill meat for 25 minutes per batch.
5) Flip the meat halfway through the cooking time.
6) Pour the marinade in a saucepan and allow to simmer until the sauce thickens.
7) Pour glaze over the meat before serving.

Nutrition information:
Calories: 634; Carbs: 32g; Protein: 32g; Fat: 42g

Grilled Steak Cubes with Charred Onions

(Servings: 3, Cooking Time: 40 minutes)

Ingredients:

- 1-pound boneless beef sirloin, cut into cubes
- 1 cup red onions, cut into wedges
- Salt and pepper to taste
- 1 tablespoon dry mustard
- 1 tablespoon olive oil

Directions for Cooking:

1) Preheat the air fryer at 390°F.
2) Place the grill pan accessory in the air fryer.
3) Toss all ingredients in a bowl and mix until everything is coated with the seasonings.
4) Place on the grill pan and cook for 40 minutes.
5) Halfway through the cooking time, give a stir to cook evenly.

Nutrition information:
Calories: 260; Carbs: 5.2g; Protein: 35.7g; Fat: 10.7g

Trip Tip Roast with Grilled Avocado

(Servings: 4, Cooking Time: 50 minutes)

Ingredients:
- 1 teaspoon onion powder
- 1 teaspoon garlic powder
- 1-pound beef tri-tip
- ½ cup red wine vinegar
- 3 tablespoons olive oil
- 3 avocadoes, seeded and sliced

Directions for Cooking:
1) In a Ziploc bag, place all ingredients except for the avocado slices.
2) Allow to marinate in the fridge for 2 hours.
3) Preheat the air fryer at 330°F.
4) Place the grill pan accessory in the air fryer.
5) Grill the avocado for 2 minutes while the beef is marinating. Set aside.
6) After two hours, grill the beef for 50 minutes. Flip the beef halfway through the cooking time.
7) Serve the beef with grilled avocadoes

Nutrition information:
Calories: 515; Carbs: 8g; Protein: 33g; Fat: 39g

Bourbon Grilled Beef

(Servings: 4, Cooking Time: 60 minutes)

Ingredients:
- 2 pounds beef steak, pounded
- ¼ cup bourbon
- ¼ cup barbecue sauce
- 1 tablespoon Worcestershire sauce
- Salt and pepper to taste

Directions for Cooking:
1) Place all ingredients in a Ziploc bag and allow to marinate in the fridge for at least 2 hours.
2) Preheat the air fryer at 390°F.
3) Place the grill pan accessory in the air fryer.
4) Place on the grill pan and cook for 20 minutes per batch.
5) Halfway through the cooking time, give a stir to cook evenly.
6) Meanwhile, pour the marinade on a saucepan and allow to simmer until the sauce thickens.
7) Serve beef with the bourbon sauce.

Nutrition information:
Calories: 346; Carbs: 9.8g; Protein: 48.2g; Fat: 12.6g

Paprika Beef Flank Steak

(Servings: 4, Cooking Time: 40 minutes)

Ingredients:

- 1 ¼ pounds beef flank steak, sliced thinly
- Salt and pepper to taste
- 3 tablespoons paprika powder
- 1 tablespoon cayenne pepper
- 1 tablespoon garlic powder
- 1 tablespoon onion powder
- 1 red bell pepper, julienned
- 1 yellow bell pepper, julienned
- 3 tablespoons olive oil

Directions for Cooking:

1) Preheat the air fryer at 390°F.
2) Place the grill pan accessory in the air fryer.
3) In a bowl, toss all ingredients to coat everything with the seasonings.
4) Place on the grill pan and cook for 40 minutes.
5) Make sure to stir every 10 minutes for even cooking.

Nutrition information:
Calories: 334; Carbs: 9.8g; Protein: 32.5g; Fat: 18.2g

Espresso-Rubbed Steak

(Servings: 3, Cooking Time: 50 minutes)

Ingredients:

- 2 teaspoons chili powder
- Salt and pepper to taste
- 1 teaspoon instant espresso powder
- ½ teaspoon garlic powder
- 1 ½ pounds beef flank steak
- 2 tablespoons olive oil

Directions for Cooking:

1) Preheat the air fryer at 390°F.
2) Place the grill pan accessory in the air fryer.
3) Make the dry rub by mixing the chili powder, salt, pepper, espresso powder, and garlic powder.
4) Rub all over the steak and brush with oil.
5) Place on the grill pan and cook for 40 minutes.
6) Halfway through the cooking time, flip the beef to cook evenly.

Nutrition information:
Calories: 249; Carbs: 4g; Protein: 20g; Fat: 17g

New York Beef Strips

(Servings: 4, Cooking Time: 50 minutes)

Ingredients:

- 4 boneless beef top loin steaks
- Salt and pepper to taste
- 2 tablespoons butter, softened
- 2 pounds crumbled blue cheese
- 2 tablespoons cream cheese
- 1 tablespoon pine nuts, toasted

Directions for Cooking:

1) Preheat the air fryer at 390°F.
2) Place the grill pan accessory in the air fryer.
3) Season the beef with salt and pepper. Brush all sides with butter.
4) Grill for 25 minutes per batch making sure to flip halfway through the cooking time.
5) Slice the beef and serve with blue cheese, cream cheese and pine nuts.

Nutrition information:
Calories: 682; Carbs: 1g; Protein: 75g; Fat: 42g

Perfect Yet Simple Grilled Steak

(Servings: 2, Cooking Time: 50 minutes)

Ingredients:

- 2 large ribeye strip steaks
- Salt and pepper to taste
- 1 teaspoon liquid smoke seasoning, hickory

Directions for Cooking:

1) Preheat the air fryer at 390°F.
2) Place the grill pan accessory in the air fryer.
3) Season the beef with salt, pepper, and liquid seasoning.
4) Grill for 25 minutes per batch.
5) Flip the meat halfway through the cooking time for even browning.

Nutrition information:
Calories: 476; Carbs: 7g; Protein: 49g; Fat: 28g

Smoked Beef Chuck

(Servings: 6, Cooking Time: 1 hour and 30 minutes)

Ingredients:

- 3 pounds beef chuck roll, scored with knife
- 2 ounces black peppercorns
- 3 tablespoons salt
- 2 tablespoons olive oil

Directions for Cooking:

1) Preheat the air fryer at 390°F.
2) Place the grill pan accessory in the air fryer.
3) Season the beef chuck roll with black peppercorns and salt.
4) Brush with olive oil and cover top with foil.
5) Grill for 1 hour and 30 minutes.
6) Flip the beef every 30 minutes for even grilling on all sides.

Nutrition information:
Calories: 360; Carbs: 1.4g; Protein: 46.7g; Fat: 18g

Sous Vide Smoked Brisket

(Servings: 6, Cooking Time: 1 hour)

Ingredients:

- 3 pounds flat-cut brisket
- ¼ teaspoon liquid smoke
- Salt and pepper to taste
- 1 cup dill pickles

Directions for Cooking:

1) Preheat the air fryer at 390°F.
2) Place the grill pan accessory in the air fryer.
3) Season the brisket with liquid smoke, salt, and pepper.
4) Place on the grill pan and cook for 30 minutes per batch.
5) Flip the meat halfway through cooking time for even grilling.
6) Serve with dill pickles.

Nutrition information:
Calories: 309; Carbs: 1.2g; Protein: 49g; Fat:12 g

Skirt Steak with Mojo Marinade

(Servings: 4, Cooking Time: 60 minutes)

Ingredients:
- 2 pounds skirt steak, trimmed from excess fat
- 2 tablespoons lime juice
- ¼ cup orange juice
- 2 tablespoons olive oil
- 4 cloves of garlic, minced
- 1 teaspoon ground cumin
- Salt and pepper to taste

Directions for Cooking:
1) Place all ingredients in a mixing bowl and allow to marinate in the fridge for at least 2 hours
2) Preheat the air fryer at 390°F.
3) Place the grill pan accessory in the air fryer.
4) Grill for 15 minutes per batch and flip the beef every 8 minutes for even grilling.
5) Meanwhile, pour the marinade on a saucepan and allow to simmer for 10 minutes or until the sauce thickens.
6) Slice the beef and pour over the sauce.

Nutrition information:
Calories: 568; Carbs: 4.7g; Protein: 59.1g; Fat: 34.7g

Dijon-Marinated Skirt Steak

(Servings: 2, Cooking Time: 40 minutes)

Ingredients:
- ¼ cup Dijon mustard
- 1-pound skirt steak, trimmed
- 2 tablespoons champagne vinegar
- 1 tablespoon rosemary leaves
- Salt and pepper to taste

Directions for Cooking:
1) Place all ingredients in a Ziploc bag and marinate in the fridge for 2 hours.
2) Preheat the air fryer at 390°F.
3) Place the grill pan accessory in the air fryer.
4) Grill the skirt steak for 20 minutes per batch.
5) Flip the beef halfway through the cooking time.

Nutrition information:
Calories: 516; Carbs: 4.2g; Protein: 60.9g; Fat: 28.4g

Grilled Carne Asada Steak

(Servings: 2, Cooking Time: 50 minutes)

Ingredients:
- 2 slices skirt steak
- 1 dried ancho chilies, chopped
- 1 chipotle pepper, chopped
- 2 tablespoons of fresh lemon juice
- 2 tablespoons olive oil
- 3 cloves of garlic, minced
- 1 tablespoons soy sauce
- 2 tablespoons Asian fish sauce
- 1 tablespoon cumin
- 1 tablespoon coriander seeds
- 2 tablespoons brown sugar

Directions for Cooking:
1) Place all ingredients in a Ziploc bag and marinate in the fridge for 2 hours.
2) Preheat the air fryer at 390°F.
3) Place the grill pan accessory in the air fryer.
4) Grill the skirt steak for 20 minutes.
5) Flip the steak every 10 minutes for even grilling.

Nutrition information:
Calories: 697; Carbs: 10.2g; Protein:62.7 g; Fat: 45g

Chimichurri-Style Steak

(Servings: 6, Cooking Time: 60 minutes)

Ingredients:
- 3 pounds steak
- Salt and pepper to taste
- 1 cup commercial chimichurri

Directions for Cooking:
1) Place all ingredients in a Ziploc bag and marinate in the fridge for 2 hours.
2) Preheat the air fryer at 390°F.
3) Place the grill pan accessory in the air fryer.
4) Grill the skirt steak for 20 minutes per batch.
5) Flip the steak every 10 minutes for even grilling.

Nutrition information:
Calories: 507; Carbs: 2.8g; Protein: 63g; Fat: 27g

Strip Steak with Cucumber Yogurt Sauce

(Servings: 2, Cooking Time: 50 minutes)

Ingredients:
- 2 New York strip steaks
- Salt and pepper to taste
- 3 tablespoons olive oil
- 1 cucumber, seeded and chopped
- 1 cup Greek yogurt
- ½ cup parsley, chopped

Directions for Cooking:
1) Preheat the air fryer at 390°F.
2) Place the grill pan accessory in the air fryer.
3) Season the strip steaks with salt and pepper. Drizzle with oil.
4) Grill the steak for 20 minutes per batch and make sure to flip the meat every 10 minutes for even grilling.
5) Meanwhile, combine the cucumber, yogurt, and parsley.
6) Serve the beef with the cucumber yogurt.

Nutrition information:
Calories: 460; Carbs: 5.2g; Protein: 50.8g; Fat: 26.3g

Grilled BBQ Sausages

(Servings: 3, Cooking Time: 30 minutes)

Ingredients:
- 6 sausage links
- ½ cup prepared BBQ sauce

for Cooking:
1) Preheat the air fryer at 390°F.
2) Place the grill pan accessory in the air fryer.
3) Place the sausage links and grill for 30 minutes.
4) Flip halfway through the cooking time.
5) Before serving brush with prepared BBQ sauce.

Nutrition information:
Calories: 265; Carbs: 6.4g; Protein: 27.7g; Fat: 14.2g

Medium Rare Simple Salt and Pepper Steak

(Servings: 3, Cooking Time: 30 minutes)

Ingredients:
- 1 ½ pounds skirt steak
- Salt and pepper to taste

Directions for Cooking:
1) Preheat the air fryer at 390°F.
2) Place the grill pan accessory in the air fryer.
3) Season the skirt steak with salt and pepper.
4) Place on the grill pan and cook for 15 minutes per batch.
5) Flip the meat halfway through the cooking time.

Nutrition information:
Calories: 469; Carbs: 1g; Protein: 60g; Fat: 25g

Pounded Flank Steak with Tomato Salsa

(Servings: 4, Cooking Time: 40 minutes)

Ingredients:
- 1 ½ pounds flank steak, pounded
- Salt and pepper to taste
- 2 cups chopped tomatoes
- ¼ cup chopped cilantro
- 1 red onion, chopped
- 1 teaspoon coriander powder

Directions for Cooking:
1) Preheat the air fryer at 390°F.
2) Place the grill pan accessory in the air fryer.
3) Season the flank steak with salt and pepper.
4) Grill for 20 minutes per batch and make sure to flip the beef halfway through the cooking time.
5) Meanwhile, prepare the salsa by mixing in a bowl the tomatoes, cilantro, onions, and coriander. Season with more salt and pepper to taste.

Nutrition information:
Calories: 243; Carbs: 4g; Protein: 37.4g; Fat: 8.6g

Strip Steak with Japanese Dipping Sauce

(Servings: 2, Cooking Time: 40 minutes)

Ingredients:
- 2 strip steaks
- Salt and pepper to taste
- 1 tablespoon olive oil
- ½ cup soy sauce
- ½ cup rice wine vinegar
- ¼ cup grated daikon radish

Directions for Cooking:
1) Preheat the air fryer at 390°F.
2) Place the grill pan accessory in the air fryer.
3) Season the steak with salt and pepper.
4) Brush with oil.
5) Grill for 20 minutes per piece and make sure to flip the beef halfway through the cooking time
6) Prepare the dipping sauce by combining the soy sauce and vinegar.
7) Serve the steak with the sauce and daikon radish.

Nutrition information:
Calories: 510; Carbs:19.3 g; Protein: 54g; Fat: 24g

Chi Spacca's Bistecca

(Servings: 4, Cooking Time: 45 minutes)

Ingredients:
- 2 pounds bone-in rib eye steak
- Salt and pepper to taste
- 1 packet Italian herb mix
- 1 tablespoon olive oil

Directions for Cooking:
1) Preheat the air fryer at 390°F.
2) Place the grill pan accessory in the air fryer.
3) Season the steak with salt, pepper, Italian herb mix, and olive oil. Cover top with foil.
4) Grill for 45 minutes and flip the steak halfway through the cooking time.

Nutrition information:
Calories: 481; Carbs:1.1 g; Protein: 50.9g; Fat: 30.3g

Grilled Steak with Parsley Salad

(Servings: 4, Cooking Time: 45 minutes)

Ingredients:
- 1 ½ pounds flatiron steak
- 3 tablespoons olive oil
- Salt and pepper to taste
- 2 cups parsley leaves
- ½ cup parmesan cheese, grated
- 1 tablespoon fresh lemon juice

Directions for Cooking:
1) Preheat the air fryer at 390°F.
2) Place the grill pan accessory in the air fryer.
3) Mix together the steak, oil, salt and pepper.
4) Grill for 15 minutes per batch and make sure to flip the meat halfway through the cooking time.
5) Meanwhile, prepare the salad by combining in a bowl the parsley leaves, parmesan cheese and lemon juice. Season with salt and pepper.

Nutrition information:
Calories: 595; Carbs: 4.9g; Protein: 47g; Fat: 43g

Korean Grilled Skirt Steak

(Servings: 1, Cooking Time: 30 minutes)

Ingredients:
- 3 tablespoons gochujang sauce
- 3 tablespoons olive oil
- 3 tablespoons rice vinegar
- Salt and pepper to taste
- 1 skirt steak, halved

Directions for Cooking:
1) Preheat the air fryer at 390°F.
2) Place the grill pan accessory in the air fryer.
3) Rub all spices and seasonings on the skirt steak.
4) Place on the grill and cook for 15 minutes per batch.
5) Flip the steak halfway through the cooking time.
6) Serve with more gochujang or kimchi.

Nutrition information:
Calories: 467; Carbs: 8.3g; Protein:9.3 g; Fat: 44g

Onion Marinated Skirt Steak

(Servings: 3, Cooking Time: 45 minutes)

Ingredients:
- 1 large red onion, grated or pureed
- 2 tablespoons brown sugar
- 1 tablespoon vinegar
- 1 ½ pounds skirt steak
- Salt and pepper to taste

Directions for Cooking:
1) Place all ingredients in a Ziploc bag and allow to marinate in the fridge for at least 2 hours.
2) Preheat the air fryer at 390°F.
3) Place the grill pan accessory in the air fryer.
4) Grill for 15 minutes per batch.
5) Flip every 8 minutes for even grilling.

Nutrition information:
Calories: 512; Carbs: 6g; Protein: 60.1g; Fat: 27.5g

Grilled Beef Steak with Herby Marinade

(Servings: 2, Cooking Time: 40 minutes)

Ingredients:
- 2 porterhouse steaks
- Salt and pepper to taste
- ¼ cup fish sauce
- 2 tablespoons marjoram
- 2 tablespoons thyme
- 2 tablespoons sage

Directions for Cooking:
1) Place all ingredients in a Ziploc bag and allow to marinate in the fridge for at least 2 hours.
2) Preheat the air fryer at 390°F.
3) Place the grill pan accessory in the air fryer.
4) Grill for 20 minutes per batch.
5) Flip every 10 minutes for even grilling.

Nutrition information:
Calories: 1189; Carbs: 6.3g; Protein: 112.5g; Fat: 79.3g

Breakfast Casserole Recipes

Mushroom & Ham Omelet

(Servings: 2, Cooking Time: 8 minutes)

Ingredients:

- 2 eggs
- 1/4 cup milk
- Pinch of salt
- ½ cup ham, diced
- 2 mushrooms, sliced
- 1 stalk green onions, chopped
- 1 teaspoon McCormick Good Morning Breakfast Seasoning – Garden Herb
- 1/4 cup shredded cheese

Directions for Cooking:

1) Lightly grease baking pan of air fryer with cooking spray. Spread ham on bottom, followed by mushrooms and cheese.
2) In a bowl, whisk eggs well. Season with salt and McCormick. Add milk and whisk well. Pour over mixture in air fryer pan.
3) For 8 minutes, cook on 330°F.
4) Sprinkle green onions and let it rest for a minute or two.
5) Serve and enjoy.

Nutrition Information:
Calories: 209; Carbs: 3.5g; Protein: 21.5g; Fat: 12.1g

Breakfast Pastry Pie

(Servings: 3, Cooking Time: 18 minutes)

Ingredients:

- one box puff pastry sheets
- 5 eggs
- 1/2 cup sausage crumbles, cooked
- 1/2 cup bacon, cooked
- 1/2 cup cheddar cheese, shredded

Directions for Cooking:

1) Scramble the eggs and cook.
2) Lightly grease baking pan of air fryer with cooking spray.
3) Evenly spread half of the puff sheets on bottom of pan.
4) Spread eggs, cooked sausage, crumbled bacon, and cheddar cheese.
5) Top with remaining puff pastry and gently push down with a fork.
6) Cover top of baking pan with foil.
7) For 8 minutes, cook on 330°F. Remove foil and continue cooking for another 5 minutes or until tops of puff pastry is golden brown.
8) Serve and enjoy.

Nutrition Information:
Calories: 355; Carbs: 9.4g; Protein: 18.6g; Fat: 26.9g

Turkey & Greens Frittata

(Servings: 2, Cooking Time: 20 minutes)

Ingredients:
- 1/2-pound breakfast turkey sausage
- 2-oz hash browns frozen, shredded
- 5-oz pre-cut mixed greens (kale, spinach, swiss chard or whatever else you can find)
- ½ cup cheddar cheese finely grated, extra sharp
- 3 eggs
- ½ cup milk skimmed
- 1/4 tsp cayenne pepper
- 1/4 tsp garlic powder
- salt to taste
- green onions for serving

Directions for Cooking:
1) Lightly grease baking pan of air fryer with cooking spray and add turkey sausage.
2) For 5 minutes, cook on 360°F. Open halfway and break up sausage.
3) Meanwhile in a bowl whisk well eggs. Season with salt, cayenned, and garlic powder. Add milk and whisk well.
4) Remove basket and break sausage some more. Stir in frozen hash brown and continue cooking for 5 minutes.
5) Toss in mixed greens and cheese.
6) Pour egg mixture over hash brown mixture.
7) Cook for another 10 minutes until eggs are set to desired doneness.
8) Sprinkle green onions and let it rest for a minute.
9) Serve and enjoy.

Nutrition Information:
Calories: 616; Carbs: 39.8g; Protein: 39.7g; Fat: 33.1g

Low-Calorie Frittata

(Servings: 2, Cooking Time: 15 minutes)

Ingredients:
- 1 cup egg whites
- 2 Tbsp skim milk
- ¼ cup sliced tomato
- ¼ cup sliced mushrooms
- 2 Tbsp chopped fresh chives
- Salt and Black pepper, to taste

Directions for Cooking:
1) Lightly grease baking pan of air fryer with cooking spray.
2) Spread mushrooms and tomato on bottom of pan.
3) In a bowl, whisk well egg whites, milk, chives, pepper and salt. Pour into baking pan.
4) For 15 minutes, cook on 330°F.
5) Remove basket and let it sit for a minute.
6) Serve and enjoy.

Nutrition Information:
Calories: 231; Carbs: 35.1g; Protein: 21.5g; Fat: 0.5g

Cheesy Tomato-Broccoli Quiche

(Servings: 2, Cooking Time: 24 minutes)

Ingredients:

- 1 small Broccoli, cut into florets
- 1 Large Carrot, peeled and diced
- 1 Large Tomato, chopped
- ½ cup Cheddar Cheese grated
- 2 tbsp Feta Cheese
- ½ cup Whole Milk
- 2 Large Eggs
- 1 Tsp Parsley
- 1 Tsp Thyme
- Salt & Pepper

Directions for Cooking:

1) Lightly grease baking pan of air fryer with cooking spray.
2) Spread carrots, broccoli, and tomato in baking pan.
3) For 10 minutes, cook on 330°F.
4) Meanwhile, in a medium bowl whisk well eggs and milk. Season generously with pepper and salt. Whisk in parsley and thyme.
5) Remove basket and toss the mixture a bit. Sprinkle cheddar cheese. Pour egg mixture over vegetables and cheese.
6) Cook for another 12 minutes or until set to desired doneness.
7) Sprinkle feta cheese and let it sit for 2 minutes.
8) Serve and enjoy.

Nutrition Information:
Calories: 363; Carbs: 23.7g; Protein: 21.0g; Fat: 20.4g

Easy Italian Frittata

(Servings: 1, Cooking Time: 16 minutes)

Ingredients:

- 3 eggs
- ½ Italian sausage, sliced into ¼-inch thick
- 4 cherry tomatoes (in half)
- 1 tablespoon olive oil
- Chopped parsley
- Grano Padano cheese (or parmesan)
- Salt/Pepper

Directions for Cooking:

1) Lightly grease baking pan of air fryer with cooking spray.
2) Add Italian sausage and cook for 5 minutes at 360°F.
3) Add olive oil and cherry tomatoes. Cook for another 6 minutes.
4) Meanwhile, whisk well eggs, parsley, cheese, salt, and pepper in a bowl.
5) Remove basket and toss the mixture a bit. Pour eggs over mixture.
6) Cook for another 5 minutes.
7) Serve and enjoy.

Nutrition Information:
Calories: 295; Carbs: 7.8g; Protein: 14.4g; Fat: 22.9g

Chili-Hot Brekky Casserole

(Servings: 4, Cooking Time: 27 minutes)

Ingredients:
- 1 cup sage sausage
- 6 strips of bacon
- 1 cup Mexican blend shredded cheese
- 2 cups freshly grated white Yukon gold potatoes
- 1 cup freshly grated sweet potato
- 4 jumbo eggs, boiled, peeled and mashed
- 1 stalk scallions, diced
- 1 large Anaheim chili peppers, chopped
- Salt to taste

Directions for Cooking:
1) Place bacon on baking pan of air fryer.
2) For 5 minutes, cook on 390°F. Remove bacon.
3) Add sausage and cook for 5 minutes at same temperature. Halfway through, remove basket and crumble sausage and stir. Continue cooking.
4) Meanwhile crumble bacon.
5) Remove basket and toss the mixture a bit. Stir in bacon, shredded Yukon potatoes and sweet potatoes. Return to air fryer and cook for 4 minutes.
6) Meanwhile, in a medium bowl, whisk well eggs, chili peppers, and scallions. Season generously with salt.
7) Remove basket, toss well mixture, sprinkle cheese evenly, and pour eggs.
8) Cook for another 13 minutes at 330°F.
9) Serve and enjoy.

Nutrition Information:
Calories: 295; Carbs: 19.1g; Protein: 17.7g; Fat: 17.3g

Sausage & Hash Brown Egg Casserole

(Servings: 4, Cooking Time: 20 minutes)

Ingredients:
- 1 Lb Hash Browns
- 1 Lb Ground Breakfast Sausage
- 1 Green Bell Pepper Diced
- 1 Red Bell Pepper Diced
- 1 Yellow Bell Pepper Diced
- 1/4 Cup Sweet Onion Diced
- 4 Eggs

Directions for Cooking:
1) Lightly grease baking pan of air fryer with cooking spray and place hash browns, spreading evenly.
2) Spread uncooked sausage, followed by peppers and onion.
3) For 10 minutes, cook on 360°F.
4) Remove basket and toss the mixture a bit.
5) Crack eggs on top, season lightly with pepper and salt.
6) Cook for another 10 minutes.
7) Serve and enjoy.

Nutrition Information:
Calories: 510; Carbs: 37.4g; Protein: 31.2g; Fat: 26.1g

Biscuit, Sausage 'n Egg Layer Casserole

(Servings: 4, Cooking Time: 30 minutes)

Ingredients:
- 1 can of Pillsbury Grand Biscuits
- 6 eggs
- ½ cup of milk
- 1½ cups of shredded cheddar cheese
- ½-lb breakfast sausage, cut into ½-inch lengths

Directions for Cooking:
1) Lightly grease baking pan of air fryer with cooking spray. Add sliced sausages and cook for 8 minutes at 330°F. Give a good stir halfway through cooking time.
2) Once done cooking remove sausages and discard any oil.
3) Slice biscuits evenly and layer on bottom of pan. For 5 minutes, cook on 330°F.
4) Meanwhile, in a bowl whisk egg well. Stir in milk.
5) Once dough is done cooking, layer sausages on top, then sprinkle cheese, and then pour eggs over.
6) Cook for another 17 minutes or until eggs are set.
7) Serve and enjoy.

Nutrition Information:
Calories: 439; Carbs: 7.0g; Protein: 28.7g; Fat: 32.8g

Creamy Broccoli Egg Scramble

(Servings: 2, Cooking Time: 20 minutes)

Ingredients:
- 3 Eggs
- 1/2 cup Broccoli small florets
- 1/2 cup Bell Pepper cut into small pieces
- 2 tbsp Cream
- 2 tbsp Parmesan Cheese grated or cheddar cheese
- Salt to taste
- Black Pepper to taste

Directions for Cooking:
1) Lightly grease baking pan of air fryer with cooking spray. Spread broccoli florets and bell pepper on bottom and for 7 minutes, cook on 360°F.
2) Meanwhile, in a bowl whisk eggs. Stir in cream. Season with pepper and salt.
3) Remove basket and toss the mixture a bit. Pour egg mixture over.
4) Cook for another 10 minutes.
5) Sprinkle cheese and let it rest for 3 minutes.
6) Serve and enjoy.

Nutrition Information:
Calories: 273; Carbs: 5.6g; Protein: 16.1g; Fat: 20.6g

Easy Brekky Frittata

(Servings: 2, Cooking Time: 20 minutes)

Ingredients:
- 1/4-lb breakfast sausage
- 4 eggs
- ½ cup shredded Cheddar-Monterey Jack cheese blend
- 2 tbsp red bell pepper, diced
- 1 green onion, chopped
- 1 pinch cayenne pepper

Directions for Cooking:
1) Lightly grease baking pan of air fryer with cooking spray.
2) Add sausage and for 8 minutes, cook on 390°F. Halfway through, crumble sausage and stir well.
3) Meanwhile, whisk eggs in a bowl and stir in bell pepper, green onion, and cayenne.
4) Remove basket and toss the mixture a bit. Evenly spread cheese and pour eggs on top.
5) Cook for another 12 minutes at 330°F or until eggs are set to desired doneness.
6) Serve and enjoy.

Nutrition Information:
Calories: 383; Carbs: 2.9g; Protein: 31.2g; Fat: 27.4g

Vegan Approved Brekky Casserole

(Servings: 2, Cooking Time: 30 minutes)

Ingredients:
- 1 tsp olive oil
- 1 small onion, diced
- 1 tsp garlic, minced
- 1 large carrot, peeled and chopped
- 2 small celery stalks, chopped
- ½ cup diced bell pepper
- ½ cup shiitake mushrooms, diced
- 1 tsp dried oregano
- ½ tsp salt
- ½ tsp black pepper
- ½ tsp dill
- ½ tsp red pepper flakes
- ½ tsp ground cumin
- 7-oz extra firm tofu, drained
- 2 tbsp yeast
- 2 tbsp soy yogurt, plain
- 2 tbsp water
- 1 tbsp lemon juice
- ½ cup cooked quinoa

Directions for Cooking:
1) Lightly grease baking pan of air fryer with olive oil. Add garlic and onion.
2) For 2 minutes, cook on 390°F.
3) Remove basket, stir in bell pepper, celery, and carrots. Cook for 3 minutes.
4) Remove basket, give a quick stir. Then add cumin, red pepper flakes, dill, pepper, salt, oregano, and mushrooms. Mix well. Cook for 5 minutes. Mixing halfway through cooking time.
5) Meanwhile, in a food processor pulse lemon juice, water, yogurt, yeast, and tofu. Process until creamy.
6) Transfer creamy tofu mixture into air fryer basket. Add quinoa and give a good stir.
7) Cook for another 15 minutes at 330°F or until golden brown.
8) Let it rest for 5 minutes.
9) Serve and enjoy.

Nutrition Information:
Calories: 280; Carbs: 28.6g; Protein: 18.5g; Fat: 10.1g

Loaded Breakfast Hash Browns

(Servings: 4, Cooking Time: 20 minutes)

Ingredients:
- 3 russet potatoes, peeled and grated
- 1/4 cup chopped green peppers
- 1/4 cup chopped red peppers
- 1/4 cup chopped onions
- 2 garlic cloves chopped
- 1 teaspoon paprika
- salt and pepper to taste
- 1 teaspoon canola oil
- 1 teaspoon olive oil

Directions for Cooking:
1) For 20 minutes, soak the grated potatoes in a bowl of cold water to make it crunchy and remove the starch. Then drain well and completely dry with paper towels.
2) Lightly grease baking pan of air fryer with cooking spray.
3) Add grated potatoes in air fryer. Season with garlic, paprika, salt, and pepper. Add canola and olive oil. Toss well to coat.
4) For 10 minutes, cook on 390°F.
5) Remove basket and toss the mixture a bit. Stir in green and red peppers, and onions.
6) Cook for another 10 minutes.
7) Serve and enjoy.

Nutrition Information:
Calories: 263; Carbs: 53.2g; Protein: 6.5g; Fat: 2.6g

Breakfast Biscuits, Eggs 'n Bacon

(Servings: 4, Cooking Time: 28 minutes)

Ingredients:
- 5 eggs
- ¼ cup milk
- ½ of 16-ounces refrigerated breakfast biscuits
- 4 scallions, chopped
- 1 cup shredded extra sharp cheddar cheese
- 8 slices cooked center cut bacon

Directions for Cooking:
1) In baking pan cook bacon for 8 minutes at 360°F or until crisped. Remove bacon and discard excess fat.
2) Evenly spread biscuits on bottom. For 5 minutes, cook at same temperature.
3) Meanwhile, whisk eggs, milk, and scallions.
4) Remove basket, evenly layer bacon on top of biscuit, sprinkle cheese on top, and pour eggs.
5) Cook for another 15 minutes or until eggs are set.
6) Serve and enjoy.

Nutrition Information:
Calories: 241; Carbs: 4.3g; Protein: 22.6g; Fat: 23.7g

Hash Brown, Sausage 'n Cauliflower Bake

(Servings: 3, Cooking Time: 27 minutes)

Ingredients:
- 1-pound hot pork sausage, diced
- 1/2 (30 ounce) package frozen hash brown potatoes, thawed
- ½ cup shredded Cheddar cheese
- 1 teaspoons salt
- 1/2 teaspoon ground black pepper
- ½ cup milk
- 1 small cauliflower, riced
- 3 large eggs

Directions for Cooking:
1) Lightly grease baking pan of air fryer with cooking spray. And add diced sausage and cook for 10 minutes on 360ºF.
2) Add hash brown and riced cauliflower. Cook for another 5 minutes.
3) Meanwhile, whisk well eggs, salt, pepper, and milk.
4) Remove basket and toss the mixture a bit. Evenly spread cheese and pour eggs.
5) Cook for another 12 minutes or until set
6) Serve and enjoy.

Nutrition Information:
Calories: 612; Carbs: 33.4g; Protein: 49.2g; Fat: 44.6g

Cauliflower-Broccoli Egg Bake

(Servings: 3, Cooking Time: 20 minutes)

Ingredients:
- 1/2-pound hot pork sausage, diced
- ½ cup shredded Cheddar cheese
- 1 teaspoons salt
- 1/2 teaspoon ground black pepper
- ½ cup milk
- 1 cup cauliflower, riced
- 1 cup broccoli, cut into little bits or riced
- 3 large eggs

Directions for Cooking:
1) Lightly grease baking pan of air fryer with cooking spray. And cook pork sausage for 5 minutes at 360ºF.
2) Remove basket and toss the mixture a bit. Stir in riced cauliflower and broccoli. Cook for another 5 minutes.
3) Meanwhile, whisk well eggs, salt, pepper, and milk. Stir in cheese.
4) Remove basket and pour in egg mixture.
5) Cook for another 10 minutes.
6) Serve and enjoy.

Nutrition Information:
Calories: 434; Carbs: 6.5g; Protein: 27.3g; Fat: 33.2g

Raisin 'n Apple French Toast

(Servings: 6, Cooking Time: 40 minutes)

Ingredients:
- ½-lb loaf cinnamon raisin bread, cubed
- 4-oz cream cheese, diced
- ½ cup diced peeled apples
- 4 eggs
- 1 ¼ cups half-and-half cream
- 3 tbsp butter, melted
- 2 tbsp maple syrup

Directions for Cooking:
1) Lightly grease baking pan of air fryer with cooking spray.
2) Evenly spread half of the bread on bottom of pan. Sprinkle evenly the cream cheese and apples. Add remaining bread on top.
3) In a large bowl, whisk well eggs, cream, butter, and maple syrup. Pour over bread mixture.
4) Cover air fryer baking pan with plastic wrap and refrigerate for two hours.
5) Preheat air fryer to 325°F.
6) Cook for 40 minutes.
7) Serve and enjoy while warm.

Nutrition Information:
Calories: 362; Carbs: 28.3g; Protein: 10.1g; Fat: 23.1g

Overnight French Toast with Blueberries

(Servings: 5, Cooking Time: 45 minutes)

Ingredients:
- 6 slices day-old bread, cut into 1-inch cubes
- 1 (8 ounce) package cream cheese, cut into 1-inch cubes
- 1 cup fresh blueberries, divided
- 6 eggs, beaten
- 1 cup milk
- 1/2 teaspoon vanilla extract
- 2 tablespoons and 2 teaspoons maple syrup
- 1/2 cup white sugar
- 1 tablespoon cornstarch
- 1/2 cup water
- 1-1/2 teaspoons butter

Directions for Cooking:
1) Lightly grease baking pan of air fryer with cooking spray.
2) Evenly spread half of the bread on bottom of pan. Sprinkle evenly the cream cheese and ½ cup blueberries. Add remaining bread on top.
3) In a large bowl, whisk well eggs, milk, syrup, and vanilla extract. Pour over bread mixture.
4) Cover air fryer baking pan with foil and refrigerate overnight.
5) Preheat air fryer to 330°F.
6) Cook for 25 minutes covered in foil, remove foil and cook for another 20 minutes or until middle is set.
7) Meanwhile, make the sauce by mixing cornstarch, water, and sugar in a saucepan and bring to a boil. Stir in remaining blueberries and simmer until thickened and blueberries have burst.
8) Serve and enjoy with blueberry syrup.

Nutrition Information:
Calories: 492; Carbs: 51.9g; Protein: 15.1g; Fat: 24.8g

Eggs Benedict in an Overnight Casserole

(Servings: 5, Cooking Time: 40 minutes)

Ingredients:

- 4 large eggs
- 1 cup milk
- 1 stalk green onions, chopped
- ½ tsp onion powder
- 1/2 teaspoon salt
- 6-ounces Canadian bacon, cut into 1/2-inch dice
- 3 English muffins, cut into 1/2-inch dice
- 1/4 teaspoon paprika
- 1/2 (.9 ounce) package hollandaise sauce mix
- 1/2 cup milk
- 2 tablespoons margarine

Directions for Cooking:

1) Lightly grease baking pan of air fryer with cooking spray.
2) Place half of the bacon on bottom of pan, evenly spread died English muffins on top. Evenly spread remaining bacon on top.
3) In a large bowl, whisk well eggs, 1 cup milk, green onions, onion powder, and salt. Pour over English muffin mixture. Sprinkle top with paprika. Cover with foil and refrigerate overnight.
4) Preheat air fryer to 390°F.
5) Cook in air fryer covered in foil for 25 minutes. Remove foil and continue cooking for another 15 minutes or until set.
6) Meanwhile, make the hollandaise sauce by melting margarine in a sauce pan. Mix remaining milk and hollandaise sauce in a small bowl and whisk into melted margarine. Simmer until thickened while continuously stirring.
7) Serve and enjoy with sauce.

Nutrition Information:
Calories: 282; Carbs: 21.2g; Protein: 17.5g; Fat: 14.1g

Egg-Substitute 'n Bacon Casserole

(Servings: 4. Cooking Time: 35 minutes)

Ingredients:

- 4 frozen hash brown patties
- 1 (6 ounce) package Canadian bacon, quartered
- 2 cups shredded Cheddar-Monterey Jack cheese blend
- 3/4 cup and 2 tablespoons egg substitute (such as Egg Beaters® Southwestern Style)
- 1/2 cup 2% milk
- 1/4 teaspoon salt
- 1/4 teaspoon ground mustard

Directions for Cooking:

1) Lightly grease baking pan of air fryer with cooking spray.
2) Evenly spread hash brown patties on bottom of pan. Top evenly with bacon and then followed by cheese.
3) In a bowl, whisk well mustard, salt, milk, and egg substitute. Pour over bacon mixture.
4) Cover air fryer baking pan with foil.
5) Preheat air fryer to 330°F.
6) Cook for another 20 minutes, remove foil and continue cooking for another 15 minutes or until eggs are set.
7) Serve and enjoy.

Nutrition Information:
Calories: 459; Carbs: 21.0g; Protein: 29.4g; Fat: 28.5g

Country style Brekky Casserole

(Servings: 4, Cooking Time: 45 minutes)

Ingredients:
- 8-ounce bulk breakfast sausage
- 1 stalk green onion, chopped
- 8-ounce package hash brown potatoes
- 1 cup shredded Cheddar cheese
- 3 eggs, lightly beaten
- 1/2 cup milk
- 1/2 (2.64-ounce) package country gravy mix
- A dash of paprika or to taste (optional)

Directions for Cooking:
1) Lightly grease baking pan of air fryer with cooking spray.
2) For 10 minutes, cook sausage and crumble at 360°F. Halfway through cooking time, open air fryer and continue crumbling sausage.
3) Once done cooking remove excess oil.
4) Stir in green onions and evenly spread crumbled sausage. Spread hash brown on top and sprinkle evenly with cheese.
5) In a bowl, whisk well gravy, milk, and eggs until smooth. Pour over cheese mixture. Sprinkle top with paprika.
6) Cover pan with foil.
7) Cook for 20 minutes, remove foil and cook for another 10 minutes.
8) Let it stand for 5 minutes.
9) Serve and enjoy.

Nutrition Information:
Calories: 406; Carbs: 13.3g; Protein: 21.7g; Fat: 29.5g

Amish Style Brekky Casserole

(Servings: 6, Cooking Time: 45 minutes)

Ingredients:
- 1/2-pound sliced bacon, diced
- 1/2 sweet onion, chopped
- 2 cups frozen shredded hash brown potatoes, thawed
- 5 medium eggs, lightly beaten
- 1 cup shredded Cheddar cheese
- 3/4 cup small curd cottage cheese
- 1/2 cup and 2 tablespoons shredded Swiss cheese

Directions for Cooking:
1) Lightly grease baking pan of air fryer with cooking spray.
2) For 10 minutes, cook on 330°F the onion and bacon. Discard excess fat.
3) Meanwhile, in a bowl, whisk well Swiss cheese, cottage cheese, cheddar cheese, eggs, and potatoes. Pour into pan of cooked bacon and mix well.
4) Cook for another 25 minutes.
5) Let it stand in air fryer for another 10 minutes.
6) Serve and enjoy.

Nutrition Information:
Calories: 341; Carbs: 12.1g; Protein: 21.7g; Fat: 22.8g

Baked Cornbread and Eggs

(Servings: 3, Cooking Time: 45 minutes)

Ingredients:
- 1/2 cup chopped onion
- 1 stalk celery, diced
- 2 cups diced cooked ham
- 1/2 (14.5 ounce) can chicken broth
- 1/4 cup water
- 1/4 cup butter
- 1/2 (14-ounce) package seasoned cornbread stuffing mix
- 3 eggs
- 3/4 cup shredded Cheddar cheese
- 1/4 teaspoon paprika, for garnish

Directions for Cooking:
1) Lightly grease baking pan of air fryer with cooking spray. Add celery and onions.
2) For 5 minutes, cook on 360°F. Open and stir in ham. Cook for another 5 minutes.
3) Open and stir in butter, water, and chicken broth. Mix well and continue cooking for another 5 minutes.
4) Toss in stuffing mix and toss well to coat. Cover pan with foil.
5) Cook for another 15 minutes.
6) Remove foil and make 3 indentation in the stuffing to hold an egg. Break an egg in each hole.
7) Cook uncovered for another 10 minutes or until egg is cooked to desired doneness.
8) Sprinkle with cheese and paprika. Let it stand in air fryer for another 5 minutes.
9) Serve and enjoy.

Nutrition Information:
Calories: 847; Carbs: 54.4g; Protein: 37.5g; Fat: 53.2g

Feta and Spinach Brekky Pie

(Servings: 3, Cooking Time: 30 minutes)

Ingredients:
- 1 1/2 teaspoons butter
- 1/2-pound fresh spinach
- 6 eggs
- salt and freshly ground black pepper to taste
- 1/2 pinch cayenne pepper
- 3 slices bacon, chopped
- 1/4 onion, diced
- 1/2 pinch salt
- 1-1/2 ounces crumbled feta cheese

Directions for Cooking:
1) Lightly grease baking pan of air fryer with butter. Add spinach and for 2 minutes, cook on 360°F.
2) Drain well the spinach and squeeze dry. Chop and set aside.
3) Add bacon in air fryer pan and cook for 6 minutes or until crisped. Discard excess fat.
4) Stir in onion and season with salt. Cook for another 5 minutes. Stir in chopped spinach and cook for another 5 minutes to heat through.
5) Meanwhile, in a bowl whisk well eggs, cayenne pepper, black pepper, and salt.
6) Remove basket, evenly spread mixture in pan, and pour in eggs. Sprinkle feta cheese on top.
7) Cook for another 15 minutes, until eggs are cooked to desired doneness.
8) Serve and enjoy.

Nutrition Information:
Calories: 273; Carbs: 5.1g; Protein: 20.3g; Fat: 19.0g

Cheesy-Bacon Casserole

(Servings: 6, Cooking Time: 50 minutes)

Ingredients:
- 4 slices bread, crusts removed
- 1 1/2 cups skim milk
- 1 cup egg substitute (such as Egg Beaters®)
- 1 tablespoon chopped fresh chives
- 6 slices cooked bacon, crumbled
- 1 cup Cheddar cheese

Directions for Cooking:
1) Cook bacon in baking pan of air fryer for 10 minutes at 360°F. Once done, discard excess fat and then crumble bacon.
2) In a bowl, whisk well eggs. Stir in milk and chives.
3) In same air fryer baking pan, evenly spread bread slices. Pour egg mixture over it. Top with bacon. Cover pan with foil and let it rest in the fridge for at least an hour.
4) Preheat air fryer to 330°F.
5) Cook while covered in foil for 20 minutes. Remove foil and sprinkle cheese. Continue cooking uncovered for another 15 minutes.
6) Serve and enjoy.

Nutrition Information:
Calories: 207; Carbs: 12.1g; Protein: 15.3g; Fat: 10.8g

Mixed Vegetable Frittata

(Servings: 6, Cooking Time: 45 minutes)

Ingredients:
- 8-ounces frozen mixed vegetables (bell peppers, broccoli, etc.), thawed
- ½-pound breakfast sausage
- 1 cup cheddar cheese shredded
- 6 eggs
- 1/2 cup milk or cream
- 1 teaspoon kosher salt
- 1/2 teaspoon black pepper

Directions for Cooking:
1) Lightly grease baking pan of air fryer with cooking spray. For 10 minutes, cook on 360°F the breakfast sausage and crumble. Halfway through cooking time, crumble sausage some more until it looks like ground meat. Once done cooking, discard excess fat.
2) Stir in thawed mixed vegetables and cook for 7 minutes or until heated through, stirring halfway through cooking time.
3) Meanwhile, in a bowl, whisk well eggs, cream, salt, and pepper.
4) Remove basket, evenly spread vegetable mixture, and pour in egg mixture. Cover pan with foil.
5) Cook for another 15 minutes, remove foil and continue cooking for another 5-10 minutes or until eggs are set to desired doneness.
6) Serve and enjoy.

Nutrition Information:
Calories: 187; Carbs: 7.0g; Protein: 15.0g; Fat: 11.0g

Breakfast Chicken Casserole

(Servings: 2, Cooking Time: 35 minutes)

Ingredients:
- 1-1/4 cups cooked chopped broccoli
- 1 cup shredded, cooked chicken meat
- 1 (4.5 ounce) can mushrooms, drained
- 1/2 (8 ounce) can water chestnuts, drained (optional)
- 1 (10.75 ounce) can condensed cream of chicken soup
- 1/2 cup mayonnaise
- 1/2 teaspoon lemon juice
- 1/8 teaspoon curry powder
- 1 1/2 teaspoons melted butter
- 1/4 cup shredded Cheddar cheese

Directions for Cooking:
1) Lightly grease baking pan of air fryer with cooking spray.
2) Evenly spread broccoli on bottom of pan. Sprinkle chicken on top, followed by water chestnuts and mushrooms.
3) In a bowl, whisk well melted butter, curry powder, lemon juice, mayonnaise, and soup. Pour over chicken mixture in pan. Cover pan with foil.
4) For 25 minutes, cook on 360°F.
5) Remove foil from pan and cook for another 10 minutes or until top is a golden brown.
6) Serve and enjoy.

Nutrition Information:
Calories: 532; Carbs: 18.0g; Protein: 20.0g; Fat: 42.2g

Rice Casserole Mexican Style

(Servings: 4, Cooking Time: 50 minutes)

Ingredients:
- 1-1/3 cups water
- 2/3 cup uncooked long grain white rice
- 1/2-pound ground pork breakfast sausage
- 8-ounce picante sauce
- 4-ounce sour cream
- 1/4-pound Cheddar cheese, shredded

Directions for Cooking:
1) Lightly grease baking pan of air fryer with cooking spray. For 10 minutes, cook on 360°F the sausage. Crumble sausage halfway through cooking time.
2) Meanwhile, add water in a saucepan and bring to a boil. Once boiling, stir in rice. Cover and cook on low fire for 20 minutes.
3) Once sausage is done cooking, discard excess fat. Stir in sour cream and picante sauce. Mix well.
4) Once rice is done cooking, fluff rice and mix into sour cream mixture. Toss well to coat. Sprinkle cheese on top. Cover pan with foil.
5) Cook for 15 minutes, remove foil and cook for another 5 minutes.
6) Serve and enjoy.

Nutrition Information:
Calories: 452; Carbs: 31.0g; Protein: 18.9g; Fat: 28.0g

Broccoli, Ham 'n Potato Casserole

(Servings: 3, Cooking Time: 35 minutes)

Ingredients:
- 6-ounce frozen French fries
- 6-ounce frozen chopped broccoli
- 3/4 cup 3/cooked, cubed ham
- 1/3 cup canned condensed cream of mushroom soup
- 1/3 cup milk
- 1 1/2 tablespoon mayonnaise
- 1/3 cup grated Parmesan cheese

Directions for Cooking:
1) Lightly grease baking pan of air fryer with cooking spray.
2) Evenly spread French fries on bottom of pan. Place broccoli on top in a single layer. Evenly spread ham.
3) In a bowl, whisk well mayonnaise, milk, and soup. Pour over fries mixture.
4) Sprinkle cheese and over pan with foil.
5) For 25 minutes, cook on 390°F. Remove foil and continue cooking for another 10 minutes.
6) Serve and enjoy.

Nutrition Information:
Calories: 511; Carbs: 34.7g; Protein: 22.8g; Fat: 31.2g

Cheeseburger and Bacon Casserole

(Servings: 4, Cooking Time: 40 minutes)

Ingredients:
- 1 cup ground beef
- 1 clove garlic, minced
- 1/8 teaspoon onion powder
- 4 slices of bacon, cut into small pieces
- 3 eggs
- 1/3 cup heavy whipping cream
- 1/8 teaspoon salt
- 1/8 teaspoon ground black pepper
- 4.5-ounce shredded Cheddar cheese, divided

Directions for Cooking:
1) Lightly grease baking pan of air fryer with cooking spray. Add ground beef, garlic, and onion powder. For 10 minutes, cook on 360°F. Stirring halfway through cooking time.
2) Drain excess fat.
3) Evenly spread ground beef. Place bacon slices on top.
4) In a bowl, whisk well pepper, salt, cream, and eggs. Pour over bacon. Sprinkle cheese on top.
5) Cover pan with foil.
6) Cook for 20 minutes, remove foil and continue cooking for another 10 minutes.
7) Serve and enjoy.

Nutrition Information:
Calories: 454; Carbs: 1.6g; Protein: 28.7g; Fat: 36.9g

Main Meal Casserole Recipes

Fried Rice with Chicken

(Servings: 3, Cooking Time: 20 minutes)

Ingredients:
- 3 cups cold cooked white rice
- 1 cup frozen peas & carrots
- 6 tbsp soy sauce
- 1 tbsp vegetable oil
- 1 packed cup cooked chicken, diced
- 1/2 cup onion, diced

Directions for Cooking:
1) Lightly grease baking pan of air fryer with vegetable oil. Add frozen carrots and peas.
2) For 5 minutes, cook on 360ºF.
3) Stir in chicken and cook for another 5 minutes.
4) Add remaining ingredients and toss well to mix.
5) Cook for another 10 minutes, while mixing halfway through.
6) Serve and enjoy.

Nutrition Information:
Calories: 445; Carbs: 59.4g; Protein: 20.0g; Fat: 14.1g

Tasty Turkey Goulash

(Servings: 3, Cooking Time: 35 minutes)

Ingredients:
- 1/2-pound lean ground turkey
- 7-ounce can stewed, diced tomatoes
- 2 cloves garlic, minced
- 1/2 cup tomato sauce
- 1 teaspoon white sugar
- 1/4 teaspoon dried basil
- 8-ounce bow tie pasta, cooked according to manufacturer's Directions for Cooking:

Directions for Cooking:
1) Lightly grease baking pan of air fryer with cooking spray. Add ground turkey and garlic.
2) For 10 minutes, cook on 360ºF. Halfway through cooking time stir and crumble ground turkey.
3) Stir in basil, sugar, tomato sauce, and stewed tomatoes. Mix well.
4) Cook for another 10 minutes, mixing well halfway through cooking time.
5) Stir in cooked pasta and mix well.
6) Cook for another 5 minutes, mix well.
7) Serve and enjoy.

Nutrition Information:
Calories: 316; Carbs: 46.9g; Protein: 18.3g; Fat: 6.1g

Meatloaf in Air Fryer

(Servings: 3, Cooking Time: 30 minutes)

Ingredients:

- 1-pound lean ground beef (93% fat free), raw
- ½ medium onion, chopped
- 1/3 cup Kellogg's corn flakes crumbs
- 1-2 tsp salt
- 1-2 tsp freshly ground black pepper
- 1 tsp (or 2 cloves) minced garlic
- 8-oz tomato sauce, divided
- 1 tsp dried basil
- 5 Tbsp Heinz reduced-sugar ketchup
- 3 tsp Splenda (or Truvia) brown sugar blend
- 1 Tbsp Worcestershire sauce
- ½ Tbsp lightly dried (or fresh chopped) Parsley

Directions for Cooking:

1) Lightly grease baking pan of air fryer with cooking spray.

2) In a large bowl, mix well 6-oz tomato sauce, garlic, pepper, salt, corn flake crumbs, and onion. Stir in ground beef and mix well with hands.
3) Evenly spread ground beef mixture in pan, ensuring that it is lumped altogether.
4) In a medium bowl, whisk all remaining Ingredients: together to make a glaze. Pour on top of ground beef.
5) Cover pan with foil.
6) For 15 minutes, cook on 360°F. Remove foil and continue cooking for another 10 minutes.
7) Let it stand for 5 minutes.
8) Serve and enjoy.

Nutrition Information:
Calories: 427; Carbs: 25.7g; Protein: 42.5g; Fat: 17.1

Tuna Casserole Quickie

(Servings: 4, Cooking Time: 20 minutes)

Ingredients:

- 1-1/2 cups cooked macaroni
- 1/2 (5 ounce) can tuna, drained
- 1/2 (10.75 ounce) can condensed cream of chicken soup
- 1/2 cup shredded Cheddar cheese
- 3/4 cup French fried onions

Directions for Cooking:

1) Lightly grease baking pan of air fryer with cooking spray.

2) Mix soup, tuna, and macaroni in pan. Sprinkle cheese on top.
3) For 15 minutes, cook on 360°F.
4) Remove basket and toss the mixture a bit. Sprinkle fried onions.
5) Cook for another 5 minutes.
6) Serve and enjoy.

Nutrition Information:
Calories: 411; Carbs: 37.1g; Protein: 11.5g; Fat: 28.5g

Potato 'n Burger Casserole

(Servings: 3, Cooking Time: 55 minutes)

Ingredients:

- 1/2-pound lean ground beef
- 1-1/2 cups peeled and thinly sliced potatoes
- 1/2 (10.75 ounce) can condensed cream of mushroom soup
- 1/4 cup chopped onion
- 1/4 cup and 2 tablespoons milk
- salt to taste
- freshly ground pepper, to taste
- 1/2 cup shredded Cheddar cheese

Directions for Cooking:

1) Lightly grease baking pan of air fryer with cooking spray. Add ground beef. For 10 minutes, cook on 360°F. Stir and crumble halfway through cooking time.
2) Meanwhile, in a bowl, whisk well pepper, salt, milk, onion, and mushroom soup. Mix well.
3) Drain fat off ground beef and transfer beef to a plate.
4) In same air fryer baking pan, layer ½ of potatoes on bottom, then ½ of soup mixture, and then ½ of beef. Repeat process.
5) Cover pan with foil.
6) Cook for 30 minutes. Remove foil and cook for another 15 minutes or until potatoes are tender.
7) Serve and enjoy.

Nutrition Information:
Calories: 399; Carbs: 17.1g; Protein: 22.1g; Fat: 26.9g

Oh-So Good! Turkey Tetrazzini

(Servings: 4, Cooking Time: 40 minutes)

Ingredients:

- 8-ounce spaghetti, cooked according to manufacturer's Directions for Cooking:
- 1/4 cup butter
- 1/4 cup all-purpose flour
- 1-1/2 cups chicken broth
- 1 cup milk
- 3/4 cup grated Parmesan cheese
- 2 cups chopped cooked turkey

Directions for Cooking:

1) Lightly grease baking pan of air fryer with butter. Melt for 2 minutes at 360°F. Stir in four, cook for 2 minutes. Mix well and stir in milk and chicken broth. Cook for 10 minutes or until it boils, while stirring frequently. Stir in Parmesan.
2) Stir in spaghetti and turkey. Mix well.
3) Cover with foil.
4) Cook for 15 minutes. Uncover and cook for another 10 minutes.
5) Serve and enjoy.

Nutrition Information:
Calories: 557; Carbs: 51.7g; Protein: 37.6g; Fat: 22.1g

Grits Casserole Southern Style

(Servings: 4, Cooking Time: 30 minutes)

Ingredients:

- 1-1/2 cups water
- 1/2 cup uncooked grits
- 2 tablespoons butter, divided
- 3/4 cup shredded Cheddar cheese, divided
- 1/4-pound ground pork sausage
- 3 eggs
- 2 tablespoons milk
- salt and pepper to taste

Directions for Cooking:

1) In a large saucepan bring water to a boil. Stir in grits and simmer until liquid is absorbed, around 5 minutes. Stir in ¼ cup cheese and 1 tbsp butter. Mix well until thoroughly incorporated.
2) Lightly grease baking pan of air fryer with cooking spray. Add pork sausage and for 5 minutes, cook on 360ºF. Crumble sausage and discard excess fat.
3) Transfer grits into pan of sausage.
4) In a bowl whisk well, milk and eggs and pour into pan. Mix well.
5) Dot the top with butter and sprinkle cheese. Season with pepper and salt.
6) Cook until tops are browned, around 20 minutes.
7) Serve and enjoy.

Nutrition Information:
Calories: 403; Carbs: 16.8g; Protein: 16.5g; Fat: 29.9g

Rice 'n Chicken Bake

(Servings: 2, Cooking Time: 40 minutes)

Ingredients:

- 1/2 (10.75 ounce) can Campbell's® Condensed Cream of Mushroom Soup (Regular, 98% Fat Free or 25% Less Sodium)
- 1/2 cup water*
- 1/4 cup and 2 tablespoons uncooked regular long-grain white rice
- 1/8 teaspoon paprika and more
- 1/8 teaspoon ground black pepper and more
- 2 skinless, boneless chicken breasts

Directions for Cooking:

1) Lightly grease baking pan of air fryer with cooking spray.
2) Mix in pepper, paprika, rice, water, and soup. Stir well.
3) Season chicken with paprika and pepper. Place chicken on top of rice mixture.
4) Cover with foil.
5) For 25 minutes, cook on 360ºF.
6) Remove foil and cook for another 10 minutes.
7) Let it stand for 5 minutes.
8) Serve and enjoy.

Nutrition Information:
Calories: 394; Carbs: 23.8g; Protein: 55.8g; Fat: 8.4g

Cheeseburger Low-Carb Casserole

(Servings: 4, Cooking Time: 35 minutes)

Ingredients:

- 1-pound ground beef
- 1 clove garlic, minced
- 1/4 teaspoon onion powder
- 1/2-pound bacon, cut into small pieces
- 4 eggs
- 1/2 cup heavy whipping cream
- 1/4 teaspoon salt
- 1/8 teaspoon ground black pepper
- 6-ounce shredded Cheddar cheese, divided

Directions for Cooking:

1) Lightly grease baking pan of air fryer with cooking spray. Add beef, onion powder, and garlic. For 10 minutes, cook on 360°F. stirring and crumbling halfway through cooking time.
2) Discard excess fat and evenly spread ground beef on bottom of pan. Top with evenly spread bacon slices. Sprinkle half of the cheese on top.
3) In a bowl, whisk well pepper, salt, heavy cream, and eggs. Pour over bacon.
4) Sprinkle remaining cheese on top of eggs.
5) Cover pan with foil and cook for 15 minutes.
6) Uncover and cook for another 10 minutes until tops are browned and eggs are set.
7) Serve and enjoy.

Nutrition Information:
Calories: 454; Carbs: 1.6g; Protein: 28.7g; Fat: 36.9g

Turkey 'n Broccoli Bake

(Servings: 4, Cooking Time: 40 minutes)

Ingredients:

- 1/2 cup uncooked white rice
- 1 cup cooked, chopped turkey meat
- 1/2 (10 ounce) package frozen broccoli, thawed
- 1/2 cup shredded Cheddar cheese
- 1/2 (7 ounce) package whole wheat crackers, crushed
- 1 tablespoon and 1-1/2 teaspoons butter, melted

Directions for Cooking:

1) Bring to a boil 2 cups of water in a saucepan. Stir in rice and simmer for 20 minutes. Turn off fire and set aside.
2) Lightly grease baking pan of air fryer with cooking spray. Mix in cooked rice, cheese, broccoli, and turkey. Toss well to mix.
3) Mix well melted butter and crushed crackers in a small bowl. Evenly spread on top of rice.
4) For 20 minutes, cook on 360°F until tops are lightly browned.
5) Serve and enjoy.

Nutrition Information:
Calories: 269; Carbs: 23.7g; Protein: 17.0g; Fat: 11.8g

Penne Chicken Pesto Bake

(Servings: 3, Cooking Time: 25 minutes)

Ingredients:

- 2 tablespoons seasoned bread crumbs
- 2 tablespoons grated Parmesan cheese
- 3/4 teaspoon olive oil
- 4-ounce penne pasta, cooked according to manufacturer's Directions for Cooking:
- 1-1/2 cups cubed cooked chicken
- 1 cup shredded Italian cheese blend
- 3/4 cup fresh baby spinach
- 1/4 (15 ounce) can crushed tomatoes
- 1/4 (15 ounce) jar Alfredo sauce
- 1/4 (15 ounce) jar pesto sauce
- 1/3 cup milk

Directions for Cooking:

1) In a small bowl, whisk well olive oil, Parmesan, and bread crumbs. Set aside.
2) Lightly grease baking pan of air fryer with cooking spray. Mix in milk, pesto sauce, alfredo sauce, tomatoes, spinach, and Italian cheese blend. Mix well. Toss in cooked pasta and toss well to coat. Evenly sprinkle bread crumb mixture on top.
3) For 25 minutes, cook on 360°F until tops are lightly browned.
4) Serve and enjoy.

Nutrition Information:
Calories: 729; Carbs: 40.7g; Protein: 45.4g; Fat: 47.2g

Green Bean ' Chicken Stuffing Bake

(Servings: 3, Cooking Time: 20 minutes)

Ingredients:

- 1 cup cooked, cubed chicken breast meat
- 1/2 (10.75 ounce) can condensed cream of chicken soup
- 1/2 (14.5 ounce) can green beans, drained
- salt and pepper to taste
- 6-ounce unseasoned dry bread stuffing mix
- 1/2 cup shredded Cheddar cheese

Directions for Cooking:

1) Mix well pepper, salt, soup, and chicken in a medium bowl.
2) Make the stuffing according to package Directions for Cooking.
3) Lightly grease baking pan of air fryer with cooking spray. Evenly spread chicken mixture on bottom of pan. Top evenly with stuffing. Sprinkle cheese on top.
4) Cover pan with foil.
5) For 15 minutes, cook on 390°F.
6) Remove foil and cook for 5 minutes at 390°F until tops are lightly browned.
7) Serve and enjoy.

Nutrition Information:
Calories: 418; Carbs: 48.8g; Protein: 27.1g; Fat: 12.7g

Cheesy Broccoli-Rice Bake

(Servings: 4, Cooking Time: 28 minutes)

Ingredients:
- 1 cup water
- 1 cup uncooked instant rice
- 1 (10 ounce) can chunk chicken, drained
- 1/2 (10.75 ounce) can condensed cream of mushroom soup
- 1/2 (10.75 ounce) can condensed cream of chicken soup
- 2 tablespoons butter
- 1/2 cup milk
- 8-ounce frozen chopped broccoli
- 1/2 small white onion, chopped
- 1/2-pound processed cheese food

Directions for Cooking:

1) Lightly grease baking pan of air fryer with cooking spray. Add water and bring to a boil at 390°F. Stir in rice and cook for 3 minutes.
2) Stir in processed cheese, onion, broccoli, milk, butter, chicken soup, mushroom soup, and chicken. Mix well.
3) Cook for 15 minutes at 390°F, fluff mixture and continue cooking for another 10 minutes until tops are browned.
4) Serve and enjoy.

Nutrition Information:
Calories: 752; Carbs: 82.7g; Protein: 36.0g; Fat: 30.8g

Rice Casserole Mexican Style

(Servings: 4, Cooking Time: 45 minutes)

Ingredients:
- 1-1/3 cups water
- 2/3 cup uncooked long grain white rice
- 1/2-pound ground pork breakfast sausage
- 1/2 (16 ounce) jar picante sauce
- 1/2 (8 ounce) container sour cream
- 1/4-pound Cheddar cheese, shredded

Directions for Cooking:
1) Ring water to a boil in a saucepan and stir in rice. Cover and simmer for 20 minutes until all liquid is absorbed. Turn off fire and fluff rice.

2) Lightly grease baking pan of air fryer with cooking spray. Add sausage and cook for 10 minutes at 360°F. Halfway through cooking time, crumble and stir sausage.
3) Stir in cooked rice, sour cream, and picante sauce. Mix well. Sprinkle cheese on top
4) Cook for 15 minutes at 390°F until tops are lightly browned.
5) Serve and enjoy.

Nutrition Information:
Calories: 452; Carbs: 31.0g; Protein: 18.9g; Fat: 28.0g

Mouth-WateringTaco Bake

(Servings: 5, Cooking Time: 25 minutes)

Ingredients:

- 1/2-pound lean ground beef
- 1/4-pound macaroni, cooked according to manufacturer's Directions for Cooking:
- 1/4 cup chopped onion
- 1/2 (10.75 ounce) can condensed tomato soup
- 1/2 (14.5 ounce) can diced tomatoes
- 1/2 (1.25 ounce) package taco seasoning mix
- 1-ounce shredded Cheddar cheese
- 1-ounce shredded Monterey Jack cheese
- 1/2 cup crushed tortilla chips
- 1/4 cup sour cream (optional)
- 2 tablespoons chopped green onions

Directions for Cooking:

1) Lightly grease baking pan of air fryer with cooking spray. Add onion and ground beef. For 10 minutes, cook on 360ºF. Halfway through cooking time, stir and crumble ground beef.
2) Add taco seasoning, diced tomatoes, and tomato soup. Mix well. Mix in pasta.
3) Sprinkle crushed tortilla chips. Sprinkle cheese.
4) Cook for 15 minutes at 390ºF until tops are lightly browned and cheese is melted.
5) Serve and enjoy.

Nutrition Information:
Calories: 329; Carbs: 28.2g; Protein: 15.6g; Fat: 17.0g

A Different Rice-Chik'n Bake

(Servings: 3, Cooking Time: 45 minutes)

Ingredients:

- 3 chicken breasts, cut into cubes
- 2 cups water
- 2 cups instant white rice
- 1 (10.75 ounce) can cream of chicken soup
- 1 (10.75 ounce) can cream of celery soup
- 1 (10.75 ounce) can cream of mushroom soup
- salt and ground black pepper to taste
- 1/2 cup butter, sliced into pats

Directions for Cooking:

1) Lightly grease baking pan of air fryer with cooking spray.
2) In pan, mix cream of mushroom, celery soup, chicken soup, rice, water and chicken. Mix well.
3) Season with pepper and salt. Top with butter pats.
4) Cover pan with foil and for 35 minutes, cook on 360ºF.
5) Let it stand for 10 minutes.
6) Serve and enjoy.

Nutrition Information:
Calories: 439; Carbs: 36.7g; Protein: 16.8g; Fat: 25.0g

Chicken Florentine Bake

(Servings: 2, Cooking Time: 40 minutes)

Ingredients:
- 2 skinless, boneless chicken breast halves
- 2 tablespoons butter
- 1-1/2 teaspoons minced garlic
- 1-1/2 teaspoons lemon juice
- 1/2 (10.75 ounce) can condensed cream of mushroom soup
- 1-1/2 teaspoons Italian seasoning
- 1/4 cup half-and-half
- 1/4 cup grated Parmesan cheese
- 1 (13.5 ounce) can spinach, drained
- 2 ounces fresh mushrooms, sliced
- 1/3 cup bacon bits
- 1 cup shredded mozzarella cheese

Directions for Cooking:
1) Lightly grease baking pan of air fryer with cooking spray. Add chicken breast and for 20 minutes, cook on 360°F. Halfway through cooking time, turnover chicken breast. Once done, transfer to a plate and set aside.
2) In same baking pan, melt butter. Stir in Parmesan cheese, half and half, Italian seasoning, mushroom soup, lemon juice, and garlic. Mix well and cook for 5 minutes or until heated through.
3) Stir in spinach and chicken. Tope with bacon bits and mozzarella cheese.
4) Cook for 15 minutes at 390°F until tops are lightly browned.
5) Serve and enjoy.

Nutrition Information:
Calories: 659; Carbs: 17.6g; Protein: 61.6g; Fat: 38.0g

Sea Scallop Bake

(Servings: 4, Cooking Time: 10 minutes)

Ingredients:
- 16 sea scallops, rinsed and drained
- 5 tablespoons butter, melted
- 5 cloves garlic, minced
- 2 shallots, chopped
- 3 pinches ground nutmeg
- salt and pepper to taste
- 1 cup bread crumbs
- 4 tablespoons olive oil
- 1/4 cup chopped parsley

Directions for Cooking:
1) Lightly grease baking pan of air fryer with cooking spray.
2) Mix in shallots, garlic, melted butter, and scallops. Season with pepper, salt, and nutmeg.
3) In a small bowl, whisk well olive oil and bread crumbs. Sprinkle over scallops.
4) For 10 minutes, cook on 390°F until tops are lightly browned.
5) Serve and enjoy with a sprinkle of parsley.

Nutrition Information:
Calories: 452; Carbs: 29.8g; Protein: 15.2g; Fat: 30.2g

Shrimp Casserole Louisiana Style

(Servings: 2, Cooking Time: 35 minutes)

Ingredients:

- 3/4 cup uncooked instant rice
- 3/4 cup water
- 1/2 teaspoon vegetable oil
- 1/2-pound small shrimp, peeled and deveined
- 1 tablespoon butter
- 1/2 (4 ounce) can sliced mushrooms, drained
- 1/2 (10.75 ounce) can condensed cream of shrimp soup
- 1/2 (8 ounce) container sour cream
- 1/3 cup shredded Cheddar cheese

Directions for Cooking:

1) Lightly grease baking pan of air fryer with cooking spray. Add rice, water, mushrooms, and butter. Cover with foil. For 20 minutes, cook on 360°F.
2) Open foil cover, stir in shrimps, return foil and let it rest for 5 minutes.
3) Remove foil completely and stir in sour cream. Mix well and evenly spread rice.
4) Top with cheese.
5) Cook for 7 minutes at 390°F until tops are lightly browned.
6) Serve and enjoy.

Nutrition Information:
Calories: 569; Carbs: 38.5g; Protein: 31.8g; Fat: 31.9g

Cheesy Zucchini-Squash Bake

(Servings: 4, Cooking Time: 30 minutes)

Ingredients:

- 1/2-pound yellow squash, sliced
- 1/2-pound zucchini, sliced
- 1/4 onion, diced
- 1/2 cup shredded Cheddar cheese
- 1/4 cup biscuit baking mix (such as Bisquick®)
- 1/4 cup butter
- 1 egg
- 1-1/2 teaspoons white sugar
- 1/2 teaspoon salt
- 5 saltine crackers, or as needed, crushed
- 2 tablespoons bread crumbs

Directions for Cooking:

1) Lightly grease baking pan of air fryer with cooking spray. Add onion, zucchini, and yellow squash. Cover pan with foil and for 15 minutes, cook on 360°F or until tender.
2) Stir in salt, sugar, egg, butter, baking mix, and cheddar cheese. Mix well. Fold in crushed crackers. Top with bread crumbs.
3) Cook for 15 minutes at 390°F until tops are lightly browned.
4) Serve and enjoy.

Nutrition Information:
Calories: 285; Carbs: 16.4g; Protein: 8.6g; Fat: 20.5g

Portuguese Bacalao Tapas

(Servings: 4, Cooking Time: 26 minutes)

Ingredients:
- 1-pound cod fish filet, chopped
- 2 Yukon Gold potatoes, peeled and diced
- 2 tablespoon butter
- 1 yellow onions, thinly sliced
- 1 clove garlic, chopped, divided
- 1/4 cup chopped fresh parsley, divided
- 1/4 cup olive oil
- 3/4 teaspoon red pepper flakes
- freshly ground pepper to taste
- 2 hard cooked eggs, chopped
- 5 pitted green olives
- 5 pitted black olives

Directions for Cooking:

1) Lightly grease baking pan of air fryer with cooking spray. Add and melt butter at 360ºF. Stir in onions and cook for 6 minutes until caramelized.
2) Stir in black pepper, red pepper flakes, half of parsley, garlic, olive oil, diced potatoes and chopped fish. For 10 minutes, cook on 360ºF. Halfway through cooking time, stir well to mix.
3) Cook for 10 minutes at 390ºF until tops are lightly browned.
4) Garnish with remaining parsley, eggs, black and green olives.
5) Serve and enjoy with chips.

Nutrition Information:
Calories: 691; Carbs: 25.2g; Protein: 77.1g; Fat: 31.3g

Zucchini & Carrot Bake

(Servings: 4, Cooking Time: 25 minutes)

Ingredients:
- 1/2-pound carrots, sliced
- 1-1/2 zucchinis, sliced
- 1/4 cup water
- 1/4 cup mayonnaise
- 1 tablespoon grated onion
- 1/4 teaspoon prepared horseradish
- 1/4 teaspoon salt
- 1/4 teaspoon ground black pepper
- 1/4 cup Italian bread crumbs
- 2 tablespoons butter, melted

Directions for Cooking:
1) Lightly grease baking pan of air fryer with cooking spray. Add carrots. For 8 minutes, cook on 360ºF. Add zucchini and continue cooking for another 5 minutes.
2) Meanwhile, in a bowl whisk well pepper, salt, horseradish, onion, mayonnaise, and water. Pour into pan of veggies. Toss well to coat.
3) In a small bowl mix melted butter and bread crumbs. Sprinkle over veggies.
4) Cook for 10 minutes at 390ºF until tops are lightly browned.
5) Serve and enjoy.

Nutrition Information:
Calories: 223; Carbs: 13.8g; Protein: 2.7g; Fat: 17.4g

Cheesy-Creamy Broccoli Bake

(Servings: 2, Cooking Time: 30 minutes)

Ingredients:
- 1-pound fresh broccoli, coarsely chopped
- 1/2 large onion, coarsely chopped
- 1/4 cup water
- 2 tablespoons all-purpose flour
- 1/2 (14 ounce) can evaporated milk, divided
- salt to taste
- 1/2 cup cubed sharp Cheddar cheese
- 1 tablespoon dry bread crumbs, or to taste
- 1-1/2 teaspoons butter, or to taste

Directions for Cooking:
1) Lightly grease baking pan of air fryer with cooking spray. Mix in half of the milk and flour in pan and for 5 minutes, cook on 360°F. Halfway through cooking time, mix well. Add broccoli and remaining milk. Mix well and cook for another 5 minutes.
2) Stir in cheese and mix well until melted.
3) In a small bowl mix well, butter and bread crumbs. Sprinkle on top of broccoli.
4) Cook for 20 minutes at 360°F until tops are lightly browned.
5) Serve and enjoy.

Nutrition Information:
Calories: 444; Carbs: 37.3g; Protein: 23.1g; Fat: 22.4g

Mushroom 'n Spinach Casserole

(Servings: 3, Cooking Time: 25 minutes)

Ingredients:
- 1 tablespoon butter
- 1/2-pound fresh mushrooms, sliced
- 1 (10 ounce) package fresh spinach, rinsed and stems removed
- 1/2 teaspoon salt
- 2 tablespoons butter, melted
- 2 tablespoons finely chopped onion
- 3/4 cup shredded Cheddar cheese, divided

Directions for Cooking:
1) Lightly grease baking pan of air fryer with butter and melt for 2 minutes at 360°F. Stir in mushrooms and cook for 10 minutes. Halfway through cooking time, stir and mix around.
2) Stir in spinach and cook until wilted, around 5 minutes. Stirring halfway through cooking time.
3) Stir in remaining ingredients and give it a good mix.
4) Cook for 15 minutes at 390°F until tops are lightly browned.
5) Serve and enjoy.

Nutrition Information:
Calories: 229; Carbs: 7.5g; Protein: 11.3g; Fat: 21.5g

Potato Casserole Twice Baked

(Servings: 4, Cooking Time: 45 minutes)

Ingredients:

- 1 teaspoon vegetable oil, or as needed
- 1/2-pound unpeeled russet potatoes, scrubbed
- 1-1/2 cups sour cream
- 1 cup shredded Monterey Jack cheese
- 1 cup shredded Cheddar cheese
- 2-1/2 ounces cooked bacon, crumbled
- 2-1/2 green onions, chopped
- 1/8 teaspoon salt
- 1/8 teaspoon ground black pepper

Directions for Cooking:

1) Lightly grease baking pan of air fryer with cooking spray.
2) Pierce potatoes many times with fork and place in pan. For 30 minutes, cook on 390°F.
3) Remove potatoes and when cool enough to handle, chop into 1-inch cubes.
4) In same pan, mix in pepper, salt, green onions, bacon, cheddar cheese, Monterey Jack cheese, and sour cream. Mix well. Toss in potatoes and toss well to coat.
5) Cook for 15 minutes at 390°F until tops are lightly browned.
6) Serve and enjoy.

Nutrition Information:
Calories: 567; Carbs: 15.1g; Protein: 25.0g; Fat: 45.1g

Chili Rellenos Bake

(Servings: 3, Cooking Time: 30 minutes)

Ingredients:

- 1 (7 ounce) can whole green Chile peppers, drained
- 1/4-pound Monterey Jack cheese, shredded
- 1/4-pound Longhorn or Cheddar cheese, shredded
- 1 egg, beaten
- 1/2 (5 ounce) can evaporated milk
- 1 tablespoon all-purpose flour
- 1/4 cup milk
- 1/2 (8 ounce) can tomato sauce

Directions for Cooking:

1) Lightly grease baking pan of air fryer with cooking spray. Evenly spread chilies and sprinkle cheddar and Jack cheese on top.
2) In a bowl whisk well flour, milk, and eggs. Pour over chilies.
3) For 20 minutes, cook on 360°F.
4) Add tomato sauce on top.
5) Cook for 10 minutes at 390°F until tops are lightly browned.
6) Serve and enjoy.

Nutrition Information:
Calories: 392; Carbs: 12.0g; Protein: 23.9g; Fat: 27.6g

Spicy Zucchini Bake Mexican Style

(Servings: 4, Cooking Time: 30 minutes)

Ingredients:
- 1 tablespoon olive oil
- 1-1/2 pounds zucchini, cubed
- 1/2 cup chopped onion
- 1/2 teaspoon garlic salt
- 1/2 teaspoon paprika
- 1/2 teaspoon dried oregano
- 1/2 teaspoon cayenne pepper, or to taste
- 1/2 cup cooked long-grain rice
- 1/2 cup cooked pinto beans
- 1-1/4 cups salsa
- 3/4 cup shredded Cheddar cheese

Directions for Cooking:
1) Lightly grease baking pan of air fryer with olive oil. Add onions and zucchini and for 10 minutes, cook on 360°F. Halfway through cooking time, stir.
2) Season with cayenne, oregano, paprika, and garlic salt. Mix well.
3) Stir in salsa, beans, and rice. Cook for 5 minutes.
4) Stir in cheddar cheese and mix well.
5) Cover pan with foil.
6) Cook for 15 minutes at 390°F until bubbly.
7) Serve and enjoy.

Nutrition Information:
Calories: 263; Carbs: 24.6g; Protein: 12.5g; Fat: 12.7g

Feta-Spinach 'n Pita Casserole

(Servings: 3, Cooking Time: 5 minutes)

Ingredients:
- 3-ounce sun-dried tomato pesto
- 3 (6 inch) whole wheat pita breads
- 1 roma (plum) tomatoes, chopped
- 1/2 bunch spinach, rinsed and chopped
- 2 fresh mushrooms, sliced
- 1/4 cup crumbled feta cheese
- 1 tablespoon grated Parmesan cheese
- 1 tablespoon and 1-1/2 teaspoons olive oil
- ground black pepper to taste

Directions for Cooking:
1) Lightly grease baking pan of air fryer with cooking spray.
2) Evenly spread tomato pesto on one side of pita bread. Place one pita bread on bottom of pan, add 1/3 each of Parmesan, feta, mushrooms, spinach, and tomatoes. Season with pepper and drizzle with olive oil.
3) Cook for 5 minutes at 390°F until tops crisped.
4) Repeat process for remaining pita bread.
5) Serve and enjoy.

Nutrition Information:
Calories: 367; Carbs: 41.6g; Protein: 11.6g; Fat: 17.1g

Chicken Deluxe Tetrazzini

(Servings: 3, Cooking Time: 30 minutes)

Ingredients:
- 4-ounce linguine pasta, cooked following manufacturer's Directions for Cooking:
- 2 tablespoons butter
- 3/4 cup sliced fresh mushrooms
- 1/4 cup minced onion
- 1/4 cup minced green bell pepper
- 1/2 (10.75 ounce) can condensed cream of mushroom soup
- 1/2 cup chicken broth
- 1/2 cup shredded sharp Cheddar cheese
- 1/4 (10 ounce) package frozen green peas
- 2 tablespoons cooking sherry
- 1/4 teaspoon Worcestershire sauce
- 1/4 teaspoon salt
- 1/8 teaspoon ground black pepper
- 1 cup chopped cooked chicken breast
- 1/4 cup grated Parmesan cheese

Directions for Cooking:
1) Lightly grease baking pan of air fryer and melt butter for 2 minutes at 360°F. Stir in bell pepper, onion, and mushrooms. Cook for 5 minutes.
2) Add chicken broth and mushroom soup, mix well. Cook for 5 minutes.
3) Mix in chicken, pepper, salt, Worcestershire sauce, sherry, peas, cheddar cheese, and pasta. Sprinkle paprika and Parmesan on top.
4) Cook for 15 minutes at 390°F until tops are lightly browned.
5) Serve and enjoy.

Nutrition Information:
Calories: 494; Carbs: 39.0g; Protein: 28.8g; Fat: 24.7g

Nutritious Cabbage Roll Bake

(Servings: 6, Cooking Time: 50 minutes)

Ingredients:
- 1-pound ground beef
- 1/2 cup chopped onion
- 1/2 (29 ounce) can tomato sauce
- 1-3/4 pounds chopped cabbage
- 1/2 cup uncooked white rice
- 1/2 teaspoon salt
- 1 (14 ounce) can beef broth

Directions for Cooking:
1) Lightly grease baking pan of air fryer with cooking spray. Add beef and for 10 minutes, cook on 360°F. Halfway through cooking time, stir and crumble beef.
2) Meanwhile, in a large bowl whisk well salt, rice, cabbage, onion, and tomato sauce. Add to pan of meat and mix well. Pour broth.
3) Cover pan with foil.
4) Cook for 25 minutes at 330°F, uncover, mix and cook for another 15 minutes.
5) Serve and enjoy.

Nutrition Information:
Calories: 356; Carbs: 25.5g; Protein: 17.1g; Fat: 20.6g

Mixed Veggie-Chicken 'n Pasta Casserole

(Servings: 3, Cooking Time: 30 minutes)

Ingredients:

- 1/2 cup dry fusilli pasta, cooked according to manufacturer's Directions for Cooking:
- 1 tablespoon olive oil
- 3 chicken tenderloins, cut into chunks
- 1-1/2 teaspoons dried minced onion
- salt and pepper to taste
- garlic powder to taste
- 1-1/2 teaspoons dried basil
- 1-1/2 teaspoons dried parsley
- 1/2 (10.75 ounce) can condensed cream of chicken soup
- 1/2 (10.75 ounce) can condensed cream of mushroom soup
- 1 cup frozen mixed vegetables
- 1/2 cup dry bread crumbs
- 1 tablespoon grated Parmesan cheese
- 1 tablespoon butter, melted

Directions for Cooking:

1) Lightly grease baking pan of air fryer with olive oil. Add chicken. Season with parsley, basil, garlic powder, pepper, salt, and minced onion.
2) For 10 minutes, cook on 360°F. Stir chicken halfway through cooking time.
3) Remove basket and toss the mixture a bit. Stir in mixed vegetables, cream of mushroom soup, cream of chicken soup, and cooked pasta. Mix well.
4) Mix melted butter, parmesan, and bread crumbs in a small bowl. Evenly spread on top of casserole.
5) Cook for 20 minutes at 390°F.
6) Serve and enjoy.

Nutrition Information:

Calories: 399; Carbs: 35.4g; Protein: 19.8g; Fat: 19.8g

Chicken ala King Casserole

(Servings: 4, Cooking Time: 40 minutes)

Ingredients:

- 1-1/2 teaspoons vegetable oil
- 1/2 white onion, diced
- 1/2 red bell pepper, diced
- 1/2 green bell pepper, diced
- 1/2 (10.75 ounce) can condensed cream of mushroom soup
- 1/2 (10.75 ounce) can condensed cream of chicken soup
- 1/2 (10 ounce) can diced tomatoes with green chile peppers (such as RO*TEL®)
- 1/2 cup chicken broth
- 1 tablespoon sour cream
- 1 teaspoon ground cumin
- 1/2 teaspoon ancho chile powder
- 1/4 teaspoon dried oregano
- 1/8 teaspoon chipotle chile powder
- 1/2 cooked chicken, torn into shreds or cut into chunks
- 1/4-pound shredded Cheddar cheese
- 4 corn tortillas, cut into quarters

Directions for Cooking:

1) Lightly grease baking pan of air fryer with vegetable oil. Add bell pepper, red bell pepper, and onion. For 5 minutes, cook on 360°F.
2) Meanwhile, in a large bowl, whisk well chipotle chile powder, oregano, ancho chile powder, cumin, sour cream, chicken broth, diced tomatoes, cream of chicken soup, and cream of mushroom soup.

3) Once bell peppers are done cooking, pour into bowl of sauce and mix well.
4) Add a few scoops of sauce on bottom of air fryer baking pan. Place ½ of chicken on top of sauce, top with1/3 cheese, cover with a layer of torn tortilla. Repeat process until all Ingredients: are used up.
5) Cover pan with foil.
6) Cook for 25 minutes. Uncover and continue cooking for another 10 minutes.
7) Serve and enjoy.

Nutrition Information:
Calories: 482; Carbs: 25.1g; Protein: 32.1g; Fat: 28.1g

Enchilada in Air Fryer

(Servings: 3, Cooking Time: 50 minutes)

Ingredients:
- 1-pound skinless, boneless chicken breast meat, cooked and shredded
- 1/2 (10.75 ounce) can condensed cream of chicken soup
- 1/2 cup sour cream
- 1/8 teaspoon chili powder
- 1-1/2 teaspoons butter
- 1/2 small onion, chopped
- 1/2 (4 ounce) can chopped green chilies, drained
- 1/2 (1.25 ounce) package mild taco seasoning mix
- 1/2 bunch green onions, chopped, divided
- 1/2 cup water
- 1/2 teaspoon lime juice
- 1/4 teaspoon onion powder
- 1/4 teaspoon garlic powder
- 3 (12 inch) flour tortillas
- 1-1/2 cups Cheddar cheese, shredded, divided
- 1/2 (10 ounce) can enchilada sauce
- 1/2 (6 ounce) can sliced black olives

Directions for Cooking:
1) Lightly grease baking pan of air fryer with butter. Add onion and for 5 minutes, cook on 360°F.
2) Stir in water, green onions, taco seasoning, green chilies, and shredded chicken. Cook for another 10 minutes.
3) Stir in garlic powder, onion powder, and lime juice. Cook for 5 minutes more.
4) In a bowl whisk well chili powder, sour cream, and cream of chicken soup. Pour a cup of the mixture in the baking pan and mix well.
5) Evenly divide the chicken mixture into the flour tortillas, sprinkle with ½ of the cheese and roll.
6) Pour remaining soup mixture into air fryer baking pan. Place tortillas seam side down. Pour enchilada sauce on top and sprinkle remaining cheese.
7) Cover pan with foil.
8) Cook for another 20 minutes, remove foil and continue cooking another 10 minutes.
9) Serve and enjoy.

Nutrition Information:
Calories: 706; Carbs: 52.5g; Protein: 42.2g; Fat: 36.3g

Air Fryed Traditional Spaghetti

(Servings: 4, Cooking Time: 40 minutes)

Ingredients:
- 8- ounce spaghetti, cooked according to manufacturer's Directions for Cooking:
- 1/2-pound ground beef
- 1/2 onion, chopped
- 1/2 (32 ounce) jar meatless spaghetti sauce
- 1/4 teaspoon seasoned salt
- 1 egg
- 3 tablespoons grated Parmesan cheese
- 3 tablespoons butter, melted
- 1 cup small curd cottage cheese, divided
- 2 cups shredded mozzarella cheese, divided

Directions for Cooking:
1) Lightly grease baking pan of air fryer with cooking spray. Add ground beef and onion. For 10 minutes, cook on 360°F. Crumble and mix well halfway through cooking time. Discard excess fat.
2) Mix in seasoned salt and spaghetti sauce. Mix well and transfer to a bowl.
3) In a large bowl, whisk well butter, parmesan cheese, and eggs.
4) In same air fryer baking pan, spread evenly half of the pasta, add half the spaghettis sauce, and then half of the mozzarella and cottage cheese. Repeat layering.
5) Cover pan with foil.
6) Cook for another 20 minutes, remove foil and cook for another 10 minutes.
7) Serve and enjoy.

Nutrition Information:
Calories: 720; Carbs: 61.9g; Protein: 42.5g; Fat: 33.6g

Traditional Ground Beef Casserole

(Servings: 3, Cooking Time: 45 minutes)

Ingredients:
- 1/2-pound ground beef
- 1/2 teaspoon white sugar
- 1/2 teaspoon salt
- 1/2 teaspoon garlic salt
- 1 (15 ounce) can tomato sauce
- 4-ounce egg noodles, cooked according to manufacturer's directions
- 1/2 cup sour cream
- 1.5-ounce cream cheese
- 1/2 large white onion, diced
- 1/4 cup shredded sharp Cheddar cheese, or more to taste

Directions for Cooking:
1) Lightly grease baking pan of air fryer with cooking spray. Add ground beef, for 10 minutes cook on 360°F. Halfway through cooking time crumble beef.
2) When done cooking, discard excess fat.
3) Stir in tomato sauce, garlic salt, salt, and sugar. Mix well and cook for another 15 minutes. Transfer to a bowl.
4) In another bowl, whisk well onion, cream cheese, and sour cream.
5) Place half of the egg noodles on bottom of air fryer baking pan. Top with half of the sour cream mixture, then half the tomato sauce mixture.

Repeat layering. And then top off with cheese.
6) Cover pan with foil.
7) Cook for another 15 minutes. Uncover and cook for another 5 minutes.

8) Serve and enjoy.

Nutrition Information:
Calories: 524; Carbs: 39.4g; Protein: 24.5g; Fat: 29.8g

Cajun Style Jambalaya

(Servings: 4, Cooking Time: 40 minutes)

Ingredients:
- 1-1/2 teaspoons olive oil
- 1/4-pound smoked sausage (such as Conecuh©), cut into 1/4-inch thick slices
- 1/2 large onion, chopped
- 1/2 cup chopped green bell pepper
- 1/2 cup chopped celery
- salt to taste
- 1/4 teaspoon Cajun seasoning, or to taste
- 1/2 cup uncooked white rice
- 1/2 (14.5 ounce) can diced tomatoes with juice
- 1-1/2 teaspoons minced garlic
- 1 cup chicken broth
- 1-1/2 bay leaves
- 1/8 teaspoon dried thyme leaves
- 1/2 pound peeled and deveined medium shrimp (30-40 per pound)

Directions for Cooking:
1) Lightly grease baking pan of air fryer with olive oil. Add sausage and for 5 minutes, cook on 360°F. Stir in Cajun seasoning, salt, celery, bell pepper, and onion. Cook for another 5 minutes.
2) Add the rice and mix well. Stir in thyme leaves, bay leaves, chicken broth, garlic, vegetable mixture, and tomatoes with juice. Cover with foil.
3) Cook for another 15 minutes.
4) Remove foil, stir in shrimp. Cook for 8 minutes.
5) Let it stand for 5 minutes.
6) Serve and enjoy.

Nutrition Information:
Calories: 276; Carbs: 24.6g; Protein: 18.4g; Fat: 11.5g

Yummy Lamb Shepherd's Pie

(Servings: 4, Cooking Time: 50 minutes)

Ingredients:

- 1-1/2 teaspoons olive oil
- 1-1/2 teaspoons butter
- 1/2 onion, diced
- 1-pound lean ground lamb
- 2 tablespoons and 2 teaspoons all-purpose flour
- salt and ground black pepper to taste
- 1 teaspoon minced fresh rosemary
- 1/2 teaspoon paprika
- 1/8 teaspoon ground cinnamon
- 1-1/2 teaspoons ketchup
- 1-1/2 cloves garlic, minced
- 1-1/4 cups water, or as needed
- 1/2 (12 ounce) package frozen peas and carrots, thawed
- 1-1/4 pounds Yukon Gold potatoes, peeled and halved
- 1-1/2 teaspoons butter
- 1/2 pinch ground cayenne pepper
- 2 tablespoons cream cheese
- 2 ounces Irish cheese (such as Dubliner®), shredded
- salt and ground black pepper to taste
- 1/2 egg yolk
- 1 tablespoon milk

Directions for Cooking:

1) Bring a large pan of salted water to boil and add potatoes. Simmer for 15 minutes until tender.

2) Meanwhile, lightly grease baking pan of air fryer with butter. Melt for 2 minutes at 360°F.
3) Add ground lamb and onion. Cook for 10 minutes, stirring and crumbling halfway through cooking time.
4) Add garlic, ketchup, cinnamon, paprika, rosemary, black pepper, salt, and flour. Mix well and cook for 3 minutes.
5) Add water and deglaze pan. Continue cooking for 6 minutes.
6) Stir in carrots and peas. Evenly spread mixture in pan.
7) Once potatoes are done, drain well and transfer potatoes to a bowl. Mash potatoes and stir in Irish cheese, cream cheese, cayenne pepper, and butter. Mix well. Season with pepper and salt to taste.
8) In a small bowl, whisk well milk and egg yolk. Stir into mashed potatoes.
9) Top the ground lamb mixture with mashed potatoes.
10) Cook for another 15 minutes or until tops of potatoes are lightly browned.
11) Serve and enjoy.

Nutrition Information:
Calories: 485; Carbs: 28.3g; Protein: 29.2g; Fat: 28.3g

Tasty Turkey Shepherd's Pie

(Servings: 2, Cooking Time: 50 minutes)

Ingredients:

- 1-1/2 large potatoes, peeled
- 1 tablespoon butter, room temperature
- 2 tablespoons warm milk
- 1-1/2 teaspoons olive oil
- 1/2 onion, chopped
- 1/2-pound ground turkey
- 1/2 large carrot, shredded
- 4.5-ounce can sliced mushrooms
- 1-1/2 teaspoons chopped fresh parsley
- 1/8 teaspoon dried thyme
- 1/2 clove garlic, minced
- 1/2 teaspoon chicken bouillon powder
- 1-1/2 teaspoons all-purpose flour
- salt to taste
- ground black pepper to taste

Directions for Cooking:

1) Until tender, boil potatoes. Drain and transfer to a bowl. Mash with milk and butter until creamy. Set aside.
2) Lightly grease baking pan of air fryer with olive oil. Add onion and for 5 minutes, cook on 360ºF. Add chicken bouillon, garlic, thyme, parsley, mushrooms, carrot, and ground turkey. Cook for 10 minutes while stirring and crumbling halfway through cooking time.
3) Season with pepper and salt. Stir in flour and mix well. Cook for 2 minutes.
4) Evenly spread turkey mixture. Top with mashed potatoes, evenly.
5) Cook for 20 minutes or until potatoes are lightly browned.
6) Serve and enjoy.

Nutrition Information:
Calories: 342; Carbs: 38.0g; Protein: 18.3g; Fat: 12.9g

Vegan Approved Shepherd's Pie

(Servings: 3, Cooking Time: 35 minutes)

Top Layer Ingredients:
- 2-1/2 russet potatoes, peeled and cut into 1-inch cubes
- 1/4 cup vegan mayonnaise
- 1/4 cup soy milk
- 2 tablespoons olive oil
- 1 tablespoon and 1-1/2 teaspoons vegan cream cheese substitute (such as Tofutti ®)
- 1 teaspoon salt

Bottom Layer Ingredients:
- 1-1/2 teaspoons vegetable oil
- 1/2 large yellow onion, chopped
- 1 carrot, chopped
- 1-1/2 stalks celery, chopped
- 1/4 cup frozen peas
- 1/2 tomato, chopped
- 1/2 teaspoon Italian seasoning
- 1/2 clove garlic, minced, or more to taste
- 1/2 pinch ground black pepper to taste
- 1/2 (14 ounce) package vegetarian ground beef substitute
- 1/4 cup shredded Cheddar-style soy cheese

Directions for Cooking:
1) Boil potatoes until tender. Drain and transfer to a bowl. Mash potatoes with

salt, vegan cream cheese, olive oil, soy milk, and vegan mayonnaise. Mix well until smooth. Set aside.
2) Lightly grease baking pan of air fryer with cooking spray. Add carrot, celery, onions, tomato, and peas. For 10 minutes, cook on 360°F. Stirring halfway through cooking time.
3) Stir in pepper, garlic, and Italian seasoning.
4) Stir in vegetarian ground beef substitute. Cook for 5 minutes while halfway through cooking time

crumbling and mixing the beef substitute.
5) Evenly spread the beef and veggie mixture in pan. Top evenly with mashed potato mixture.
6) Cook for another 20 minutes or until mashed potatoes are lightly browned.
7) Serve and enjoy.

Nutrition Information:
Calories: 559; Carbs: 64.5g; Protein: 20.2g; Fat: 24.4g

Enchilada Leftovers Casserole

(Servings: 3, Cooking Time: 45 minutes)

Ingredients:
- 1/2 (15 ounce) can tomato sauce
- 2 tablespoons water
- 1/2 envelope taco seasoning mix
- 2-1/4 teaspoons chili powder
- 1-1/2 teaspoons vegetable oil
- 1/2-pound chicken breast tenderloins
- 1/2 (15 ounce) can black beans, drained
- 2 tablespoons cream cheese
- 1/2 cup shredded Mexican-style cheese blend, or more to taste
- 1/2 (7.5 ounce) package corn bread mix
- 1 egg
- 3 tablespoons milk

Directions for Cooking:
1) Lightly grease baking pan of air fryer with vegetable oil. Add chicken and cook for 5 minutes per side at 360°F.

2) Stir in chili powder, taco seasoning mix, water, and tomato sauce. Cook for 10 minutes, while stirring and turning chicken halfway through cooking time.
3) Remove chicken from pan and shred with two forks. Return to pan and stir in cream cheese and black beans. Mix well.
4) Top with Mexican cheese.
5) In a bowl, whisk well egg and milk. Add corn bread mix and mix well. Pour over chicken.
6) Cover pan with foil.
7) Cook for another 15 minutes. Remove foil and cook for 10 minutes more or until topping is lightly browned.
8) Let it rest for 5 minutes.
9) Serve and enjoy.

Nutrition Information:
Calories: 487; Carbs: 45.9g; Protein: 31.2g; Fat: 19.8g

Rice, Chicken 'n Salsa Casserole

(Servings: 4, Cooking Time: 65 minutes)

Ingredients:
- 2/3 cup uncooked white rice
- 1-1/3 cups water
- 2 skinless, boneless chicken breast halves
- 1 cup shredded Monterey Jack cheese
- 1 cup shredded Cheddar cheese
- 1/2 (10.75 ounce) can condensed cream of chicken soup
- 1/2 (10.75 ounce) can condensed cream of mushroom soup
- 1/2 onion, chopped
- 3/4 cup mild salsa

Directions for Cooking:
1) Lightly grease baking pan of air fryer with cooking spray. Add water, rice, and chicken. Cover with foil and for 25 minutes, cook on 360°F.
2) Remove foil and remove chicken and cut into bite sized pieces. Fluff rice and transfer to plate.
3) In a bowl mix well, cheeses. In another bowl whisk well salsa, onion, cream of mushroom, and cream of chicken.
4) In same air fryer baking pan evenly spread ½ of rice on bottom, top with ½ of chicken, ½ of soup mixture, and then ½ of cheese. Repeat layering process.
5) Cover with foil and cook for another 25 minutes. Remove foil and cook until top is browned, around 15 minutes.
6) Serve and enjoy.

Nutrition Information:
Calories: 475; Carbs: 34.8g; Protein: 30.0g; Fat: 23.9g

Veggie-Pasta 'n chicken Bake

(Servings: 3, Cooking Time: 30 minutes)

Ingredients:
- 1/2 cup dry fusilli pasta, cooked according to manufacturer's Directions for Cooking:
- 1 tablespoon and 1-1/2 teaspoons olive oil
- 3 chicken tenderloins, cut into chunks
- 1-1/2 teaspoons dried minced onion
- salt and pepper to taste
- garlic powder to taste
- 1-1/2 teaspoons dried basil
- 1-1/2 teaspoons dried parsley
- 1/2 (10.75 ounce) can condensed cream of chicken soup
- 1/2 (10.75 ounce) can condensed cream of mushroom soup
- 1 cup frozen mixed vegetables
- 1/2 cup dry bread crumbs
- 1 tablespoon grated Parmesan cheese
- 1 tablespoon butter, melted

Directions for Cooking:
1) Lightly grease baking pan of air fryer with oil. Add chicken and season with parsley, basil, garlic powder, pepper, salt, and minced onion. For 10 minutes, cook on 360°F. Stirring halfway through cooking time.
2) Then stir in mixed vegetables, mushroom soup, chicken soup, and cooked pasta. Mix well.
3) Mix well butter, Parmesan cheese, and bread crumbs in a small bowl and spread on top of casserole.

4) Cook for 20 minutes or until tops are lightly browned.
5) Serve and enjoy.

Nutrition Information:
Calories: 399; Carbs: 35.4g; Protein: 19.8g; Fat: 19.8g

Yummy Mac 'n Cheese

(Servings: 3, Cooking Time: 32 minutes)

Ingredients:

- 8-ounce elbow macaroni, cooked according to package Directions for Cooking:
- 2 tablespoons butter
- 2 tablespoons all-purpose flour
- 1/8 teaspoon dried thyme
- 1/8 teaspoon cayenne pepper
- 1/8 teaspoon white pepper
- 1-1/2 cups milk
- 1/2 pinch ground nutmeg
- 1/8 teaspoon Worcestershire sauce
- 1/2 teaspoon salt
- 1-1/2 cups shredded sharp Cheddar cheese, divided
- 1/2 teaspoon Dijon mustard
- 1/4 cup panko bread crumbs
- 1-1/2 teaspoons butter, melted

Directions for Cooking:

1) Melt 2 tbsp butter in baking pan of air fryer for 2 minutes at 360°F. Stir in flour and cook for 3 minutes, stirring every now and then. Stir in white pepper, cayenne pepper, and thyme. Cook for 2 minutes. Stir in a cup of milk and whisk well. Cook for 5 minutes while mixing constantly.
2) Mix in salt, Worcestershire sauce, and nutmeg . Mix well. Cook for 5 minutes or until thickened while stirring frequently.
3) Add cheese and mix well. Cook for 3 minutes or until melted and thoroughly mixed.
4) Stir in Dijon mustard and mix well. Add macaroni and toss well to coat. Sprinkle remaining cheese on top.
5) In a small bowl mix well 1 ½ tsp butter and panko. Sprinkle on top of cheese.
6) Cook for 15 minutes at 390°F until tops are lightly browned.
7) Serve and enjoy.

Nutrition Information:
Calories: 700; Carbs: 72.8g; Protein: 29.4g; Fat: 32.3g

Black Bean and Brown Rice Bake

(Servings: 4, Cooking Time: 62 minutes)

Ingredients:
- 3 tablespoons brown rice
- 1/2 cup vegetable broth
- 1-1/2 teaspoons olive oil
- 2 tablespoons and 2 teaspoons diced onion
- 1/2 medium zucchini, thinly sliced
- 1 cooked skinless boneless chicken breast halves, chopped
- 1/4 cup sliced mushrooms
- 1/4 teaspoon cumin
- salt to taste
- ground cayenne pepper to taste
- 1/2 (15 ounce) can black beans, drained
- 1/2 (4 ounce) can diced green chile peppers, drained
- 3 tablespoons shredded carrots
- 1 cup shredded Swiss cheese

Directions for Cooking:
1) Lightly grease baking pan of air fryer with cooking spray. Add rice and broth. Cover pan with foil cook for 10 minutes at 390ºF. Lower heat to 300ºF and fluff rice. Cook for another 10 minutes. Let it stand for 10 minutes and transfer to a bowl and set aside.
2) Add oil to same baking pan. Stir in onion and cook for 5 minutes at 330ºF.
3) Stir in mushrooms, chicken, and zucchini. Mix well and cook for 5 minutes.
4) Stir in cayenne pepper, salt, and cumin. Mix well and cook for another 2 minutes.
5) Stir in ½ of the Swiss cheese, carrots, chiles, beans, and rice. Toss well to mix. Evenly spread in pan. Top with remaining cheese.
6) Cover pan with foil.
7) Cook for 15 minutes at 390ºF and then remove foil and cook for another 5 to 10 minutes or until tops are lightly browned.
8) Serve and enjoy.

Nutrition Information:
Calories: 337; Carbs: 11.5g; Protein: 25.3g; Fat: 21.0g

Herb and Zucchini Bake

(Servings: 3, Cooking Time: 52 minutes)

Ingredients:
- 3 tablespoons uncooked long grain white rice
- 1/3 cup water
- 1 tablespoon vegetable oil
- 3/4-pound zucchini, cubed
- 1/2 cup sliced green onions
- 1/2 clove garlic, minced
- 1/2 teaspoon garlic salt
- 1/4 teaspoon basil
- 1/4 teaspoon sweet paprika
- 1/4 teaspoon dried oregano
- 3/4 cup seeded, chopped tomatoes
- 1 cup shredded sharp Cheddar cheese, divided

Directions for Cooking:
1) Lightly grease baking pan of air fryer with cooking spray. Add rice and water. Cover pan with foil cook for 10

minutes at 390°F. Lower heat to 300°F and fluff rice. Cook for another 10 minutes. Let it stand for 10 minutes and transfer to a bowl and set aside.

2) Add oil to same air fryer baking pan and add garlic, green onions, and zucchini. For 5 minutes, cook on 360°F. Halfway through cooking time, stir veggies.

3) Season with oregano, paprika, basil, and garlic salt. Cook for 2 minutes.

4) Add half cup cheese, tomatoes, and the cooked rice. Toss well to mix. Cook for 5 minutes.

5) Sprinkle remaining cheese on top.

6) Cook for 10 minutes at 390°F until tops are lightly browned.

7) Serve and enjoy.

Nutrition Information:
Calories: 274; Carbs: 16.5g; Protein: 12.4g; Fat: 17.5g

Lobster Lasagna Maine Style

(Servings: 6, Cooking Time: 50 minutes)

Ingredients:
- 1/2 (15 ounce) container ricotta cheese
- 1 egg
- 1 cup shredded Cheddar cheese
- 1/2 cup shredded mozzarella cheese
- 1/2 cup grated Parmesan cheese
- 1/2 medium onion, minced
- 1-1/2 teaspoons minced garlic
- 1 tablespoon chopped fresh parsley
- 1/2 teaspoon freshly ground black pepper
- 1 (16 ounce) jar Alfredo pasta sauce
- 8 no-boil lasagna noodles
- 1 pound cooked and cubed lobster meat
- 5-ounce package baby spinach leaves

Directions for Cooking:
1) Mix well half of Parmesan, half of mozzarella, half of cheddar, egg, and ricotta cheese in a medium bowl. Stir in pepper, parsley, garlic, and onion.

2) Lightly grease baking pan of air fryer with cooking spray.

3) On bottom of pan, spread ½ of the Alfredo sauce, top with a single layer of lasagna noodles. Followed by 1/3 of lobster meat, 1/3 of ricotta cheese mixture, 1/3 of spinach. Repeat layering process until all Ingredients: are used up.

4) Sprinkle remaining cheese on top. Shake pan to settle lasagna and burst bubbles. Cover pan with foil.

5) For 30 minutes, cook on 360°F.

6) Remove foil and cook for 10 minutes at 390°F until tops are lightly browned.

7) Let it stand for 10 minutes.

8) Serve and enjoy.

Nutrition Information:
Calories: 558; Carbs: 20.4g; Protein: 36.8g; Fat: 36.5g

Rice and Tuna Puff

(Servings: 6, Cooking Time: 60 minutes)

Ingredients:

- 2/3 cup uncooked white rice
- 1 1/3 cups water
- 1/3 cup butter
- 1/4 cup all-purpose flour
- 1 teaspoon salt
- 1/4 teaspoon ground black pepper
- 1 1/2 cups milk
- 2 egg yolks1 (12 ounce) can tuna, undrained
- 2 tablespoons grated onion
- 1 tablespoon lemon juice
- 2 egg whites

Directions for Cooking:

1) In a saucepan bring water to a boil. Stir in rice, cover and cook on low fire until liquid is fully absorbed, around 20 minutes.
2) In another saucepan over medium fire, melt butter. Stir in pepper, salt, and flour. Cook for 2 minutes. Whisking constantly, slowly add milk. Continue cooking and stirring until thickened.
3) In medium bowl, whisk egg yolks. Slowly whisk in half of the thickened milk mixture. Add to pan of remaining milk and continue cooking and stirring for 2 more minutes. Stir in lemon juice, onion, tuna, and rice.
4) Lightly grease baking pan of air fryer with cooking spray. And transfer rice mixture.
5) Beat egg whites until stiff peak forms. Slowly fold into rice mixture.
6) Cover pan with foil.
7) For 20 minutes, cook on 360ºF.
8) Cook for 15 minutes at 390ºF until tops are lightly browned and the middle has set.
9) Serve and enjoy.

Nutrition Information:
Calories: 302; Carbs: 24.1g; Protein: 20.6g; Fat: 13.6g

Yellow Squash Bake, Low Carb

(Servings: 4, Cooking Time: 30 minutes)

Ingredients:

- 1-1/2 teaspoons olive oil
- 1/2 teaspoon butter
- 1/2 small onion, chopped
- 1 clove garlic, minced
- 2 cups peeled and cubed yellow squash
- 1/2 teaspoon kosher salt
- 1/4 teaspoon freshly ground black pepper
- 2 tablespoons and 2 teaspoons finely chopped raw almonds
- 1/2 cup shredded Colby-Monterey Jack cheese, divided
- 1/4 cup heavy whipping cream
- 1 egg
- 3 tablespoons coarsely chopped roasted, salted almonds

Directions for Cooking:

1) Lightly grease baking pan of air fryer with cooking spray. Add garlic and onion. For 5 minutes, cook on 360ºF. Halfway through cooking time, stir pan.

2) Stir in pepper, salt, and squash. Cook for another 8 minutes.
3) Mix in half of cheese and raw almonds.
4) In a small bowl, whisk well eggs and cream. Pour into pan and mix well.
5) Evenly spread squash and top with cheese and roasted almonds.
6) Cook for 15 minutes at 360°F until tops are lightly browned.
7) Serve and enjoy.

Nutrition Information:
Calories: 238; Carbs: 6.7g; Protein: 8.6g; Fat: 19.6g

Eggplant-Parm Bake

(Servings: 3, Cooking Time: 45 minutes)

Ingredients:
- 1 large eggplants
- 1 tablespoon olive oil
- 1/2 pinch salt, or as needed
- 1-1/2 teaspoons olive oil
- 1 clove garlic, sliced
- 1/4 teaspoon red pepper flakes
- 1-1/2 cups prepared marinara sauce
- 1/4 cup water, plus more as needed
- 1/4 cup and 2 tablespoons ricotta cheese
- 1/4 cup grated Parmesan cheese
- 2 tablespoons shredded pepper jack cheese
- salt and freshly ground black pepper to taste
- 1/4 cup and 2 tablespoons dry bread crumbs
- 1/4 cup grated Parmesan cheese
- 1 tablespoon olive oil

Directions for Cooking:
1) Cut eggplant crosswise in 5 pieces. Peel and chop two pieces into ½-inch cubes.
2) Lightly grease baking pan of air fryer with 1 tbsp olive oil. For 5 minutes, heat oil at 390°F. Add half eggplant strips and cook for 2 minutes per side. Transfer to a plate.
3) Add 1 ½ tsp olive oil and add garlic. Cook for a minute. Add chopped eggplants. Season with pepper flakes and salt. Cook for 4 minutes. Lower heat to 330°F and continue cooking eggplants until soft, around 8 minutes more.
4) Stir in water and marinara sauce. Cook for 7 minutes until heated through. Stirring every now and then. Transfer to a bowl.
5) In a bowl, whisk well pepper, salt, pepper jack cheese, Parmesan cheese, and ricotta. Evenly spread cheeses over eggplant strips and then fold in half.
6) Lay folded eggplant in baking pan. Pour marinara sauce on top.
7) In a small bowl whisk well olive oil, and bread crumbs. Sprinkle all over sauce.
8) Cook for 15 minutes at 390°F until tops are lightly browned.
9) Serve and enjoy.

Nutrition Information:
Calories: 405; Carbs: 41.1g; Protein: 12.7g; Fat: 21.4g

Seven Layers of Tortilla Pie

(Servings: 6, Cooking Time: 30 minutes)

Ingredients:

- 2 (15 ounce) cans pinto beans, drained and rinsed
- 1 cup salsa, divided
- 2 cloves garlic, minced
- 2 tablespoons chopped fresh cilantro
- 1 (15 ounce) can black beans, rinsed and drained
- 1/2 cup chopped tomatoes
- 7 (8 inch) flour tortillas
- 2 cups shredded reduced-fat Cheddar cheese
- 1 cup salsa
- 1/2 cup sour cream

Directions for Cooking:

1) Mash pinto beans in a large bowl and mix in garlic and salsa.
2) In another bowl whisk together tomatoes, black beans, cilantro, and ¼ cup salsa.
3) Lightly grease baking pan of air fryer with cooking spray. Spread 1 tortilla, spread ¾ cup pinto bean mixture evenly up to ½-inch away from the edge of tortilla, spread ¼ cup cheese on top. Cover with another tortilla, spread 2/3 cup black bean mixture, and then ¼ cup cheese. Repeat twice the layering process. Cover with the last tortilla, top with pinto bean mixture and then cheese.
4) Cover pan with foil.
5) Cook for 25 minutes at 390ºF, remove foil and cook for 5 minutes or until tops are lightly browned.
6) Serve and enjoy.

Nutrition Information:
Calories: 409; Carbs: 54.8g; Protein: 21.1g; Fat: 11.7g

Penne Pasta 'n Portobello Bake

(Servings: 4, Cooking Time: 30 minutes)

Ingredients:

- 4-ounce penne pasta, cooked according to manufacturer's Directions for Cooking:
- 1 tablespoon vegetable oil
- 1/4-pound portobello mushrooms, thinly sliced
- 1/4 cup margarine
- 2 tablespoons all-purpose flour
- 1 large clove garlic, minced
- 1/4 teaspoon dried basil
- 1 cup milk
- 1 cup shredded mozzarella cheese
- 5-ounce frozen chopped spinach, thawed
- 2 tablespoons soy sauce

Directions for Cooking:

1) Lightly grease baking pan of air fryer with oil. For 2 minutes, heat on 360ºF. Add mushrooms and cook for a minute. Transfer to a plate.
2) In same pan, melt margarine for a minute. Stir in basil, garlic, and flour. Cook for 3 minutes. Stir and cook for another 2 minutes. Stir in half of milk slowly while whisking continuously. Cook for another 2 minutes. Mix well. Cook for another 2 minutes. Stir in remaining milk and cook for another 3 minutes.

3) Add cheese and mix well.
4) Stir in soy sauce, spinach, mushrooms, and pasta. Mix well. Top with remaining cheese.
5) Cook for 15 minutes at 390°F until tops are lightly browned.

6) Serve and enjoy.

Nutrition Information:
Calories: 482; Carbs: 32.1g; Protein: 16.0g; Fat: 32.1g

Southwest Style Meaty Casserole

(Servings: 6, Cooking Time: 45 minutes)

Ingredients:
- 1 cup uncooked elbow macaroni, cooked according to manufacturer's instructions
- 1-pound ground beef
- 1 large onion, chopped
- 2 garlic cloves, minced
- 1 can (14-1/2 ounces each) diced tomatoes, undrained
- 1/2 can (16 ounces) kidney beans, rinsed and drained
- 1/2 can (6 ounces) tomato paste
- 1/2 can (4 ounces) chopped green chilies, drained
- 1 teaspoons salt
- 1 teaspoon chili powder
- 1/2 teaspoon ground cumin
- 1/2 teaspoon pepper
- 1 cup shredded Monterey Jack cheese
- 1 jalapeno pepper, seeded and chopped

Directions for Cooking:
1) Lightly grease baking pan of air fryer with cooking spray. Add ground beef, onion, and garlic. For 10 minutes, cook on 360°F. Halfway through cooking time, stir and crumble beef.
2) Mix in diced tomatoes, kidney beans, tomato paste, green chilies, salt, chili powder, cumin, and pepper. Mix well. Cook for another 10 minutes.
3) Stir in macaroni and mix well. Top with jalapenos and cheese.
4) Cover pan with foil.
5) Cook for 15 minutes at 390°F, remove foil and continue cooking for another 10 minutes until tops are lightly browned.
6) Serve and enjoy.

Nutrition Information:
Calories: 323; Carbs: 23.0g; Protein: 24.0g; Fat: 15.0g

Easy-Bake Spanish Rice

(Servings: 3, Cooking Time: 50 minutes)

Ingredients:

- 1/2-pound lean ground beef
- 1/4 cup finely chopped onion
- 2 tablespoons chopped green bell pepper
- 1/2 (14.5 ounce) can canned tomatoes
- 1/2 cup water
- 1/3 cup uncooked long grain rice
- 1/4 cup chile sauce
- 1/2 teaspoon salt
- 1/2 teaspoon brown sugar
- 1/4 teaspoon ground cumin
- 1/4 teaspoon Worcestershire sauce
- 1/2 pinch ground black pepper
- 1/4 cup shredded Cheddar cheese
- 1 tablespoon chopped fresh cilantro

Directions for Cooking:

1) Lightly grease baking pan of air fryer with cooking spray. Add ground beef. For 10 minutes, cook on 360°F. Halfway through cooking time, stir and crumble beef. Discard excess fat,
2) Stir in pepper, Worcestershire sauce, cumin, brown sugar, salt, chile sauce, rice, water, tomatoes, green bell pepper, and onion. Mix well. Cover pan with foil and cook for 25 minutes. Stirring occasionally.
3) Give it one last good stir, press down firmly and sprinkle cheese on top.
4) Cook uncovered for 15 minutes at 390°F until tops are lightly browned.
5) Serve and enjoy with chopped cilantro.

Nutrition Information:
Calories: 346; Carbs: 24.9g; Protein: 18.5g; Fat: 19.1g

Brown Rice 'n Chicken Curry Casserole

(Servings: 3, Cooking Time: 45 minutes)

Ingredients:

- 1/2 cup water
- 1/2 (8 ounce) can stewed tomatoes
- 1/4 cup and 2 tablespoons quick-cooking brown rice
- 1/4 cup raisins
- 1-1/2 teaspoons lemon juice
- 1-1/2 teaspoons curry powder
- 1/2 cube chicken bouillon
- 1/4 teaspoon ground cinnamon
- 1/8 teaspoon salt
- 1 clove garlic, minced
- 1/2 bay leaf (optional)
- 6 ounces skinless, boneless chicken breast halves - cut into 1-inch cubes

Directions for Cooking:

1) Lightly grease baking pan of air fryer with cooking spray.
2) Stir in bay leaf, garlic, salt, cinnamon, bouillon, curry powder, lemon juice, raisins, brown rice, stewed tomatoes, and water. For 20 minutes, cook on 360°F. Halfway through cooking time, stir in chicken and mix well.
3) Cover pan with foil.
4) Cook for 15 minutes at 390°F, remove foil, cook for 10 minutes until tops are lightly browned.
5) Serve and enjoy.

Nutrition Information:
Calories: 247; Carbs: 34.5g; Protein: 22.7g; Fat: 2.0g

Skewer Recipes

Shrimp Kebabs Cajun Flavor

(Servings: 2, Cooking Time: 10 minutes)

Ingredients:
- 12 pcs XL shrimp
- 2 tbsp olive oil
- 1 tsp kosher salt
- 1 tsp cayenne
- 1 tsp paprika
- 1 tsp garlic powder
- 1 tsp onion powder
- 1 tsp oregano
- 2 lemons, sliced thinly crosswise

Directions for Cooking:

1) In a bowl, mix all Ingredients: except for sliced lemons. Marinate for 10 minutes.
2) Thread 3 shrimps per steel skewer.
3) Place in skewer rack.
4) Cook for 5 minutes at 390°F.
5) Serve and enjoy with freshly squeezed lemon.

Nutrition Information:
Calories: 232; Carbs: 7.9g; Protein: 15.9g; Fat: 15.1g

Teriyaki Steak BBQ

(Servings: 2, Cooking Time: 15 minutes)

Ingredients:
- 14 oz lean diced steak, with fat trimmed
- 1 tbsp soy sauce
- 1 tbsp mirin
- 1 tbsp honey
- 1 thumb-sized piece of fresh ginger, grated

Directions for Cooking:
1) Mix all Ingredients: in a bowl and marinate for at least an hour. Turning over halfway through marinating time.
2) Thread mead into skewers. Place on skewer rack.
3) Cook for 5 minutes at 390°F or to desired doneness.
4) Serve and enjoy.

Nutrition Information:
Calories: 460; Carbs: 10.6g; Protein: 55.8g; Fat: 21.6g

India's Chicken Tikka

(Servings: 4, Cooking Time: 20 minutes)

Ingredients:
- 1 boneless, skinless chicken breast, cut into bite sized pieces
- 1 cup thick yogurt
- 1 medium bell pepper, cut into bite sized pieces
- 8 cherry tomatoes
- 1 tbsp fresh ginger paste
- 2 tbsp red chili powder
- 1 tsp turmeric powder
- 2 tbsp coriander powder
- 2 tbsp cumin powder
- 2 tsp olive oil
- Salt to taste
- 1 tsp Garam masala

Directions for Cooking:

1) In a bowl, whisk well all Ingredients: except for chicken breast, bell pepper, and tomatoes. Add chicken and marinate for at least 30 minutes.
2) With 4 steel skewers, skewer a piece of chicken, bell pepper, chicken, cherry tomato, chicken, and then tomato and pepper. Repeat for remaining skewers.
3) Place skewer in skewer rack, for 10 minutes, cook on 390°F. Halfway through cooking time, turnover skewer to cook evenly.
4) Serve and enjoy.

Nutrition Information:
Calories: 273; Carbs: 17.4g; Protein: 20.3g; Fat: 13.5g

Grilled Pepper-Garlic Shrimp

(Servings: 4, Cooking Time: 10 minutes)

Ingredients:
- 1 fresh red Chile (such as Fresno), seeds removed, finely grated
- 3 garlic cloves, finely grated
- 1 tablespoon coarsely ground pepper
- 1 tablespoon fresh lime juice
- 2 tablespoons vegetable oil, plus more for grill
- 1-pound large shrimp, peeled, deveined
- Kosher salt
- Lime wedges and Kashmiri chili powder or paprika (for serving)

Directions for Cooking:
1) In a large bowl, mix well oil, lime juice, pepper, garlic, and Chile. Add shrimp and marinate for at least 10 minutes. Season with salt.
2) Thread shrimp into steel skewers.
3) Place in skewer rack.
4) Cook for 5 minutes at 390°F.
5) Serve and enjoy with chili powder and lime wedges.

Nutrition Information:
Calories: 144; Carbs: 2.2g; Protein: 15.6g; Fat: 8.0g

Lamb BBQ with Garlic-Yogurt Dip

(Servings: 4, Cooking Time: 25 minutes)

BBQ Ingredients:

- 2 tablespoons cumin seeds
- 1 tablespoon Sichuan peppercorns or 1 teaspoon black peppercorns
- 2 teaspoons caraway seeds
- 2 teaspoons crushed red pepper flakes
- 1 teaspoon sugar
- 1 1/4 pounds boneless lamb shoulder, cut into 1-inch pieces
- Kosher salt, freshly cracked pepper
- Finely grated lemon zest (for serving)

For the Garlic Yogurt Dip:

- 1 garlic clove, grated
- 1/2 teaspoon finely grated lemon zest
- 1 tablespoon fresh lemon juice
- 1 cup plain Greek yogurt
- Kosher salt, freshly ground pepper

Directions for Cooking:

1) In a food processor, process cumin seeds, peppercorns, caraway seeds, pepper flakes, and sugar until smooth.
2) Thread lamb pieces into skewers. Season with salt. Rub paste all over meat pieces.
3) Place on skewer rack.
4) Cook for 5 minutes at 390°F or to desired doneness.
5) Meanwhile, in a medium bowl whisk well dip Ingredients: and set aside.
6) Serve and enjoy with dip.

Nutrition Information:

Calories: 265; Carbs: 7.6g; Protein: 34.3g; Fat: 10.8g

Ranch Potatoes on Air Fryer

(Servings: 2, Cooking Time: 15 minutes)

Ingredients:

- 1-lb baby potatoes, halved
- ½ tbsp extra virgin olive oil
- ½ lemon, juiced
- ¼ packet ranch seasoning
- Salt and pepper to taste
- Ranch dressing for drizzling
- Chopped fresh chives for garnish

Directions for Cooking:

1) Whisk well ranch seasoning, lemon juice, and olive oil. Add potatoes and toss well to mix.
2) Thread potatoes in skewers. Place on skewer rack.
3) Cook for 15 minutes at 330°F until tender.
4) Serve and enjoy with a drizzle of ranch dressing and chives.

Nutrition Information:

Calories: 280; Carbs: 45.6g; Protein: 5.4g; Fat: 8.4g

Miso-Ginger Glazed Chicken Meatballs

(Servings: 4, Cooking Time: 10 minutes)

Ingredients:

- 3/4-pound ground chicken
- 1 large egg
- 1/4 cup panko (Japanese breadcrumbs), or fresh breadcrumbs
- 2 tablespoons sliced scallions
- 2 teaspoons low-sodium soy sauce
- 1 1/2 teaspoons white miso paste
- 1 teaspoon finely grated ginger
- 1/4 teaspoon kosher salt

Directions for Cooking:

1) In a medium bowl, whisk well soy sauce, miso paste, and ginger. Set aside.
2) In a large bowl, mix well with hands ground chicken, large egg, scallions, and salt. Add panko and half of the sauce. Mix well.
3) Evenly divide into 12 balls. Thread into 4 skewers equally.
4) Place on skewer rack.
5) Cook for 2 minutes at 390°F. Baste with remaining sauce, turnover and cook for another 2 minutes. Baste with sauce on more time and cook for another minute.
6) Serve and enjoy.

Nutrition Information:
Calories: 145; Carbs: 4.2g; Protein: 17.4g; Fat: 8.2g

Turkish Lamb Kebab

(Servings: 2, Cooking Time: 15 minutes)

Ingredients:

- 1-lb lamb meat, cut into 2-inch cubes
- 1/2 cup extra-virgin olive oil, divided
- Kosher salt
- Freshly cracked black pepper
- 1/2 cup dried apricots, cut into medium dice
- 2 tablespoons Maras pepper, or 2 teaspoons other dried chili powder mixed with 1 tablespoon paprika
- 1 teaspoon minced garlic
- 2 tablespoons roughly chopped fresh mint

Directions for Cooking:

1) In a bowl, mix pepper, salt, and half of olive oil. Add lamb and toss well to coat. Thread lamb into 4 skewers.
2) Cook for 5 minutes at 390°F or to desired doneness.
3) In a large bowl, mix well remaining oil, mint, garlic, Maras pepper, and apricots. Add cooked lamb. Season with salt and pepper. Toss well to coat
4) Serve and enjoy.

Nutrition Information:
Calories: 602; Carbs: 25.8g; Protein: 40.3g; Fat: 37.5g

Satay Tofu Air Fryed

(Servings: 4, Cooking Time: 30 minutes)

Ingredients:
- 2 tablespoons soy sauce
- juice of 1 fresh lime
- 1 tablespoon maple syrup
- 2 teaspoons fresh ginger no need to peel, coarsely chopped
- 1 teaspoon sriracha sauce
- 2 cloves of garlic
- 1 block tofu, cut into strips

Peanut Butter Sauce Ingredients:
- 2-inch piece of fresh ginger coarsely chopped
- 2 cloves of garlic
- 1/2 cup creamy peanut butter
- 1 tablespoon soy sauce
- juice of 1/2 a fresh lemon
- 1-2 teaspoons Sriracha sauce to taste
- 6 tablespoons of water

Directions for Cooking:
1) In a blender, blend all peanut butter sauce Ingredients: until smooth and creamy. Transfer to a medium bowl and set aside for dipping sauce.
2) In same blender, blend garlic, sriracha, ginger, maple syrup, lime juice, and soy sauce until smooth. Pour into a bowl and add strips of tofu, Marinate for 30 minutes.
3) With the steel skewer, skewer tofu strips.
4) Place on skewer rack and air fry for 15 minutes at 370ºF.
5) Serve and enjoy.

Nutrition Information:
Calories: 347; Carbs: 16.6g; Protein: 16.6g; Fat: 23.8g

Honeyed & Grilled Strawberries

(Servings: 2, Cooking Time: 20 minutes)

Ingredients:
- 1-lb large strawberries
- 3 tbsp melted butter
- 1 tbsp honey
- 1 tsp lemon zest
- Pinch kosher salt
- Lemon wedges

Directions for Cooking:
1) Thread strawberries in 4 skewers.
2) In a small bowl, mix well remaining Ingredients: except for lemon wedges. Brush all over strawberries.
3) Place skewer on air fryer skewer rack.
4) For 10 minutes, cook on 360ºF. Halfway through cooking time, brush with honey mixture and turnover skewer.
5) Serve and enjoy with a squeeze of lemon.

Nutrition Information:
Calories: 281; Carbs: 27.9g; Protein: 1.8g; Fat: 18.0g

Aleppo Pepper-Yogurt Marinade on Chicken Kebab

(Servings: 2, Cooking Time: 20 minutes)

Ingredients:

- 1 tablespoon Aleppo pepper
- 1/3 cup plain whole-milk Greek-style yogurt
- 1 tablespoon extra-virgin olive oil
- 1 tablespoon red wine vinegar
- 1 tablespoon tomato paste
- 1 teaspoon coarse kosher salt
- 1 teaspoon freshly ground black pepper
- 3 garlic cloves, peeled, flattened
- 1 unpeeled lemon; 1/2 thinly sliced into rounds, 1/2 cut into wedges for serving
- 1-pound skinless boneless chicken (thighs and/or breast halves), cut into 1 1/4-inch cubes

Directions for Cooking:

1) Mix all Ingredients: in a bowl. Marinate in the ref for at least an hour.
2) Thread chicken in skewers and place in air fryer skewer rack.
3) For 10 minutes, cook on 360°F. Halfway through cooking time, turnover skewers.
4) Serve and enjoy with lemon wedges.

Nutrition Information:
Calories: 336; Carbs: 7.0g; Protein: 53.6g; Fat: 10.4g

Grilled & Spiced Salmon

(Servings: 4 Cooking Time: 15 minutes)

Ingredients:

- 2 tablespoons chopped fresh oregano
- 2 teaspoons sesame seeds
- 1 teaspoon ground cumin
- 1 teaspoon kosher salt
- 1/4 teaspoon crushed red pepper flakes
- 1 1/2 pounds skinless salmon fillet (preferably wild), cut into 1" pieces
- 2 lemons, very thinly sliced into rounds
- 2 tablespoons olive oil

Directions for Cooking:

1) In a small bowl, mix well oregano, sesame seeds, cumin, salt, and pepper flakes.
2) Thread salmon and folded lemon slices in a skewer. Brush with oil and sprinkle with spice.
3) Place skewers on air fryer skewer rack.
4) For 5 minutes, cook on 360°F. If needed, cook in batches.
5) Serve and enjoy.

Nutrition Information:
Calories: 313; Carbs: 2.3g; Protein: 34.3g; Fat: 18.5g

Tater Tot in Skewers

(Servings: 6, Cooking Time: 20 minutes)

Ingredients:

- 1-lb frozen tater tots, defrosted
- 12 slices bacon
- ½ cup shredded Cheddar
- 2 tbsp chives
- Ranch dressing, for serving

Directions for Cooking:

1) Thread one end of bacon in a skewer, followed by one tater, snuggly thread the bacon around tater like a snake, and then another tater, and then snake the bacon again until you reach the end. Repeat with the rest of the Ingredients.
2) For 10 minutes, cook on 360°F. Halfway through cooking time, turnover skewers. If needed cook in batches.
3) Place skewers on a serving platter and sprinkle cheese and chives on top.
4) Serve and enjoy with ranch dressing on the side.

Nutrition Information:
Calories: 337; Carbs: 17.2g; Protein: 11.5g; Fat: 29.1g

Chicken-Grill Moroccan Style

(Servings: 4, Cooking Time: 20 minutes)

Ingredients:

- 4 garlic cloves, finely chopped
- Kosher salt
- 1/3 cup olive oil
- 3 tablespoons plain yogurt
- 1-pound skinless, boneless chicken thighs, cut into 2" pieces
- 2 garlic cloves, chopped
- 1/2 cup finely chopped fresh flat-leaf parsley
- 2 teaspoons ground cumin
- 2 teaspoons paprika
- 1/4 teaspoon crushed red pepper flakes
- Kosher salt
- Vegetable oil (for grilling)
- Warm pita bread, labneh (Lebanese strained yogurt),chopped tomatoes, and fresh mint leaves (for serving)

Directions for Cooking:

1) In food processor, process garlic, salt, and oil until creamy. Add yogurt and continue pulsing until emulsified. Transfer to a bowl, set aside in the ref.
2) In a large bowl, marinate chicken in red pepper flakes, paprika, cumin, parsley, and garlic. Marinate for at least two hours in the ref.
3) Thread chicken in skewers and place in skewer rack of air fryer.
4) For 10 minutes, cook on 390°F. Halfway through cooking time, turnover skewers.
5) Serve and enjoy with the dip on the side.

Nutrition Information:
Calories: 343; Carbs: 8.1g; Protein: 28.0g; Fat: 22.0g

Salmon-Grill with Miso Glaze

(Servings: 4, Cooking Time: 16 minutes)

Ingredients:
- 1/4 cup yellow miso paste
- 2 teaspoons dashi powder
- 2 tablespoons mirin (Japanese rice wine)
- 2 teaspoons superfine sugar
- 1 1/4 pounds skinless salmon fillets, thinly sliced
- Amaranth leaves (optional), to serve
- Shichimi togarashi, to serve

Directions for Cooking:

1) In a bowl mix well sugar, mirin, dashi powder, and miso.
2) Thread salmon into skewers. Baste with miso glaze. Place on skewer rack in air fryer. If needed, cook in batches.
3) For 8 minutes, cook on 360°F. Halfway through cooking time, turnover and baste.
4) Serve and enjoy.

Nutrition Information:
Calories: 281; Carbs: 7.6g; Protein: 39.8g; Fat: 10.1g

Skewered Greek Salad on the Grill

(Servings: 6, Cooking Time: 16 minutes)

Ingredients:
- 1 big block of feta (about 12-oz.), cut into cubes
- 1/4 cup extra-virgin olive oil
- 1 tbsp lemon juice
- 1 clove garlic, smashed
- 1 tbsp Chopped fresh dill
- 1 tbsp chopped fresh parsley
- Flaky sea salt
- Freshly ground black pepper
- 12 pitted kalamata olives
- 12 cherry tomatoes
- 1 cucumber, cut into 12 large cubes

Directions for Cooking:

1) In a medium bowl, whisk well parsley, dill, garlic, lemon juice, and olive oil. Season with pepper and salt. Add feta cheese and marinate for at least 15 minutes.
2) Thread feta, olives, cherry tomatoes, and cucumber in skewers. Place on skewer rack in air fryer. If needed, cook in batches.
3) Cook for 8 minutes at 390°F.
4) Serve and enjoy.

Nutrition Information:
Calories: 217; Carbs: 7.1g; Protein: 8.8g; Fat: 17.0g

Grilled Scallion-Tomato 'n Mushrooms

(Servings: 4, Cooking Time: 20 minutes)

Ingredients:

- 2 garlic cloves, finely chopped
- 1/2 cup extra-virgin olive oil
- 1/4 cup red wine or Sherry vinegar
- 3 tablespoons chopped fresh thyme and/or rosemary leaves
- Large pinch of crushed red pepper flakes
- 1 teaspoon kosher salt, plus more to taste
- 1/2 teaspoon freshly ground black pepper, plus more to taste
- 6 scallions, cut crosswise into 2-inch pieces
- 1-pint cherry tomatoes
- 1-pint cremini, button, or other small mushrooms

Directions for Cooking:

1) In Ziploc bag, mix well black pepper, salt, red pepper flakes, thyme, vinegar, oil, and garlic. Add mushrooms, tomatoes, and scallions. Mix well and let it marinate for half an hour.
2) Thread mushrooms, tomatoes, and scallions. Reserve sauce for basting. Place on skewer rack in air fryer. If needed, cook in batches.
3) For 10 minutes, cook on 360°F. Halfway through cooking time, turnover skewers and baste with reserved sauce.
4) Serve and enjoy.

Nutrition Information:
Calories: 126; Carbs: 4.1g; Protein: 1.0g; Fat: 11.7g

Grilled Lime-Tequila Shrimp

(Servings: 3, Cooking Time: 16 minutes)

Ingredients:

- 2 tablespoons lime juice
- 2 tablespoons tequila
- 1/4 cup olive oil
- 1 pinch garlic salt
- 1 pinch ground cumin
- ground black pepper to taste
- 1-pound large shrimp, peeled and deveined
- 1 large lime, quartered

Directions for Cooking:

1) In a bowl mix well pepper, cumin, salt, olive oil, tequila and lime juice. Stir in shrimp and marinate for at least an hour. Tossing every now and then.
2) Thread shrimps in skewers. Place on skewer rack. If needed cook in batches.
3) For 8 minutes, cook on 360°F. Halfway through cooking time,
4) Serve and enjoy.

Nutrition Information:
Calories: 222; Carbs: 3.8g; Protein: 18.8g; Fat: 14.6g

Tzatziki Dip and Chicken Souvlaki

(Servings: 6, Cooking Time: 24 minutes)

Ingredients:
- 1/4 cup olive oil
- 2 tablespoons lemon juice
- 2 cloves garlic, minced
- 1 teaspoon dried oregano
- 1/2 teaspoon salt
- 1 1/2 pounds skinless, boneless chicken breast halves - cut into bite-sized pieces

Tzatziki Dip Ingredients:
- 1 (6 ounce) container plain Greek-style yogurt
- 1/2 cucumber - peeled, seeded, and grated
- 1 tablespoon olive oil
- 2 teaspoons white vinegar
- 1 clove garlic, minced
- 1 pinch salt

Directions for Cooking:
1) In a medium bowl mix well, all Tzatziki dip Ingredients. Refrigerate for at least 2 hours to allow flavors to blend.
2) In a resealable bag, mix well salt, oregano, garlic, lemon juice, and olive oil. Add chicken, squeeze excess air, seal, and marinate for at least 2 hours.
3) Thread chicken into skewers and place on skewer rack. Cook in batches.
4) For 12 minutes, cook on 360°F. Halfway through cooking time, turnover skewers and baste with marinade from resealable bag.
5) Serve and enjoy with Tzatziki dip.

Nutrition Information:
Calories: 264; Carbs: 2.6g; Protein: 25.5g; Fat: 16.8g

Pesto Glazed Grilled Shrimp

(Servings: 4, Cooking Time: 16 minutes)

Ingredients:
- 1-lb extra-large shrimp, peeled and deveined
- bamboo skewers, soaked in water
- Extra-virgin olive oil, for drizzling
- Freshly ground black pepper
- 1 cup pesto
- 1/4 cup chopped fresh basil

Directions for Cooking:

1) Thread shrimp into skewers and place on skewer rack. Drizzle with oil, season with pepper and salt.
2) For 8 minutes, cook on 360°F. Halfway through cooking time, turnover skewers and baste with pesto.
3) Serve and enjoy with a garnish of fresh basil.

Nutrition Information:
Calories: 544; Carbs: 9.6g; Protein: 7.0g; Fat: 53.0

Sausage-Shrimp Skewer BBQ

(Servings: 6, Cooking Time: 20 minutes)

Ingredients:
- 3/4 cup olive oil
- 4 large garlic cloves, pressed
- 2 tablespoons chopped fresh thyme
- 5 teaspoons smoked paprika*
- 4 teaspoons Sherry wine vinegar
- 3/4 teaspoon salt
- 1/2 teaspoon freshly ground black pepper
- 1/2 teaspoon dried crushed red pepper
- 12 uncooked extra-large shrimp (13 to 15 per pound), peeled, deveined
- 12 1-inch-long pieces andouille or other fully cooked smoked sausages (such as linguiça; about 16 ounces)
- 12 cherry tomatoes
- 12 2-layer sections of red onion wedges
- Nonstick vegetable oil spray

Directions for Cooking:
1) In medium bowl, mix well red pepper, black pepper, salt, wine vinegar, smoked paprika, thyme, garlic, and oil. Transfer half to a small bowl for dipping.
2) Thread alternately sausage and shrimp in skewers. Place on skewer rack on air fryer and baste with the paprika glaze. Cook in batches.
3) For 10 minutes, cook on 360°F. Halfway through cooking time, baste and turnover skewers.
4) Serve and enjoy with the reserved dip on the side.

Nutrition Information:
Calories: 329; Carbs: 9.8g; Protein: 8.5g; Fat: 28.4g

Chicken and Pineapple BBQ

(Servings: 5, Cooking Time: 20 minutes)

Ingredients:
- 1/2 cup pineapple juice
- 1/4 cup packed brown sugar
- 3 tablespoons light soy sauce
- 1-pound chicken breast tenderloins or strips

Directions for Cooking:
1) In a small saucepan bring to a boil pineapple juice, brown sugar, and soy sauce. Transfer to a large bowl. Stir in chicken and pineapple. Let it marinate in the fridge for an hour.
2) Thread pineapple and chicken in skewers. Place on skewer rack.
3) For 10 minutes, cook on 360°F. Halfway through cooking time, turnover chicken and baste with marinade.
4) Serve and enjoy.

Nutrition Information:
Calories: 157; Carbs: 14.7g; Protein: 19.4g; Fat: 2.2g

Sweetly Honeyed Chicken Kebabs

(Servings: 8, Cooking Time: 36 minutes)

Ingredients:
- 2 tablespoons vegetable oil
- 2 tablespoons and 2 teaspoons honey
- 2 tablespoons and 2 teaspoons soy sauce
- 1/8 teaspoon ground black pepper
- 4 skinless, boneless chicken breast halves cut into 1-inch cubes
- 1 clove garlic
- 2-1/2 small onions, cut into 2-inch pieces
- 1 red bell peppers, cut into 2-inch pieces

Directions for Cooking:
1) Whisk well pepper, soy sauce, honey, and oil. Transfer ¼ of the marinade to a small bowl for basting. Add chicken to bowl and toss well to coat. Add pepper, onion, and garlic. Toss well to mix. Let it marinate for 2 hours.
2) Thread vegetables and chicken into skewers and place on sewer rack in air fryer.
3) For 12 minutes, cook on 360°F. Halfway through cooking time, baste with marinade sauce and turnover skewers.
4) Serve and enjoy.

Nutrition Information:
Calories: 179; Carbs: 12.4g; Protein: 17.4g; Fat: 6.6g

Skewered Beef Asian Way

(Servings: 3, Cooking Time: 5 minutes)

Ingredients:
- 1 tablespoon and 1-1/2 teaspoons hoisin sauce
- 1 tablespoon and 1-1/2 teaspoons sherry
- 2 tablespoons soy sauce
- 1/2 teaspoon barbeque sauce
- 1 green onions, chopped
- 1 clove garlic, minced
- 1-1/2 teaspoons minced fresh ginger root
- 3/4-pound flank steak, thinly sliced

Directions for Cooking:
1) In a resealable bag, mix well ginger, garlic, green onions, barbecue sauce, soy sauce, sherry, and hoisin. Add steak and mix well. Remove excess air, seal, and marinate for at least 2 hours.
2) Thread steak into skewers and discard marinade.
3) For 5 minutes, cook on preheated 390°F air fryer.
4) Serve and enjoy.

Nutrition Information:
Calories: 130; Carbs: 6.7g; Protein: 14.7g; Fat: 4.9g

Chicken Kebabs Greek Way

(Servings: 4, Cooking Time: 24 minutes)

Ingredients:
- 1 (8 ounce) container fat-free plain yogurt
- 1/3 cup crumbled feta cheese with basil and sun-dried tomatoes
- 1/2 teaspoon lemon zest
- 2 tablespoons fresh lemon juice
- 2 teaspoons dried oregano
- 1/2 teaspoon salt
- 1/4 teaspoon ground black pepper
- 1/4 teaspoon crushed dried rosemary
- 1-pound skinless, boneless chicken breast halves - cut into 1-inch pieces
- 1 large red onion, cut into wedges
- 1 large green bell pepper, cut into 1 1/2-inch pieces

Directions for Cooking:
1) In a shallow dish, mix well rosemary, pepper, salt, oregano, lemon juice, lemon zest, feta cheese, and yogurt. Add chicken and toss well to coat. Marinate in the ref for 3 hours.
2) Thread bell pepper, onion, and chicken pieces in skewers. Place on skewer rack.
3) For 12 minutes, cook on 360°F. Halfway through cooking time, turnover skewers. If needed, cook in batches.
4) Serve and enjoy.

Nutrition Information:
Calories: 242; Carbs: 12.3g; Protein: 31.0g; Fat: 7.5g

Skewered Oriental Teriyaki Beef

(Servings: 6, Cooking Time: 12 minutes)

Ingredients:
- 1/4 cup and 2 tablespoons light brown sugar
- 1/4 cup soy sauce
- 2 tablespoons pineapple juice (optional)
- 2 tablespoons water
- 1 tablespoon vegetable oil
- 3/4 large garlic cloves, chopped
- 1-pound boneless round steak, cut into 1/4-inch slices

Directions for Cooking:

1) In a resealable bag, mix all Ingredients: thoroughly except for beef. Then add beef, remove excess air, and seal. Place in ref and marinate for at least a day.
2) Thread beef into skewers and place on skewer rack in air fryer. If needed, cook in batches.
3) For 6 minutes, cook on 390°F.
4) Serve and enjoy.

Nutrition Information:
Calories: 191; Carbs: 15.2g; Protein: 15.9g; Fat: 7.4g

Grilled Beef with Ginger-Hoisin

(Servings: 5, Cooking Time: 16 minutes)

Ingredients:

- 1-pound flank steak, sliced at an angle 1" x ¼" thick
- 1/4 cup hoisin sauce
- 1 tablespoon lime juice
- 1-1/2 teaspoons honey
- 1/2 clove garlic, minced
- 1/2 teaspoon kosher salt
- 1/2 teaspoon peeled and grated fresh ginger root
- 1/2 teaspoon sesame oil (optional)
- 1/2 teaspoon chile-garlic sauce (such as Sriracha®)
- 1/4 teaspoon crushed red pepper flakes
- 1/8 teaspoon ground black pepper
- 1-1/2 teaspoons toasted sesame seeds
- 1 chopped green onions

Directions for Cooking:

1) In a shallow dish, mix well pepper, red pepper flakes, chile-garlic sauce, sesame oil, ginger, salt, honey, lime juice, and hoisin sauce. Add steak and toss well to coat. Marinate in the ref for 3 hours.
2) Thread steak in skewers. Place on skewer rack in air fryer.
3) For 8 minutes, cook on 360°F. If needed, cook in batches.
4) Serve and enjoy with a drizzle of green onions and sesame seeds.

Nutrition Information:

Calories: 123; Carbs: 8.3g; Protein: 11.7g; Fat: 4.7g

Spiced Lime 'n Coconut Shrimp Skewer

(Servings: 6, Cooking Time: 12 minutes)

Ingredients:

- 2 jalapeno peppers, seeded
- 1 lime, zested and juiced
- 2 garlic cloves
- 1/3 cup chopped fresh cilantro
- 1/3 cup shredded coconut
- 1/4 cup olive oil
- 1/4 cup soy sauce
- 1-pound uncooked medium shrimp, peeled and deveined

Directions for Cooking:

1) In food processor, process until smooth the soy sauce, olive oil, coconut oil, cilantro, garlic, lime juice, lime zest, and jalapeno.
2) In a shallow dish, mix well shrimp and processed marinade. Toss well to coat and marinate in the ref for 3 hours.
3) Thread shrimps in skewers. Place on skewer rack in air fryer.
4) For 6 minutes, cook on 360°F. If needed, cook in batches.
5) Serve and enjoy.

Nutrition Information:

Calories: 172; Carbs: 4.8g; Protein: 13.4g; Fat: 10.9g

Mint-Pesto Dipped Lamb Kebabs

(Servings: 4, Cooking Time: 16 minutes)

Ingredients:
- 1 tablespoon extra-virgin olive oil plus additional for brushing
- 4 large garlic cloves, minced
- 1 teaspoon coarse kosher salt
- 1 1/2 teaspoons coriander seeds, ground in spice mill or in mortar with pestle
- 1-pound trimmed lamb meat, cut into 1 1/4-inch cubes
- 1 large red bell pepper, cut into 1-inch squares
- 1 small red onion, cut into 1-inch squares

Mint-Pesto Dip Ingredients:
- 1 cup (packed) fresh mint leaves
- 1/2 cup (packed) fresh cilantro leaves
- 2 tablespoons pine nuts
- 2 tablespoons freshly grated Parmesan cheese
- 1 tablespoon fresh lemon juice
- 1 medium garlic clove, peeled
- 1/2 teaspoon coarse kosher salt
- 1/2 cup (or more) extra-virgin olive oil

Directions for Cooking:
1) In a blender, puree all dip Ingredients: until smooth and creamy. Transfer to a bowl and set aside.
2) In a large bowl, mix well coriander, salt, garlic, and oil. Add lamb, toss well to coat. Marinate for at least an hour in the ref.
3) The thread lamb, bell pepper, and onion alternately in a skewer. Repeat until all Ingredients: re used up. Place in skewer rack in air fryer.
4) For 8 minutes, cook on 390°F. Halfway through cooking time, turnover.
5) Serve and enjoy with sauce on the side.

Nutrition Information:
Calories: 307; Carbs: 6.3g; Protein: 21.1g; Fat: 21.9

Tangy Grilled Fig-Prosciutto

(Servings: 2, Cooking Time: 8 minutes)

Ingredients:
- 2 whole figs, sliced in quarters
- 8 prosciutto slices
- Pepper and salt to taste

Directions for Cooking:
1) Wrap a prosciutto slice around one slice of fid and then thread into skewer. Repeat process for remaining Ingredients. Place on skewer rack in air fryer.
2) For 8 minutes, cook on 390°F. Halfway through cooking time, turnover skewers.
3) Serve and enjoy.

Nutrition Information:
Calories: 277; Carbs: 10.7g; Protein: 36.0g; Fat: 10.0g

Veggie Souvlaki on Air Fryer Grill

(Servings: 2, Cooking Time: 20 minutes)

Ingredients:
- 3 garlic cloves
- 1 tablespoon coriander seeds
- 1 tablespoon olive oil
- 1 teaspoon cumin
- 1 teaspoon paprika
- 1 teaspoon salt
- 1 zucchini, sliced into 1-inch thick circles
- 1 Chinese eggplant, sliced into 1-inch thick circles
- 1 medium bell pepper, cut into chunks

Directions for Cooking:

1) In a food processor, process garlic, coriander, olive oil, cumin, paprika, and salt until creamy.
2) Thread bell pepper, eggplant, and zucchini in skewers. Brush with garlic creamy paste. Place on skewer rack in air fryer.
3) For 10 minutes, cook on 360°F. Halfway through cooking time, turnover skewers. If needed, cook in batches.
4) Serve and enjoy.

Nutrition Information:
Calories: 181; Carbs: 22.4g; Protein: 4.2g; Fat: 8.2g

Swordfish with Sage on the Grill

(Servings: 2, Cooking Time: 16 minutes)

Ingredients:
- 1/2-pound swordfish, sliced into 2-inch chunks
- 1 tbsp lemon juice
- 1 tsp parsley
- salt and pepper to taste.
- 1 zucchini, peeled and then thinly sliced in lengths
- 2 tbsp olive oil
- ½ lemon, sliced thinly in rounds
- 6-8 sage leaves

Directions for Cooking:
1) In a shallow dish, mix well lemon juice, parsley, and sliced swordfish. Toss well to coat and generously season with pepper and salt. Marinate for at least 10 minutes.
2) Place one length of zucchini on a flat surface. Add one piece of fish and sage leaf. Roll zucchini and then thread into a skewer. Repeat process to remaining Ingredients.
3) Brush with oil and place on skewer rack in air fryer.
4) For 8 minutes, cook on 390°F. If needed, cook in batches.
5) Serve and enjoy with lemon slices.

Nutrition Information:
Calories: 297; Carbs: 3.7g; Protein: 22.8g; Fat: 21.2g

Peanut Dip and Chicken Satay

(Servings: 4, Cooking Time: 25 minutes)

Ingredients:

- 1/2 cup unsweetened coconut milk
- 2 teaspoons yellow curry powder
- 1 teaspoon white sugar
- 1 teaspoon fish sauce
- 1/2 teaspoon granulated garlic
- 1-pound skinless, boneless chicken breasts, cut into strips
- 2 tablespoons olive oil
- 3/4 cup unsweetened coconut milk
- 1 tablespoon yellow curry powder
- 1/2 cup chicken broth
- 1/4 cup creamy peanut butter
- 1 tablespoon white sugar
- 1 tablespoon lime juice
- 1 tablespoon fish sauce

Directions for Cooking:

1) In resealable bag, mix well garlic, 1 tsp fish sauce, 1 tsp sugar, 2 tsps. curry powder, and ½ cup coconut milk. Add chicken and toss well to coat. Remove excess air and seal bag. Marinate for 2 hours.
2) Thread chicken into skewer and place on skewer rack.
3) For 10 minutes, cook on 390°F. Halfway through cooking time, turnover skewers.
4) Meanwhile, make the peanut sauce by bringing remaining coconut milk to a simmer in a medium saucepan. Stir in curry powder and cook for 4 minutes. Add 1 tbsp fish sauce, lime juice, 1 tbsp sugar, peanut butter, and chicken broth. Mix well and cook until heated through. Transfer to a small bowl.
5) Serve and enjoy with the peanut sauce.

Nutrition Information:
Calories: 482; Carbs: 12.1g; Protein: 31.7g; Fat: 34.0g

Scallops and Bacon Grill

(Servings: 2, Cooking Time: 12 minutes)

Ingredients:

- 6 large scallops
- 6 bacon strips
- 1 teaspoon smoked paprika

Directions for Cooking:

1) Wrap one bacon around one scallop and thread in a skewer ensuring that it will not unravel. Repeat until all Ingredients: are used.
2) Season with paprika.
3) Place on skewer rack in air fryer.
4) For 12 minutes, cook on 390°F. Halfway through cooking time, turnover skewers.
5) Serve and enjoy.

Nutrition Information:
Calories: 72; Carbs: 2.4g; Protein: 1.9g; Fat: 6.0g

Grilled Chicken Shish Tanoak

(Servings: 3, Cooking Time: 20 minutes)

Ingredients:
- 2 tablespoons lemon juice
- 2 tablespoons vegetable oil
- 1/3 cup plain yogurt
- 2 cloves garlic, minced
- 1 teaspoon tomato paste
- 3/4 teaspoon salt
- 1/2 teaspoon dried oregano
- 1/8 teaspoon ground black pepper
- 1/8 teaspoon ground allspice
- 1/8 teaspoon ground cinnamon
- 1/8 teaspoon ground cardamom
- 1-pound skinless, boneless chicken breast halves cut into 2-inch pieces
- 1 onion, cut into large chunks
- 1 small green bell pepper, cut into large chunks
- 1/2 cup chopped fresh flat-leaf parsley

Directions for Cooking:
1) In a resealable plastic bag, mix cardamom, cinnamon, allspice, pepper, oregano, salt, tomato paste, garlic, yogurt, vegetable oil, and lemon juice. Add chicken, remove excess air, seal, and marinate in the ref for at least 4 hours.
2) Thread chicken into skewers, place on skewer rack and cook in batches.
3) For 10 minutes, cook on 360ºF. Halfway through cooking time, turnover skewers.
4) Serve and enjoy with a sprinkle of parsley.

Nutrition Information:
Calories: 297; Carbs: 9.8g; Protein: 34.3g; Fat: 13.4g

Grilled Chipotle Shrimp

(Servings: 2, Cooking Time: 24 minutes)

Ingredients:
- 1/4 cup barbecue sauce
- juice of 1/2 orange
- 3 tablespoons minced chipotles in adobo sauce
- salt
- ½-pound large shrimps

Directions for Cooking:
1) In a small shallow dish, mix well all Ingredients: except for shrimp. Save ¼ of the mixture for basting.
2) Add shrimp in dish and toss well to coat. Marinate for at least 10 minutes.
3) Thread shrimps in skewers. Place on skewer rack in air fryer.
4) For 12 minutes, cook on 360ºF. Halfway through cooking time, turnover skewers and baste with sauce. If needed, cook in batches.
5) Serve and enjoy.

Nutrition Information:
Calories: 179; Carbs: 24.6g; Protein: 16.6g; Fat: 1.5g

Beef Eastern Shish Kebabs

(Servings: 4, Cooking Time: 20 minutes)

Ingredients:

- 1/3 cup vegetable oil
- 1/2 cup soy sauce
- 1/4 cup lemon juice
- 1 tablespoon prepared mustard
- 1 tablespoon Worcestershire sauce
- 1 clove garlic, minced
- 1 teaspoon coarsely cracked black pepper
- 1 1/2 teaspoons salt
- 1 1/2 pounds lean beef, cut into 1-inch cubes
- 16 mushroom caps
- 2 green bell peppers, cut into chunks
- 1 red bell pepper, cut into chunks
- 1 large onion, cut into large squares

Directions for Cooking:

1) In a resealable bag, mix well salt, pepper, garlic, Worcestershire, mustard, lemon juice, soy sauce, and oil. Add beef and toss well to coat. Remove excess air and seal. Marinate for 8 hours. Add mushroom and marinate for an additional 8 hours.
2) Thread mushrooms, bell peppers, onion, and meat in skewers.
3) Pour marinade in saucepan and thicken for 10 minutes and transfer to a bowl for basting.
4) Place skewers on skewer rack in air fryer. If needed, cook in batches.
5) For 10 minutes, cook on 390°F. Halfway through cooking time, baste and turnover skewers.
6) Serve and enjoy.

Nutrition Information:
Calories: 426; Carbs: 15.8g; Protein: 26.2g; Fat: 28.6g

Dill-Rubbed Grilled Salmon

(Servings: 2, Cooking Time: 12 minutes)

Ingredients:

- 1-lb salmon filet, cut into 2-inch rectangles
- 3 tablespoons hoisin sauce
- 1 tablespoon soy sauce
- 1 tablespoon rice wine
- 1 tablespoon honey
- 1 tablespoon olive oil

Directions for Cooking:

1) In a shallow dish, mix well all Ingredients. Marinate in the ref for 3 hours.
2) Thread salmon pieces in skewers and reserve marinade for basting. Place on skewer rack in air fryer.
3) For 12 minutes, cook on 360°F. Halfway through cooking time, turnover skewers and baste with marinade. If needed, cook in batches.
4) Serve and enjoy.

Nutrition Information:
Calories: 971; Carbs: 23.0g; Protein: 139.4g; Fat: 35.7g

Turkey Meatballs in Skewer

(Servings: 4, Cooking Time: 25 minutes)

Ingredients:
- 1/3 cup cranberry sauce
- 1 1/2 tablespoons barbecue sauce
- 1 ½ tablespoons water
- 2 teaspoons cider vinegar
- 1 tsp salt and more to taste
- 1-pound ground turkey
- 1/4-pound ground bacon

Directions for Cooking:
1) In a bowl, mix well with hands the turkey, ground bacon and a tsp of salt. Evenly form into 16 equal sized balls.
2) In a small saucepan boil cranberry sauce, barbecue sauce, water, cider vinegar, and a dash or two of salt. Mix well and simmer for 3 minutes.
3) Thread meatballs in skewers and baste with cranberry sauce. Place on skewer rack in air fryer.
4) For 15 minutes, cook on 360°F. Every after 5 minutes of cooking time, turnover skewers and baste with sauce. If needed, cook in batches.
5) Serve and enjoy.

Nutrition Information:
Calories: 217; Carbs: 11.5g; Protein: 28.0g; Fat: 10.9g

Grilled Curried Chicken

(Servings: 3, Cooking Time: 12 minutes)

Ingredients:
- 2/3 cup coconut milk
- 3 tablespoons peanut butter
- 1 tablespoon Thai curry paste
- 1 tablespoon lime juice
- 1 teaspoon salt
- ½-lb boneless and skinless chicken thigh meat, cut into 2-inch chunks
- 1 medium bell pepper, seeded and cut into chunks

Directions for Cooking:
1) In a shallow dish, mix well all Ingredients: except for chicken and bell pepper. Transfer half of the sauce in a small bowl for basting.
2) Add chicken to dish and toss well to coat. Marinate in the ref for 3 hours.
3) Thread bell pepper and chicken pieces in skewers. Place on skewer rack in air fryer.
4) For 12 minutes, cook on 360°F. Halfway through cooking time, turnover skewers and baste with sauce. If needed, cook in batches.
5) Serve and enjoy.

Nutrition Information:
Calories: 282; Carbs: 10.0g; Protein: 20.0g; Fat: 18.0g

Peppered & Carbonated Sirloin Kebabs

(Servings: 4, Cooking Time: 20 minutes)

Ingredients:

- 2 tablespoons soy sauce
- 1 1/2 tablespoons light brown sugar
- 1 1/2 tablespoon distilled white vinegar
- 1/4 teaspoon garlic powder
- 1/4 teaspoon seasoned salt
- 1/4 teaspoon garlic pepper seasoning
- 1/4 cup lemon-lime flavored carbonated beverage
- 1-pound beef sirloin steak, cut into 1 1/2-inch cubes
- 1 green bell peppers, cut into 2-inch pieces
- 1/4-pound fresh mushrooms, stems removed
- 1 cup cherry tomatoes
- 1/2 fresh pineapple - peeled, cored and cubed

Directions for Cooking:

1) Whisk well carbonated beverage, garlic pepper seasoning, seasoned salt, garlic powder, white vinegar, light brown sugar, and soy sauce. Transfer 1/4 cup to a bowl for basting. Place remaining sauce in a Ziploc bag.
2) Add steak in bag and marinate for at least overnight. Ensuring to turnover at least twice.
3) Thread pineapple, tomatoes, mushrooms, green peppers, and steak in skewers. Place on skewer rack on air fryer. Cook in batches. Baste with reserved sauce.
4) For 10 minutes, cook on 360ºF. Halfway through cooking time, baste and turnover skewers.
5) Serve and enjoy.

Nutrition Information:
Calories: 330; Carbs: 19.2g; Protein: 24.0g; Fat: 17.4g

Grilled Jerk Chicken

(Servings: 2, Cooking Time: 30 minutes)

Ingredients:

- 2 whole chicken thighs
- 1/4 cup pineapple chunks
- 4 tablespoons jerk seasoning
- 1 tablespoon vegetable oil
- 3 teaspoons lime juice

Directions for Cooking:

1) In a shallow dish, mix well all Ingredients. Marinate in the ref for 3 hours.
2) Thread chicken pieces and pineapples in skewers. Place on skewer rack in air fryer.
3) For 30 minutes, cook on 360ºF. Halfway through cooking time, turnover skewers.
4) Serve and enjoy.

Nutrition Information:
Calories: 579; Carbs: 36.3g; Protein: 25.7g; Fat: 36.7g

Chicken Caesar on the Grill

(Servings: 3, Cooking Time: 24 minutes)

Ingredients:
- 1-pound ground chicken
- 2 tablespoons Caesar dressing and more for drizzling
- 1/2 cup Parmesan
- 1/4 cup breadcrumbs
- 1 teaspoon lemon zest. Form into ovals, skewer and grill.
- 2-4 romaine leaves
- ¼ cup crouton

Directions for Cooking:
1) In a shallow dish, mix well chicken, 2 tablespoons Caesar dressing, parmesan, and breadcrumbs. Mix well with hands. Form into 1-inch oval patties.
2) Thread chicken pieces in skewers. Place on skewer rack in air fryer.
3) For 12 minutes, cook on 360°F. Halfway through cooking time, turnover skewers. If needed, cook in batches.
4) Serve and enjoy on a bed of lettuce and sprinkle with croutons and extra dressing.

Nutrition Information:
Calories: 339; Carbs: 9.5g; Protein: 32.6g; Fat: 18.9g

Rosemary-Rubbed Grilled Lamb

(Servings: 2, Cooking Time: 12 minutes)

Ingredients:
- 1-lb cubed lamb leg
- 1/2 cup olive oil
- juice of 1 lemon
- fresh rosemary
- 3 smashed garlic cloves
- salt and pepper

Directions for Cooking:
1) In a shallow dish, mix well all Ingredients: and marinate for 3 hours.
2) Thread lamb pieces in skewers. Place on skewer rack in air fryer.
3) For 12 minutes, cook on 390°F. Halfway through cooking time, turnover skewers. If needed, cook in batches.
4) Serve and enjoy.

Nutrition Information:
Calories: 560; Carbs: 5.4g; Protein: 46.5g; Fat: 39.1g

Thai-Style Grilled Pork

(Servings: 3, Cooking Time: 15 minutes)

Ingredients:
- 1-pound ground pork
- 3 tablespoons chopped mint
- 3 tablespoons cilantro
- 3 tablespoons basil
- 1 minced shallot
- 1 minced hot chile
- 2 tablespoons fish sauce
- 2 tablespoons lime juice

Directions for Cooking:

1) In a shallow dish, mix well all Ingredients: with hands. Form into 1-inch ovals.
2) Thread ovals in skewers. Place on skewer rack in air fryer.
3) For 15 minutes, cook on 360°F. Halfway through cooking time, turnover skewers. If needed, cook in batches.
4) Serve and enjoy.

Nutrition Information:
Calories: 455; Carbs: 2.5g; Protein: 40.2g; Fat: 31.5g

Hungarian Style Grilled Beef

(Servings: 3, Cooking Time: 12 minutes)

Ingredients:
- 1-lb beef tri-tip, sliced to 2-inch cubes
- 1/2 cup olive oil
- 2 smashed garlic cloves
- a pinch of salt
- 1/2 teaspoon paprika
- 2 teaspoons crushed caraway seeds
- 1 medium red onion, sliced into quarters
- 1 medium bell pepper seeded and cut into chunks

Directions for Cooking:

1) In a shallow dish, mix well all Ingredients: except for bell pepper and onion. Toss well to coat. Marinate in the ref for 3 hours.
2) Thread beef, onion, and bell pepper pieces in skewers. Place on skewer rack in air fryer.
3) For 12 minutes, cook on 360°F. Halfway through cooking time, turnover skewers. If needed, cook in batches.
4) Serve and enjoy.

Nutrition Information:
Calories: 530; Carbs: 3.3g; Protein: 33.1g; Fat: 42.7g

Cajun Pork on the Grill

(Servings: 3, Cooking Time: 12 minutes)

Ingredients:
- 1-lb pork loin, sliced into 1-inch cubes
- 3 tablespoons brown sugar
- 2 tablespoons Cajun seasoning
- 1/4 cup cider vinegar
- ¼ cup brown sugar

Directions for Cooking:
1) In a shallow dish, mix well pork loin, 3 tablespoons brown sugar, and Cajun seasoning. Toss well to coat. Marinate in the ref for 3 hours.
2) In a medium bowl mix well, brown sugar and vinegar for basting.
3) Thread pork pieces in skewers. Baste with sauce and place on skewer rack in air fryer.
4) For 12 minutes, cook on 360°F. Halfway through cooking time, turnover skewers and baste with sauce. If needed, cook in batches.
5) Serve and enjoy.

Nutrition Information:
Calories: 428; Carbs: 30.3g; Protein: 39.0g; Fat: 16.7g

Grilled Buccaneer Pork

(Servings: 3, Cooking Time: 15 minutes)

Ingredients:
- 1 cup water
- 3 tablespoons each salt
- 3 tablespoons brown sugar
- 2 teaspoons pickling spices
- 4 garlic cloves
- 1 cup rum
- 1-lb pork tenderloin, sliced into 1-inch cubes
- ½ cup ready-made jerk sauce

Directions for Cooking:
1) In a saucepan, bring to a boil water salt and brown sugar. Stir in garlic and pickling spices and simmer for 3 minutes. Turn off fire and whisk in rum.
2) Transfer sauce to a shallow dish, mix well pork tenderloin and marinate in the ref for 3 hours.
3) Thread pork pieces in skewers. Baste with jerk sauce and place on skewer rack in air fryer.
4) For 12 minutes, cook on 360°F. Halfway through cooking time, turnover skewers and baste with sauce. If needed, cook in batches.
5) Serve and enjoy.

Nutrition Information:
Calories: 295; Carbs: 19.9g; Protein: 41.0g; Fat: 5.7g

Grilled Steak with Scallion Dip

(Servings: 4, Cooking Time: 20 minutes)

Ingredients:
- 1 cup canned unsweetened coconut milk
- 1/4 cup fish sauce
- 2 tablespoons packed light brown sugar
- 1 tablespoon fresh lime juice
- 6 garlic cloves
- 4 red or green Thai chiles, stemmed
- 2 lemongrass stalks, bottom third only, tough outer layers removed
- 1 1 1/2" piece ginger, peeled
- 1-pound tri-tip fat cap left on , cut into 1-inch cubes

Scallion Dip Ingredients:
- 15 scallions, very thinly sliced
- 1/4 cup fish sauce
- 3 tablespoons grapeseed oil
- 2 tablespoons black vinegar
- 2 tablespoons toasted sesame seeds

Basting Sauce Ingredients:
- 1/2 cup canned unsweetened coconut milk

- 3 tablespoons fish sauce
- 1 1/2 tablespoons fresh lime juice
- 2 garlic cloves, crushed

Directions for Cooking:
1) Except for meat, puree all Ingredients: in a blender. Transfer into a bowl and marinate beef at least overnight in the ref.
2) In a medium bowl, mix well all scallion dip Ingredients: and set aside.
3) In a separate bowl mix all basting sauce Ingredients.
4) Thread meat into skewers and place on skewer rack in air fryer. Baste with sauce.
5) Cook for 10 minutes at 390°F or to desired doneness. Halfway through cooking time, baste and turnover skewers.
6) Serve and enjoy with the dip on the side.

Nutrition Information:
Calories: 579; Carbs: 15.3g; Protein: 32.0g; Fat: 43.3g

Teriyaki 'n Hawaiian Chicken

(Servings: 4, Cooking Time: 23 minutes)

Ingredients:
- 2 boneless skinless chicken breasts, cut into 1-inch cubes
- ½ cup brown sugar
- ½ cup soy sauce
- ¼ cup pineapple juice
- 2 garlic cloves, minced
- ¼ teaspoon pepper
- ½ teaspoon salt
- 1 Tablespoon cornstarch
- 1 Tablespoon water

- 1 red bell pepper, cut into 1-inch cubes
- 1 yellow red bell pepper, cut into 1-inch cubes
- 1 green bell pepper, cut into 1-inch cubes
- 1 red onion, cut into 1-inch cubes
- 2 cups fresh pineapple cut into 1-inch cubes
- green onions, for garnish

Directions for Cooking:

1) In a saucepan, bring to a boil salt, pepper, garlic, pineapple juice, soy sauce, and brown sugar. In a small bowl whisk well, cornstarch and water. Slowly stir in to mixture in pan while whisking constantly. Simmer until thickened, around 3 minutes. Save ¼ cup of the sauce for basting and set aside.

2) In shallow dish, mix well chicken and remaining thickened sauce. Toss well to coat. Marinate in the ref for a half hour.

3) Thread bell pepper, onion, pineapple, and chicken pieces in skewers. Place on skewer rack in air fryer.

4) For 10 minutes, cook on 360°F. Halfway through cooking time, turnover skewers and baste with sauce. If needed, cook in batches.

5) Serve and enjoy with a sprinkle of green onions.

Nutrition Information:
Calories: 391; Carbs: 58.7g; Protein: 31.2g; Fat: 3.4g

Baked Recipes

Air Fried Fish with Coconut Sauce

(Servings: 4, Cooking Time: 15 minutes)

Ingredients:
- ½ pound bass fillet
- Salt and pepper to taste
- 1 tablespoon olive oil
- ¼ cup coconut milk
- 2 tablespoons lime juice, freshly squeezed
- 2 tablespoons jalapeno, chopped
- 3 tablespoons parsley, chopped

Directions for Cooking:
1) Preheat the air fryer for 5 minutes at 330°F.
2) Add the coconut milk, lime juice, jalapeno and parsley in the air fryer baking pan.
3) Season the bass with salt and pepper to taste and place in pan.
4) Brush the surface with olive oil.
5) Cook for 15 minutes at 330°F.
6) Serve and enjoy.

Nutrition information:
Calories: 139; Carbs: 2.7g; Protein: 8.7g; Fat: 10.3g

Air Fried Cod with Basil Vinaigrette

(Servings: 4, Cooking Time: 15 minutes)

Ingredients:
- 4 cod fillets
- Salt and pepper to taste
- Juice from 1 lemon, freshly squeezed
- ¼ cup olive oil
- A bunch of basil, torn

Directions for Cooking:
1) Preheat the air fryer for 5 minutes.
2) Season the cod fillets with salt and pepper to taste. Place on lightly greased air fryer baking pan.
3) Mix the rest of the ingredients in a bowl and toss to combine. Pour over fish.
4) Cook for 15 minutes at 330°F.
5) Serve and enjoy.

Nutrition information:
Calories: 235; Cars: 1.9g; Protein: 14.3g; Fat: 18.9g

Smoked Trout Frittata

(Servings: 6 Cooking Time: 15 minutes)

Ingredients:

- 2 tablespoons olive oil
- 1 onion, chopped
- 6 eggs, beaten
- 2 tablespoons coconut oil
- 2 fillets smoked trout, shredded
- Salt and pepper to taste

Directions for Cooking:

1) Preheat the air fryer for 5 minutes.
2) Place all ingredients in a mixing bowl until well-combined.
3) Pour into the air fryer baking dish.
4) Cook for 15 minutes at 390ºF.

Nutrition information:

Calories: 254; Carbs: 3.4g; Protein: 14.2g; Fat: 20.4g

Creamy Air Fried Salmon

(Servings: 2, Cooking Time: 15 minutes)

Ingredients:

- ½ pound salmon fillet
- Salt and pepper to taste
- 1 teaspoon olive oil
- 1 avocado, pitted and chopped
- ½ clove of garlic
- 2 tablespoons cashew nuts, soaked in water for 10 minutes

Directions for Cooking:

1) Preheat the air fryer for 5 minutes
2) Season the salmon fillets with salt, pepper, and olive oil.
3) Place in the air fryer and cook for 15 minutes at 390ºF.
4) Meanwhile, place the rest of the Ingredients: in a food processor. Season with salt and pulse until smooth.
5) Serve the salmon fillet with the creamy avocado sauce.

Nutrition information:

Calories: 417; Carbs: 13.7g; Protein: 23.4g; Fat: 29.8g

Baked Thai Fish

(Servings: 4, Cooking Time: 20 minutes)

Ingredients:
- 1-pound cod fillet, cut into bite-sized pieces
- ¼ cup coconut milk, freshly squeezed
- Salt and pepper to taste
- 1 tablespoon lime juice, freshly squeezed

Directions for Cooking:
1) Preheat the air fryer for 5 minutes.
2) Place all ingredients in a baking dish that will fit in the air fryer.
3) Place in the air fryer.
4) Cook for 20 minutes at 325°F.

Nutrition information:
Calories: 844; Carbs: 2.3g; Protein: 21.6g; Fat: 83.1g

Air Fried Fish in Pesto Sauce

(Servings: 3, Cooking Time: 20 minutes)

Ingredients:
- 1 cup olive oil
- Salt and pepper to taste
- 1 bunch fresh basil
- 2 cloves of garlic,
- 2 tablespoons pine nuts
- 1 tablespoon parmesan cheese, grated
- 3 white fish fillets

Directions for Cooking:

1) In a food processor, combine all ingredients except for the fish fillets.
2) Pulse until smooth.
3) Place the fish in a baking dish and pour over the pesto sauce.
4) Place in the air fryer and cook for 20 minutes at 390°F.

Nutrition information:
Calories: 191; Carbs: 9.5g; Protein: 8.2g; Fat: 13.3g

Hong Kong Style Cod Fish

(Servings: 2, Cooking Time: 15 minutes)

Ingredients:
- 2 cod fish fillets
- A dash of sesame oil
- 250 mL water
- 3 tablespoons coconut aminos
- 3 tablespoons coconut oil
- 5 slices of ginger
- Green onions for garnish

Directions for Cooking:

1) Preheat the air fryer for 5 minutes
2) Place all ingredients except for the green onions in the air fryer baking pan.
3) Place in the air fryer and cook for 15 minutes at 390°F.
4) Garnish with green onions.

Nutrition information:
Calories: 571; Carbs: 4.3g; Protein: 22.3g; Fat: 51.6g

Balsamic Roast Beef

(Servings: 10, Cooking Time: 2 hours)

Ingredients:
- 3 pounds boneless roast beef
- 1 cup beef organic beef broth
- ½ cup balsamic vinegar
- 4 tablespoons olive oil
- 1 tablespoon coconut aminos
- 1 tablespoon Worcestershire sauce
- 1 tablespoon honey
- ½ teaspoon red pepper flakes
- 4 cloves of garlic, minced

Directions for Cooking:

1) Place all ingredients in the air fryer baking pan and make sure that the entire surface of the beef is coated with the spices.
2) Place the baking dish with the beef in the air fryer. Cover pan with foil. Close.
3) Cook for 2 hours at 390°F.

Nutrition information:
Calories: 325; Carbs: 6.9g; Protein: 36.2g; Fat: 16.9g

Italian Beef Roast

(Servings: 10, Cooking Time: 3 hours)

Ingredients:
- 2 ½ pounds beef round roast
- 1 onion, sliced thinly
- 4 tablespoons olive oil
- ½ cup water
- 1 teaspoon basil
- ½ teaspoon thyme
- 1 teaspoon salt
- ¼ teaspoon black pepper

Directions for Cooking:

1) Place all ingredients in an air fryer baking pan and make sure that the entire surface of the beef is coated with the spices.
2) Place the baking dish with the beef in the air fryer. Cover pan with foil. Close.
3) Cook for 3 hours at 390°F.

Nutrition information:
Calories: 282; Carbs: 0.2g; Protein: 23.6g; Fat: 20.7g

Peppered Roast Beef with Shallots

(Servings: 9, Cooking Time: 1 hour and 30 minutes)

Ingredients:
- 3 tablespoons mixed peppercorns
- 1 boneless rib roast
- 4 tablespoons olive oil
- Salt to taste
- 1 ½ pounds medium shallots, chopped
- 4 medium shallots, chopped
- 2 tablespoons whole grain mustard
- ¼ cup flat-leaf parsley, chopped

Directions for Cooking:
1) Preheat the air fryer for 5 minutes.
2) Place all ingredients in a baking dish that will fit in the air fryer.
3) Place the dish in the air fryer and cook for 1 hour and 30 minutes at 325°F.

Nutrition information:
Calories: 451; Carbs: 15.4g; Protein: 30.5g; Fat: 29.7g

Rosemary-Pepper Beef Rib Roast

(Servings: 14, Cooking Time: 2 hours)

Ingredients:
- 3 tablespoons vegetable oil
- 6 ribs, beef rib roast
- 3 tablespoons unsalted pepper
- 1 medium shallot, chopped
- 2 cloves of garlic, minced
- 2 cups water
- 1 cup dried porcini mushrooms
- 4 sprigs of thyme
- Salt and pepper to taste

Directions for Cooking:
1) Preheat the air fryer for 5 minutes.
2) Place all ingredients in air fryer baking pan and cover with foil.
3) Place the dish in the air fryer and cook for 2 hours at 300ºF.

Nutrition information:
Calories: 320; Carbs: 0.9g; Protein: 32.4g; Fat: 20.7g

Oven-Braised Corned Beef

(Servings: 12, Cooking Time: 50 minutes)

Ingredients:
- 4 cups water
- 3 pounds corned beef brisket, cut into chunks
- 2 tablespoons Dijon mustard
- 1 onion, chopped
- Salt and pepper to taste

Directions for Cooking:
1) Preheat the air fryer for 5 minutes
2) Place all ingredients in air fryer baking pan and cover with foil.
3) Cook for 50 minutes at 390ºF.

Nutrition information:
Calories: 241; Carbs: 1.5g; Protein: 15.2g; Fat: 19.3g

Air Fried-Braised Beef Roast

(Servings: 6, Cooking Time: 2 hours)

Ingredients:

- 1-pound beef chuck roast
- 2 tablespoons olive oil
- 1 tablespoon butter
- 1 tablespoon Worcestershire sauce
- 2 cloves of garlic, minced
- 1 onion, chopped
- 3 stalks of celery, sliced
- 1 teaspoon thyme
- 1 teaspoon rosemary
- 3 cups water

Directions for Cooking:

1) Preheat the air fryer for 5 minutes.
2) Place all ingredients in air fryer baking pan and cover pan with foil.
3) Bake for 2 hours at 300°F.
4) Braise the meat with its sauce every 30 minutes until cooked.

Nutrition information:
Calories: 260; Carbs: 2.9g; Protein: 17.5g; Fat: 19.8g

Buffalo Chicken Dip Bake

(Servings: 4, Cooking Time: 20 minutes)

Ingredients:

- 1-1/2 cups diced cooked rotisserie chicken
- 1 (8 ounce) package cream cheese, softened
- 1/4 cup and 2 tablespoons hot pepper sauce (such as Frank's Reshoot®)
- 1/4 cup shredded pepper Jack cheese
- 1/4 cup blue cheese dressing
- 1/4 cup crumbled blue cheese
- 1/4 teaspoon seafood seasoning (such as Old Bay®)
- 1/2 pinch cayenne pepper, or to taste
- 1 tablespoon shredded pepper Jack cheese
- 1/2 pinch cayenne pepper, for garnish

Directions for Cooking:

1) Lightly grease baking pan of air fryer with cooking spray. Mix in cayenne pepper, seafood seasoning, crumbled blue cheese, blue cheese dressing, pepper Jack, hot pepper sauce, cream cheese, and chicken.
2) For 15 minutes, cook on 390°F.
3) Let it stand for 5 minutes and garnish with cayenne pepper.
4) Serve and enjoy.

Nutrition Information:
Calories: 405; Carbs: 3.2g; Protein: 17.1g; Fat: 35.9g

Traditional Beef Pot Pie

(Servings: 6, Cooking Time: 30 minutes)

Ingredients:
- 1-pound ground beef
- 1 green bell pepper, julienned
- 1 red bell pepper, julienned
- 1 yellow bell pepper, julienned
- 1 onion, chopped
- 2 cloves of garlic, minced
- 4 tablespoons coconut oil
- 1 tablespoon butter
- Salt and pepper to taste
- 1 cup almond flour
- 2 beaten eggs

Directions for Cooking:

1) Preheat the air fryer for 5 minutes with baking pan insert.
2) In a baking pan, combine the first 9 Ingredients. Mix well then set aside.
3) In a mixing bowl, mix the almond flour and eggs to create a dough.
4) Press the dough over the beef mixture.
5) Place in the air fryer and cook for 30 minutes at 330°F.

Nutrition information:
Calories: 363; Carbs: 5.3g; Protein: 21.3g; Fat: 28.5g

Air Fryer Beef Casserole

(Servings: 4, Cooking Time: 30 minutes)

Ingredients:
- 1-pound ground beef
- 1 onion, chopped
- 3 cloves of garlic, minced
- 3 tablespoons olive oil
- 1 green bell pepper, seeded and chopped
- Salt and pepper to taste
- 6 cups eggs, beaten

Directions for Cooking:

1) Preheat the air fryer for 5 minutes with baking pan insert.
2) In a baking dish mix the ground beef, onion, garlic, olive oil, and bell pepper. Season with salt and pepper to taste.
3) Pour in the beaten eggs and give a good stir.
4) Place the dish with the beef and egg mixture in the air fryer.
5) Bake for 30 minutes at 330oF.

Nutrition information:
Calories: 579; Carbs: 14.5g; Protein: 65.8g; Fat: 28.6g

Baked Mediterranean Veggies

(Servings: 4, Cooking Time: 30 minutes)

Ingredients:
- ½-lb Cherry Tomatoes
- 1 Large Courgette, peeled and chopped into 1-inch cubes
- 1 Green Pepper
- 1 Large Parsnip, peeled and chopped into 1-inch cubes
- 1 Medium Carrot, peeled and sliced into ½-inch circles
- 1 Tsp Mixed Herbs
- 2 Tbsp Honey
- 1 Tsp Mustard
- 2 Tsp Garlic Puree
- 6 Tbsp Olive Oil
- Salt & Pepper

Directions for Cooking:

1) Lightly grease baking pan of air fryer with cooking spray. Add courgetti on bottom, parsnip, carrot, pepper, and then cherry tomatoes. Season with mixed herbs, mustard, garlic puree, and drizzle with oil. Season with pepper and salt, generously.
2) For 15 minutes, cook on 330°F. Halfway through cooking time, stir.
3) Cook for 15 minutes at 330°F.
4) Serve and enjoy.

Nutrition Information:
Calories: 281; Carbs: 21.0g; Protein: 2.0g; Fat: 21.0g

Shrimp and Veggie Bake

(Servings: 4, Cooking Time: 20 minutes)

Ingredients:
- Small Shrimp Peeled & Deveined (Regular Size Bag about 50-80 Small Shrimp)
- 1 Bag of Frozen Mixed Vegetables
- 1 Tbsp Gluten Free Cajun Seasoning
- Olive Oil Spray
- Season with salt and pepper

Directions for Cooking:
1) Lightly grease baking pan of air fryer with cooking spray. Add all Ingredients: and toss well to coat. Season with pepper and salt, generously.
2) For 10 minutes, cook on 330°F. Halfway through cooking time, stir.
3) Cook for 10 minutes at 330°F.
4) Serve and enjoy.

Nutrition Information:
Calories: 78; Carbs: 13.2g; Protein: 2.8g; Fat: 1.5g

Orange-Caesar Dressed Roughie

(Servings: 2, Cooking Time: 15 minutes)

Ingredients:
- 2 orange roughie fillets (4 ounces each)
- 1/4 cup creamy Caesar salad dressing
- 1/2 cups crushed butter-flavored crackers
- 1/2 cup shredded cheddar cheese

Directions for Cooking:
1) Lightly grease baking pan of air fryer with cooking spray. Add filet on bottom of pan. Drizzle with dressing, sprinkle crumbled crackers.
2) For 10 minutes, cook on 390°F.
3) Sprinkle cheese and let it stand for 5 minutes.
4) Serve and enjoy.

Nutrition Information:
Calories: 341; Carbs: 5.0g; Protein: 32.6g; Fat: 21.1g

Salmon with Crisped Topped Crumbs

(Servings: 2, Cooking Time: 15 minutes)

Ingredients:
- 1-1/2 cups soft bread crumbs
- 2 tablespoons minced fresh parsley
- 1 tablespoon minced fresh thyme or 1 teaspoon dried thyme
- 2 garlic cloves, minced
- 1 teaspoon grated lemon zest
- 1/2 teaspoon salt
- 1/4 teaspoon lemon-pepper seasoning
- 1/4 teaspoon paprika
- 1 tablespoon butter, melted
- 2 salmon fillets (6 ounces each)

Directions for Cooking:
1) In a medium bowl mix well bread crumbs, fresh parsley thyme, garlic, lemon zest, salt, lemon-pepper seasoning, and paprika.
2) Lightly grease baking pan of air fryer with cooking spray. Add salmon filet with skin side down. Evenly sprinkle crumbs on tops of salmon.
3) For 10 minutes, cook on 390°F. Let it rest for 5 minutes.
4) Serve and enjoy.

Nutrition Information:
Calories: 331; Carbs: 9.0g; Protein: 31.0g; Fat: 19.0g

Crispy Baked Brussels Sprouts

(Servings: 2, Cooking Time: 12 minutes)

Ingredients:
- 3 cups halved Brussel sprouts
- 1 Tbsp olive oil
- 1/4 tsp salt
- 1/4 tsp pepper

Directions for Cooking:

1) Lightly grease baking pan of air fryer with cooking spray. Add all Ingredients: and toss well to coat.
2) For 12 minutes, cook on 330°F.
3) Serve and enjoy.

Nutrition Information:
Calories: 133; Carbs: 12.3g; Protein: 4.6g; Fat: 7.2g

Orange & Tofu Fry

(Servings: 4, Cooking Time: 25 minutes)

Ingredients:
- 1-pound extra-firm tofu drained and pressed (or use super-firm tofu), cut in cubes
- 1 Tablespoon tamari
- 1 Tablespoon cornstarch (or arrowroot powder)

Sauce Ingredients:
- 1 teaspoon orange zest
- 1/3 cup orange juice
- 1/2 cup water
- 2 teaspoons cornstarch (or arrowroot powder)
- 1/4 teaspoon crushed red pepper flakes
- 1 teaspoon fresh ginger minced
- 1 teaspoon fresh garlic minced
- 1 Tablespoon pure maple syrup

Directions for Cooking:

1) In a bowl, mix tofu with tamari and a tablespoon of cornstarch. Marinate for at least 15 minutes. Tossing well to coat every now and then.
2) In a small bowl mix all sauce Ingredients: and set aside.
3) Lightly grease baking pan of air fryer with cooking spray. Add tofu for 10 minutes, cook on 390°F. Halfway through cooking time, stir. Cook for 10 minutes more.
4) Stir in sauce, toss well to coat. Cook for another 5 minutes.
5) Serve and enjoy.

Nutrition Information:
Calories: 63; Carbs: 11.0g; Protein: 8.0g; Fat: 3.0g

Gouda-Spinach Stuffed Pork

(Servings: 2, Cooking Time: 15 minutes)

Ingredients:

- 3 tablespoons dry bread crumbs
- 2 tablespoons grated Parmesan cheese
- 2 pork sirloin cutlets (3 ounces each)
- 1/4 teaspoon salt
- 1/8 teaspoon pepper
- 2 slices smoked Gouda cheese (about 2 ounces)
- 2 cups fresh baby spinach
- 2 tablespoons horseradish mustard

Directions for Cooking:

1) Mix well Parmesan and bread crumbs in a small bowl.
2) On a flat surface, season pork with pepper and salt. Add spinach and cheese on each cutlet and fold to enclose filling. With toothpicks secure pork.
3) Brush mustard all over pork and dip in crumb mixture.
4) Lightly grease baking pan of air fryer with cooking spray. Add pork.
5) For 15 minutes, cook on 330°F. Halfway through cooking time, turnover.
6) Serve and enjoy.

Nutrition Information:

Calories: 304; Carbs: 10.0g; Protein: 30.0g; Fat: 16.0g

Perfect Air Fried Roast Beef

(Servings: 8, Cooking Time: 1 hour)

Ingredients:

- 2 pounds topside of beef
- 2 medium onions, chopped
- 2 sticks of celery, sliced
- 1 bulb of garlic, peeled and crushed
- A bunch of fresh herbs of your choice
- Salt and pepper to taste
- 3 tablespoons olive oil
- 1 tablespoon butter

Directions for Cooking:

1) Preheat the air fryer for 5 minutes.
2) In air fryer baking pan, place all the Ingredients: and give a good stir.
3) Place the dish in the air fryer and bake for 1 hour at 330°F.

Nutrition information:

Calories: 243; Carbs: 3.1g; Protein: 16.7g; Fat: 18.2g

Spiced 'n Fried Cauliflower

(Servings: 4, Cooking Time: 25 minutes)

Ingredients:
- 1 head cauliflower cut into florets
- 3/4 cup onion white, thinly sliced
- 5 cloves garlic finely sliced
- 1 1/2 tablespoons tamari or gluten free tamari
- 1 tablespoon rice vinegar
- 1/2 teaspoon coconut sugar
- 1 tablespoon Sriracha or other favorite hot sauce
- 2 scallions for garnish

Directions for Cooking:
1) Lightly grease baking pan of air fryer with cooking spray. Add cauliflower and for 10 minutes, cook on 330ºF.
2) Add onion and garlic. Stir well and cook for another 10 minutes.
3) In a small bowl, whisk well pepper, salt, sriracha, coconut sugar, rice vinegar, and soy sauce.
4) Stir in pan and cook for 5 minutes more.
5) Serve and enjoy with sprinkled scallions.

Nutrition Information:
Calories: 91; Carbs: 12.0g; Protein: 4.0g; Fat: 3.0g

Scrumptious Shrimp Scampi Fry

(Servings: 4, Cooking Time: 15 minutes)

Ingredients:
- 4 tablespoons butter
- 1 tablespoon lemon juice
- 1 tablespoon minced garlic
- 2 teaspoons red pepper flakes
- 1 tablespoon chopped chives or 1 teaspoon dried chives
- 1 tablespoon minced basil leaves plus more for sprinkling or 1 teaspoon dried basil
- 2 tablespoons chicken stock (or white wine)
- 1-lb defrosted shrimp (21-25 count)

Directions for Cooking:
1) Lightly grease baking pan of air fryer with cooking spray. Melt butter for 2 minutes at 330ºF. Stir in red pepper flakes and garlic. Cook for 3 minutes.
2) Add remaining Ingredients: in pan and toss well to coat.
3) Cook for 5 minutes at 330ºF. Stir and let it stand for another 5 minutes.
4) Serve and enjoy.

Nutrition Information:
Calories: 213; Carbs: 1.0g; Protein: 23.0g; Fat: 13.0g

Baked Cod in Air Fryer

(Servings: 2, Cooking Time: 12 minutes)

Ingredients:
- 1 tablespoon butter
- 1/4 sleeve buttery round crackers (such as Ritz®), crushed
- 1 tablespoon butter
- 1/2 pound thick-cut cod loin
- 1/4 lemon, juiced
- 2 tablespoons dry white wine
- 1-1/2 teaspoons chopped fresh parsley
- 1-1/2 teaspoons chopped green onion
- 1/2 lemon, cut into wedges

Directions for Cooking:
1) In a small bowl, melt butter in microwave. Whisk in crackers.
2) Lightly grease baking pan of air fryer with remaining butter. And melt for 2 minutes at 390°F.
3) In a small bowl whisk well lemon juice, white wine, parsley, and green onion.
4) Coat cod filets in melted butter. Pour dressing. Top with butter-cracker mixture.
5) Cook for 10 minutes at 390°F.
6) Serve and enjoy with a slice of lemon.

Nutrition Information:
Calories: 266; Carbs: 9.3g; Protein: 20.9g; Fat: 16.1g

Tender Chicken Thigh Bake

(Servings: 4, Cooking Time: 11 minutes)

Ingredients:
- 4 bone-in chicken thighs with skin
- 1/8 teaspoon garlic salt
- 1/8 teaspoon onion salt
- 1/8 teaspoon dried oregano
- 1/8 teaspoon ground thyme
- 1/8 teaspoon paprika
- 1/8 teaspoon ground black pepper

Directions for Cooking:
1) Lightly grease baking pan of air fryer with cooking spray. Place chicken with skin side touching the bottom of pan.
2) In a small bowl whisk well pepper, paprika, thyme, oregano, onion salt, and garlic salt. Sprinkle all over chicken.
3) For 1 minute, cook on 390°F.
4) Turnover chicken while rubbing on bottom and sides of pan for more seasoning.
5) Cook for 10 minutes at 390°F.
6) Serve and enjoy.

Nutrition Information:
Calories: 185; Carbs: 0.2g; Protein: 19.2g; Fat: 11.9g

Chicken Teriyaki Bake

(Servings: 2, Cooking Time: 25 minutes)

Ingredients:

- 1-1/2 teaspoons cornstarch
- 1-1/2 teaspoons cold water
- 1/4 cup white sugar
- 1/4 cup soy sauce
- 2 tablespoons cider vinegar
- 1/2 clove garlic, minced
- 1/4 teaspoon ground ginger
- 1/8 teaspoon ground black pepper
- 4 skinless chicken thighs

Directions for Cooking:

1) Lightly grease baking pan of air fryer with cooking spray. Add all Ingredients: and toss well to coat. Spread chicken in a single layer on bottom of pan.
2) For 15 minutes, cook on 390°F.
3) Turnover chicken while brushing and covering well with the sauce.
4) Cook for 15 minutes at 330°F.
5) Serve and enjoy.

Nutrition Information:
Calories: 267; Carbs: 19.9g; Protein: 24.7g; Fat: 9.8g

Meatball Pizza Bake

(Servings: 4, Cooking Time: 15 minutes)

Ingredients:

- 1 prebaked 6-inch pizza crust
- 1/2 can (8 ounces) pizza sauce
- 1 teaspoon garlic powder
- 1 teaspoon Italian seasoning
- 4 tbsp grated Parmesan cheese
- 1 small onion, halved and sliced
- 6 frozen fully cooked Italian meatballs (1/2 ounce each), thawed and halved
- 1/2 cup shredded part-skim mozzarella cheese
- 1/2 cup shredded cheddar cheese

Directions for Cooking:

1) Lightly grease baking pan of air fryer with cooking spray.
2) Place crust on bottom of pan. Spread sauce on top. Sprinkle with parmesan, Italian seasoning, and garlic powder.
3) Top with meatballs and onion. Sprinkle remaining cheese.
4) For 15 minutes, cook on preheated 390°F air fryer.
5) Serve and enjoy.

Nutrition Information:
Calories: 324; Carbs: 28.0g; Protein: 17.0g; Fat: 16.0g

Pepperoni Calzone Bake

(Servings: 4, Cooking Time: 25 minutes)

Ingredients:
- 1 cup chopped pepperoni
- 1/2 cup pasta sauce with meat
- 1/4 cup shredded part-skim mozzarella cheese
- 1 loaf (1 pound) frozen bread dough, thawed
- 1 to 2 tablespoons 2% milk
- 1 tablespoon grated Parmesan cheese
- 1/2 teaspoon Italian seasoning, optional

Directions for Cooking:
1) In a bowl mix well mozzarella cheese, pizza sauce, and pepperoni.
2) On a lightly floured surface, divide dough into four portions. Roll each into a 6-in. circle; top each with a scant 1/3 cup pepperoni mixture. Fold dough over filling; pinch edges to seal.
3) Lightly grease baking pan of air fryer with cooking spray. Place dough in a single layer and if needed, cook in batches.
4) For 25 minutes, cook on 330°F preheated air fryer or until dough is lightly browned.
5) Serve and enjoy.

Nutrition Information:
Calories: 527; Carbs: 59.0g; Protein: 21.0g; Fat: 23.0g

Comforting Beef Stew Bake

(Servings: 4, Cooking Time: 40 minutes)

Ingredients:
- 1/2 can (14-1/2 ounces) diced tomatoes, undrained
- 1/2 cup water
- 2 tablespoons quick-cooking tapioca
- 1 teaspoon sugar
- 1 teaspoons salt
- 1/2 teaspoon pepper
- 1-pound beef stew meat, cut into 1-inch cubes
- 2 medium carrots, cut into 1-inch chunks
- 1 large potato, peeled and quartered
- 1 celery rib, cut into 3/4-inch chunks
- 1 small onion, cut into chunks
- 1 slice bread, cubed

Directions for Cooking:
1) Lightly grease baking pan of air fryer with cooking spray. Add all Ingredients: and toss well to coat.
2) Cover pan with foil.
3) For 25 minutes, cook on 390°F. Halfway through cooking time, stir.
4) Remove foil, stir well, and cook for 15 minutes at 330°F.
5) Serve and enjoy.

Nutrition Information:
Calories: 296; Carbs: 31.0g; Protein: 25.0g; Fat: 8.0g

Roll-up Chicken Reuben

(Servings: 2, Cooking Time: 15 minutes)

Ingredients:

- 2 slices swirled rye and pumpernickel bread
- 2 boneless skinless chicken breast halves (4 ounces each)
- 1/4 teaspoon garlic salt
- 1/4 teaspoon pepper
- 2 slices Swiss cheese
- 2 slices deli corned beef
- 2 tablespoons Thousand Island salad dressing
- Additional Thousand Island salad dressing, optional

Directions for Cooking:

1) Tear bread into 2-inch pieces and place in blender. Pulse until crumbly. Transfer to a shallow bowl.

2) With meal mallet, pound chicken to ¼*inch thick. Season with pepper and salt. Top chicken with corned beef and cheese. Roll chicken and secure ends with toothpick.

3) Brush chicken with dressing and dip in crumbs until covered totally.

4) Lightly grease baking pan of air fryer with cooking spray. Place rollups.

5) For 15 minutes, cook on 330°F preheated air fryer.

6) Turnover rollups and continue cooking for another 10 minutes.

7) Serve and enjoy with extra dressing.

Nutrition Information:
Calories: 317; Carbs: 18.0g; Protein: 32.0g; Fat: 13.0g

Chicken Mediterranean Fry

(Servings: 2, Cooking Time: 21 minutes)

Ingredients:

- 2 boneless skinless chicken breast halves (6 ounces each)
- 1/4 teaspoon salt
- 1/4 teaspoon pepper
- 3 tablespoons olive oil
- 1/2-pint grape tomatoes
- 6 pitted Greek or ripe olives, sliced
- 2 tablespoons capers, drained

Directions for Cooking:

1) Lightly grease baking pan of air fryer with cooking spray.

2) Add chicken and season with pepper and salt.

3) Brown for 3 minutes per side in preheated 390°F air fryer.

4) Stir in capers, olives, tomatoes, and oil.

5) Cook for 15 minutes at 330°F.

6) Serve and enjoy.

Nutrition Information:
Calories: 330; Carbs: 6.0g; Protein: 36.0g; Fat: 18.0g

Crusted Fish with Dijon

(Servings: 2, Cooking Time: 15 minutes)

Ingredients:

- 3 tablespoons reduced-fat mayonnaise
- 1 tablespoon lemon juice
- 2 teaspoons Dijon mustard
- 1 teaspoon prepared horseradish
- 2 tablespoons grated Parmesan cheese, divided
- 2 tilapia fillets (5 ounces each)
- 1/4 cup dry bread crumbs
- 2 teaspoons butter, melted

Directions for Cooking:

1) Lightly grease baking pan of air fryer with cooking spray. Place tilapia in a single layer.
2) In a small bowl, whisk well mayo, lemon juice, mustard, 1 tablespoon cheese and horseradish. Spread on top of fish.
3) In another bowl, mix remaining cheese, melted butter, and bread crumbs. Sprinkle on top of fish.
4) For 15 minutes, cook on 390°F.
5) Serve and enjoy.

Nutrition Information:
Calories: 212; Carbs: 7.0g; Protein: 28.0g; Fat: 8.0g

Rosemary Pork with Apricot Glaze

(Servings: 3, Cooking Time: 30 minutes)

Ingredients:

- 2 tablespoons minced fresh rosemary or 1 tablespoon dried rosemary, crushed
- 2 tablespoons olive oil, divided
- 4 garlic cloves, minced
- 1 teaspoon salt
- 1/2 teaspoon pepper
- 1-lb pork tenderloin

Apricot Glaze Ingredients:

- 1 cup apricot preserves
- 3 tablespoons lemon juice
- 2 garlic cloves, minced

Directions for Cooking:

1) Mix well pepper, salt, garlic, oil, and rosemary. Brush all over pork. If needed cut pork crosswise in half to fit in air fryer.
2) Lightly grease baking pan of air fryer with cooking spray. Add pork.
3) For 3 minutes per side, brown pork in a preheated 390°F air fryer.
4) Meanwhile, mix well all glaze Ingredients: in a small bowl. Baste pork every 5 minutes.
5) Cook for 20 minutes at 330°F.
6) Serve and enjoy.

Nutrition Information:
Calories: 281; Carbs: 27.0g; Protein: 23.0g; Fat: 9.0g

Creamy Coconut Sauce on Jamaican Salmon

(Servings: 2, Cooking Time: 12 minutes)

Ingredients:

- 2 salmon fillets (6 ounces each)
- 1 ½ tablespoons mayonnaise
- 2 teaspoons Caribbean jerk seasoning
- 1/4 cup sour cream
- 4 tbsp cream of coconut
- 1 teaspoon grated lime zest
- 4 tbsp cup lime juice
- 1/4 cup sweetened shredded coconut, toasted

Directions for Cooking:

1) Lightly grease baking pan of air fryer with cooking spray. Add salmon with skin side down. Spread mayo on top and season with Caribbean jerk.
2) For 12 minutes, cook on 330°F.
3) On medium low fire, place a pan and bring lime juice, lime zest, cream of coconut, and sour cream to a simmer. Mix well. Transfer to a bowl for dipping.
4) Serve and enjoy.

Nutrition Information:
Calories: 490; Carbs: 16.0g; Protein: 30.0g; Fat: 34.0g

Turkey 'n Biscuit Bake

(Servings: 5, Cooking Time: 30 minutes)

Ingredients:

- 1 can (10-3/4 ounces) condensed cream of chicken soup, undiluted
- 1 cup chopped cooked turkey or chicken
- 1 can (4 ounces) mushroom stems and pieces, drained
- 1/2 cup frozen peas
- 1/4 cup 2% milk
- Dash each ground cumin, dried basil and thyme
- 1 tube (12 ounces) refrigerated buttermilk biscuits, cut into 4 equal slices

Directions for Cooking:

1) Lightly grease baking pan of air fryer with cooking spray. Add all Ingredients: and toss well to mix except for biscuits.
2) Top with biscuits. Cover pan with foil.
3) For 15 minutes, cook on 390°F.
4) Remove foil and cook for 15 minutes at 330°F or until biscuits are lightly browned.
5) Serve and enjoy.

Nutrition Information:
Calories: 325; Carbs: 38.0g; Protein: 14.0g; Fat: 13.0g

Chicken Bruschetta Bake

(Servings: 2, Cooking Time: 28 minutes)

Ingredients:
- 1/4 cup all-purpose flour
- 1/4 cup egg substitute
- 2 boneless skinless chicken breast halves (4 ounces each)
- 1/4 cup grated Parmesan cheese
- 1/4 cup dry bread crumbs
- 1 tablespoon butter, melted
- 1 large tomato, seeded and chopped
- 1 1/2 tablespoons minced fresh basil
- 1/2 tablespoon olive oil
- 2 garlic cloves, minced
- 1/2 teaspoon salt
- 1/4 teaspoon pepper

Directions for Cooking:
1) In shallow bowl, whisk well egg substitute and place flour in a separate bowl. Dip chicken in flour, then egg, and then flour. In small bowl whisk well butter, bread crumbs and cheese. Sprinkle over chicken.
2) Lightly grease baking pan of air fryer with cooking spray. Place breaded chicken on bottom of pan. Cover with foil.
3) For 20 minutes, cook on 390ºF.
4) Meanwhile, in a bowl whisk well remaining ingredient.
5) Remove foil from pan and then pour over chicken the remaining Ingredients.
6) Cook for 8 minutes.
7) Serve and enjoy.

Nutrition Information:
Calories: 311; Carbs: 22.0g; Protein: 31.0g; Fat: 11.0g

Amazingly Healthy Zucchini Bake

(Servings: 5, Cooking Time: 20 minutes)

Ingredients:
- 1 large zucchini, cut lengthwise then in half
- 1 (8 ounce) package cream cheese, softened
- 1 cup sour cream
- 1/4 cup grated Parmesan cheese
- 1 tablespoon minced garlic
- paprika to taste

Directions for Cooking:
1) Lightly grease baking pan of air fryer with cooking spray.
2) Place zucchini slices in a single layer in pan.
3) In a bowl whisk well, remaining Ingredients: except for paprika. Spread on top of zucchini slices. Sprinkle paprika.
4) Cover pan with foil.
5) For 10 minutes, cook on 390ºF.
6) Remove foil and cook for 10 minutes at 330ºF.
7) Serve and enjoy.

Nutrition Information:
Calories: 296; Carbs: 6.5g; Protein: 7.3g; Fat: 26.7g

3-Cheese Meatball Bake

(Servings: 5, Cooking Time: 40 minutes)

Ingredients:

- 1/2 package (16 ounces) mostaccioli, cooked according to package Directions for Cooking: and drained
- 1 large Egg, lightly beaten
- 1/2 carton (15 ounces) part-skim ricotta cheese
- 1/2-pound ground beef
- 1 small onion, chopped
- 1 tablespoon brown sugar
- 1 tablespoon Italian seasoning
- 1 teaspoon garlic powder
- 1/4 teaspoon pepper
- 1 jar (24 ounces) pasta sauce with meat
- 1/4 cup grated Romano cheese
- 1/2 package (12 ounces) frozen fully cooked Italian meatballs, thawed
- 1/4 cup shaved Parmesan cheese
- Minced fresh parsley or fresh baby arugula, optional

Directions for Cooking:

1) Lightly grease baking pan of air fryer with cooking spray. Add beef and onions.
2) Cook for 10 minutes at 330°F, stirring and crumbling halfway through cooking time.
3) Drain excess fat. Stir in sugar and seasoning.
4) Mix in pasta and sauce. Mix well.
5) Remove half of mixture and transfer to a plate. Evenly spread half of ricotta mixture and half of Romano cheese. Return half of pasta. Evenly spread remaining ricotta and Romano. Top with meatballs and Parmesan.
6) Cover with foil.
7) For 20 minutes, cook on 390°F.
8) Remove foil cook for 10 minutes more until tops are lightly browned.
9) Serve and enjoy.

Nutrition Information:
Calories: 563; Carbs: 55.0g; Protein: 34.0g; Fat: 23.0g

Tater Tot, Cheeseburger 'n Bacon Bake

(Servings: 6, Cooking Time: 35 minutes)

Ingredients:

- 1-pound ground beef
- 1 small onion, chopped
- 1/2 can (15 ounces) tomato sauce
- 4-ounces process cheese (Velveeta)
- 1 tablespoon ground mustard
- 1 tablespoon Worcestershire sauce
- 1/2 cup shredded cheddar cheese
- 6 bacon strips, cooked and crumbled
- 8-ounces frozen Tater Tots
- 1/2 cup grape tomatoes, chopped
- 1/4 cup sliced dill pickles

Directions for Cooking:

1) Lightly grease baking pan of air fryer with cooking spray. Add beef and half of onions.
2) For 10 minutes, cook on 390°F. Halfway through cooking time, stir and crumble beef.
3) Stir in Worcestershire, mustard, Velveeta, and tomato sauce. Mix well. Cook for 4 minutes until melted.

4) Mix well and evenly spread in pan. Top with cheddar cheese and then bacon strips.
5) Evenly top with tater tots. Cover pan with foil.
6) Cook for 15 minutes at 390°F. Uncover and bake for 10 minutes more until tops are lightly browned.

7) Serve and enjoy topped with pickles and tomatoes and remaining onion.

Nutrition Information:
Calories: 483; Carbs: 24.0g; Protein: 27.0g; Fat: 31.0g

Chicago-Style Deep Dish Pizza
(Servings: 4, Cooking Time: 25 minutes)

Ingredients:
- 1 package (1/4 ounce) active dry yeast
- 1 cup warm water (110°F to 115°F)
- 1 teaspoon sugar
- 1 teaspoon salt
- 2 tablespoons canola oil
- 2-1/2 cups all-purpose flour
- 1-pound ground beef, cooked and drained
- 1 can (10-3/4 ounces) condensed tomato soup, undiluted
- 1 teaspoon each dried basil, oregano and thyme
- 1 teaspoon dried rosemary, crushed
- 1/4 teaspoon garlic powder
- 1 small green pepper, julienned
- 1 can (8 ounces) mushroom stems and pieces, drained
- 1 cup shredded part-skim mozzarella cheese

Directions for Cooking:

1) In a large bowl, dissolve yeast in warm water. Add the sugar, salt, oil and 2 cups flour. Beat until smooth. Stir in enough remaining flour to form a soft dough. Cover and let rest for 20 minutes. Divide into two and store half in the freezer for future use.
2) On a floured surface, roll into a square the size of your air fryer. Transfer to a greased air fryer baking pan. Sprinkle with beef.
3) Mix well seasonings and soup in a small bowl and pour over beef.
4) Sprinkle top with mushrooms and green pepper. Top with cheese.
5) Cover pan with foil.
6) For 15 minutes, cook on 390°F.
7) Remove foil, cook for another 10 minutes or until cheese is melted.
8) Serve and enjoy.

Nutrition Information:
Calories: 362; Carbs: 39.0g; Protein: 20.0g; Fat: 14.0g

Dessert & Snacks Recipes

Apple-Blueberry Crumble Vegan Approved

(Servings: 2, Cooking Time: 15 minutes)

Ingredients:
- 1 medium apple, finely diced
- ½ cup frozen blueberries, strawberries, or peaches
- ¼ cup plus 1 tablespoon brown rice flour
- 2 tablespoons sugar
- ½ teaspoon ground cinnamon
- 2 tablespoons nondairy butter

Directions for Cooking:
1) Lightly grease baking pan of air fryer with cooking spray.
2) Spread frozen blueberries and apple slices on bottom of pan.
3) In a bowl, whisk well butter, cinnamon, sugar, and flour. Sprinkle over fruit. If needed, sprinkle extra flour to cover exposed fruit.
4) For 15 minutes, cook on 330°F
5) Serve and enjoy.

Nutrition Information:
Calories: 281; Carbs: 40.1g; Protein: 2.0g; Fat: 12.5g

Brownie with Salty Pistachio

(Servings: 4, Cooking Time: 25 minutes)

Ingredients:
- 1/4 cup nondairy milk
- 1/4 cup aquafaba
- 1/2 teaspoon vanilla extract
- 1/2 cup whole wheat pastry flour
- 1/2 cup vegan sugar
- 1/4 cup cocoa powder
- 1 tablespoon ground flax seeds
- 1/4 teaspoon salt

Directions for Cooking:
1) In a large bowl, whisk well all dry Ingredients. Beat in the wet Ingredients: until combined thoroughly.
2) Lightly grease baking pan of air fryer with cooking spray. Pour in batter and evenly spread.
3) For 20 minutes, cook on preheated 330°F air fryer.
4) Let it sit for 5 minutes.
5) Serve and enjoy.

Nutrition Information:
Calories: 158; Carbs: 28.2g; Protein: 4.1g; Fat: 3.2g

Caramel Dip 'n Apple Fries

(Servings: 8, Cooking Time: 16 minutes)

Ingredients:

- 3 Pink Lady or Honeycrisp apples, peeled, cored and cut into 8 wedges
- ½ cup flour
- 3 eggs, beaten
- 1 cup graham cracker crumbs
- ¼ cup sugar
- 8 ounces whipped cream cheese
- ½ cup caramel sauce, plus more for garnish

Directions for Cooking:

1) In a large bowl, toss well flour and apple slices.
2) In one bowl beat eggs. In another bowl mix well, sugar and graham crackers.
3) Dredge apple slices in egg and then roll in graham mixture.
4) Lightly grease air fryer basket with cooking spray. Add a single layer of apples. Cook in batches for 8 minutes at 390°F.
5) Meanwhile, mix caramel sauce and whipped cream cheese..
6) Serve and enjoy with the dip on the side.

Nutrition Information:

Calories: 226; Carbs: 22.4g; Protein: 6.7g; Fat: 12.1g

Biscuit Bites with Cinnamon

(Servings: 8, Cooking Time: 16 minutes)

Ingredients:

- 2/3 cup (about 2 7/8 oz.) all-purpose flour
- 2/3 cup (about 2 2/3 oz.) whole-wheat flour
- 2 tablespoons granulated sugar
- 1 teaspoon baking powder
- 1/4 teaspoon ground cinnamon
- 1/4 teaspoon kosher salt
- 4 tablespoons cold salted butter, cut into small pieces
- 1/3 cup whole milk
- 2 cups (about 8 oz.) powdered sugar
- 3 tablespoons water

Directions for Cooking:

1) In a large bowl, whisk well all dry Ingredients. Stir in wet Ingredients: and mix well. Knead well into a dough and roll into 16 equal balls.
2) Lightly grease baking pan of air fryer with cooking spray. Add the balls in a single layer. Cook in batches.
3) For 8 minutes, cook on 390°F. Halfway through cooking time, shake basket.
4) Serve and enjoy.

Nutrition Information:

Calories: 335; Carbs: 60.0g; Protein: 8.0g; Fat: 7.0g

Choco Chip Cookies

(Servings: 9, Cooking Time: 15 minutes)

Ingredients:
- 100 g Butter
- 75 g Brown Sugar
- 175 g Self Raising Flour
- 100 g Chocolate
- 2 Tbsp Honey
- 1 Tbsp Milk

Directions for Cooking:
1) In a bowl, whisk well all dry Ingredients. Stir in wet Ingredients: and mix well.
2) Lightly grease baking pan of air fryer with cooking spray. Drop cookie dough by teaspoonful, around 3-4 pieces.
3) Cook in batches for 5 minutes at 390°F.
4) Serve and enjoy.

Nutrition Information:
Calories: 253; Carbs: 32.0g; Protein: 2.0g; Fat: 13.0g

Donut Holes with Maple Cream

(Servings: 12, Cooking Time: 12 minutes)

Ingredients:
- 1 cup all-purpose flour
- 1/4 cup organic sugar
- 1 teaspoon baking powder
- 1/2 teaspoon salt
- 2 tablespoons aquafaba
- 1 tablespoon neutral oil like sunflower
- 1/4 cup brewed coffee
- 1 teaspoon coffee extract

Maple Cream Ingredients:
- 1/2 cup raw cashews quick soaked in hot water for 10-20 minutes, then drained (10 for a high-speed blender, 20 for a regular blender)
- 1/2 cup brewed coffee
- 1 1/2 tablespoons maple syrup

Directions for Cooking:
1) Mix well salt, baking powder, sugar, and flour in a large bowl. Stir in coffee extract, coffee, oil, aquafaba. Mix well. Form into 12 balls. If needed refrigerate dough for easy handling.
2) Lightly grease baking pan of air fryer with cooking spray. Add donut holes and bake in a single layer for 6 minutes at 390°F. Do not shake. Bake in batches.
3) Meanwhile, mix the maple cream Ingredients: and drizzle over cooked doughnut holes.
4) Serve and enjoy.

Nutrition Information:
Calories: 92; Carbs: 13.7g; Protein: 2.2g; Fat: 3.1g

Air Fryed Peach Pies

(Servings: 8, Cooking Time: 24 minutes)

Ingredients:

- 2 (5-oz.) fresh peaches, peeled and chopped
- 1 tablespoon fresh lemon juice (from 1 lemon)
- 3 tablespoons granulated sugar
- 1 teaspoon vanilla extract
- 1/4 teaspoon table salt
- 1 teaspoon cornstarch
- 1 (14.1-oz.) pkg. refrigerated piecrusts

Directions for Cooking:

1) In medium bowl, whisk well salt, vanilla, sugar, and lemon juice. Let stand for 15 minutes while stirring every now and then. Drain while reserving a tablespoon of the liquid.

2) In reserved liquid mix in cornstarch and then stir into drained peaches.

3) Slice crusts into 8 pieces of 4-inch circles. Add a tablespoon of peach filling. Brush sides of dough with water, fold in half and crimp edge with fork to seal dough. Repeat to remaining doughs.

4) Lightly grease air fryer basket with cooking spray. Add dough in a single layer and cook in batches.

5) For 8 minutes, cook on 390°F.

6) Serve and enjoy.

Nutrition Information:
Calories: 328; Carbs: 43.0g; Protein: 3.0g; Fat: 16.0g

Garlic Knots with Parmesan

(Servings: 12, Cooking Time: 16 minutes)

Ingredients:

- 1 13.8 oz refrigerated pizza crust
- 3 tbsp Olive oil
- 3 tbsp Minced garlic
- Garlic salt
- Parmesan cheese powder

Directions for Cooking:

1) Roll dough out onto a cutting board. Cut dough into equal ¼" strips. Wrap each strip into knots

2) Mix olive oil & garlic in a bowl. Dip each knot into the mixture.

3) Lightly grease baking pan of air fryer with cooking spray. Add knots in a single layer and cook in batches for 4 minutes at 390°F.

4) Dust with Parmesan.

5) Serve and enjoy.

Nutrition Information:
Calories: 148; Carbs: 11.0g; Protein: 4.7g; Fat: 9.4

Pecan-Cranberry Cake

(Servings: 6, Cooking Time: 25 minutes)

Ingredients:

- 1/4 cup cashew milk (or use any dairy or non-dairy milk you prefer)
- 2 large eggs
- 1/2 tsp vanilla extract
- 1 1/2 cups Almond Flour
- 1/4 cup Monk fruit (or use your preferred sweetener)
- 1 tsp baking powder
- 1/4 tsp cinnamon
- 1/8 tsp salt
- 1/2 cup fresh cranberries
- 1/4 cup chopped pecans

Directions for Cooking:

1) In blender, add all wet Ingredients: and mix well. Add all dry Ingredients: except for cranberries and pecans. Blend well until smooth.
2) Lightly grease baking pan of air fryer with cooking spray. Pour in batter. Drizzle cranberries on top and then followed by pecans.
3) For 20 minutes, cook on 330°F.
4) Let stand for 5 minutes.
5) Serve and enjoy.

Nutrition Information:
Calories: 98; Carbs: 11.7g; Protein: 1.7g; Fat: 4.9g

Strawberry Pop Tarts

(Servings: 6, Cooking Time: 25 minutes)

Ingredients:

- 2 refrigerated pie crusts
- 1 tsp cornstarch
- 1/3 cup low-sugar strawberry preserves
- 1/2 cup plain, non-fat vanilla Greek yogurt
- 1 oz reduced-fat Philadelphia cream cheese
- 1 tsp sugar sprinkles
- 1 tsp stevia
- olive oil or coconut oil spray

Directions for Cooking:

1) Cut pie crusts into 6 equal rectangles.
2) In a bowl, mix cornstarch and preserves. Add preserves in middle of crust. Fold over crust. Crimp edges with fork to seal. Repeat process for remaining crusts.
3) Lightly grease baking pan of air fryer with cooking spray. Add pop tarts in single layer. Cook in batches for 8 minutes at 370°F.
4) Meanwhile, make the frosting by mixing stevia, cream cheese, and yogurt in a bowl. Spread on top of cooked pop tart and add sugar sprinkles.
5) Serve and enjoy.

Nutrition Information:
Calories: 317; Carbs: 34.8g; Protein: 4.7g; Fat: 17.6g

Lemon Blueberry Cake

(Servings: 4, Cooking Time: 17 minutes)

Ingredients:

- 2 1/2 cups self-rising flour
- 1/2 cup Monk Fruit (or use your preferred sugar)
- 1/2 cup cream
- 1/4 cup avocado oil (any light cooking oil)
- 2 eggs
- 1 cup blueberries
- zest from 1 lemon
- juice from 1 lemon
- 1 tsp. vanilla
- brown sugar for topping (a little sprinkling on top of each muffin-less than a teaspoon)

Directions for Cooking:

1) In mixing bowl, beat well wet Ingredients. Stir in dry Ingredients: and mix thoroughly.
2) Lightly grease baking pan of air fryer with cooking spray. Pour in batter.
3) For 12 minutes, cook on 330°F.
4) Let it stand in air fryer for 5 minutes.
5) Serve and enjoy.

Nutrition Information:
Calories: 589; Carbs: 76.7g; Protein: 13.5g; Fat: 25.3g

Creamy Leche Flan

(Servings: 4, Cooking Time: 30 minutes)

Ingredients:

- 1/3 cup white sugar
- 1/2 (14 ounce) can sweetened condensed milk
- 1 cup heavy cream
- 1/2 cup milk
- 2-1/2 eggs
- 1 teaspoon vanilla extract

Directions for Cooking:

1) In blender, blend well vanilla, eggs, milk, cream, and condensed milk.
2) Lightly grease baking pan of air fryer with cooking spray. Add sugar and heat for 10 minutes at 370°F until melted and caramelized. Lower heat to 300°F and continue melting and swirling.
3) Pour milk mixture into caramelized sugar. Cover pan with foil.
4) Cook for 20 minutes at 330°F.
5) Let it cool completely in the fridge.
6) Place a plate on top of pan and invert pan to easily remove flan.
7) Serve and enjoy.

Nutrition Information:
Calories: 498; Carbs: 46.8g; Protein: 10.0g; Fat: 30.0g

Easy-Peasy Apple Pie

(Servings: 4, Cooking Time: 35 minutes)

Ingredients:
- 1 Pillsbury Refrigerator pie crust
- Baking spray
- 1 large apple, chopped
- 2 teaspoons lemon juice
- 1 tablespoon ground cinnamon
- 2 tablespoon sugar
- ½ teaspoon vanilla extract
- 1 tablespoon butter
- 1 beaten egg
- 1 tablespoon raw sugar

Directions for Cooking:
1) Lightly grease baking pan of air fryer with cooking spray. Spread pie crust on bottom of pan up to the sides.
2) In a bowl, mix vanilla, sugar, cinnamon, lemon juice, and apples. Pour on top of pie crust. Top apples with butter slices.
3) Cover apples with the other pie crust. Pierce with knife the tops of pie.
4) Spread beaten egg on top of crust and sprinkle sugar.
5) Cover with foil.
6) For 25 minutes, cook on 390°F.
7) Remove foil cook for 10 minutes at 330°F until tops are browned.
8) Serve and enjoy.

Nutrition Information:
Calories: 372; Carbs: 44.7g; Protein: 4.2g; Fat: 19.6g

Crunchy Crisped Peaches

(Servings: 4, Cooking Time: 30 minutes)

Ingredients:
- 4 cup sliced peaches, frozen
- 3 tablespoon sugar
- 2 tablespoon Flour, white
- 1 teaspoon sugar, white
- 1/4 cup Flour, white
- 1/3 cup oats, dry rolled
- 3 tablespoon butter, unsalted
- 1 teaspoon cinnamon
- 3 tablespoon pecans, chopped

Directions for Cooking:
1) Lightly grease baking pan of air fryer with cooking spray. Mix in a tsp cinnamon, 2 tbsp flour, 3 tbsp sugar, and peaches.
2) For 20 minutes, cook on 300°F.
3) Mix the rest of the Ingredients: in a bowl. Pour over peaches.
4) Cook for 10 minutes at 330°F.
5) Serve and enjoy.

Nutrition Information:
Calories: 435; Carbs: 74.1g; Protein: 4.3g; Fat: 13.4g

Five-Cheese Pull Apart Bread

(Servings: 2, Cooking Time: 15 minutes)

Ingredients:

- 1 Large Bread Loaf
- 100 g Butter
- 2 Tsp Garlic Puree
- 30 g Cheddar Cheese
- 30 g Goats Cheese
- 30 g Mozzarella Cheese
- 30 g Soft Cheese
- 30 g Edam Cheese
- 2 Tsp Chives
- Salt & Pepper

Directions for Cooking:

1) Grate hard cheese and separate into 4 piles.
2) Lightly grease baking pan of air fryer with cooking spray. Melt butter for 2 minutes at 330°F. Stir in garlic, pepper, salt, and chives and cook for 3 minutes.
3) Make slits on bread and pour melted butter into slits. Cover with soft cheese all the slits. Followed by remaining cheeses. Insert in all the slits on the bread.
4) Place bread in air fryer basket.
5) Cook for 10 minutes at 330°F.
6) Serve and enjoy.

Nutrition Information:

Calories: 518; Carbs: 13.3g; Protein: 21.4g; Fat: 42.1g

Buttery Dinner Rolls

(Servings: 9, Cooking Time: 25 minutes)

Ingredients:

- 1 cup Fresh Milk (room temperature)
- 114gn Butter (softened) and more for brushing
- 63gm Sugar
- 2 Eggs
- 1 1/2 tsp Salt
- 508gm Bread Flour
- 2 1/4 tsp Instant Yeast

Directions for Cooking:

1) In mixer, mix all wet Ingredients. Followed by dry Ingredients: and knead for at least 10 minutes. Roll dough into 9 rolls.
2) Lightly grease baking pan of air fryer with cooking spray. Place rolls in a single layer. Cover top of pan with damp cloth and rolls rise for at least an hour.
3) For 15 minutes, cook on 330°F. Halfway through cooking time, stir.
4) Add butter slices on top of rolls.
5) Serve and enjoy.

Nutrition Information:

Calories: 300; Carbs: 31.2g; Protein: 7.7g; Fat: 16.0g

Yummy Carrot Cake

(Servings: 8, Cooking Time: 40 minutes)

Ingredients:
- 225 g Self Raising
- 150 g Brown Sugar
- 1 Tsp Mixed Spice
- 2 Large Carrots peeled and grated
- 2 Medium Eggs
- 150 ml Olive Oil
- 2 Tbsp Milk
- 50 g Butter
- 1 Small Orange rind and juice
- 235 g Icing Sugar

Directions for Cooking:
1) In blender, blend all wet Ingredients. Add all dry Ingredients: except for carrots and icing sugar and orange. Mix well. Stir in carrots with a spatula.
2) Lightly grease baking pan of air fryer with cooking spray. Pour batter.
3) Cover pan with foil.
4) For 20 minutes, cook on 330°F. Remove foil and cook for 10 minutes. Let it stand for ten minutes in air fryer.
5) In a small bowl whisk well orange juice, rind, and icing sugar.
6) Once cake has cooled, pour icing on top and spread.
7) Serve and enjoy.

Nutrition Information:
Calories: 529; Carbs: 71.0g; Protein: 5.0g; Fat: 25.0g

Delightful Caramel Cheesecake

(Servings: 8, Cooking Time: 40 minutes)

Ingredients:
- 6 Digestives, crumbled
- 50 g Melted Butter
- 1 Can Dulce de Leche
- 500 g Soft Cheese
- 250 g Caster Sugar
- 4 Large Eggs
- 1 Tbsp Vanilla Essence
- 1 Tbsp Melted Chocolate

Directions for Cooking:
1) Lightly grease baking pan of air fryer with cooking spray. Mix and press crumbled digestives and melted butter on pan bottom. Spread dulce de leche.
2) In bowl, beat well soft cheese and sugar until fluffy. Stir in vanilla and egg. Pour over dulce de leche.
3) Cover pan with foil. For 15 minutes, cook on 390°F.
4) Cook for 10 minutes at 330°F. And then 15 minutes at 300°F.
5) Let it cool completely in air fryer. Refrigerate for at least 4 hours before slicing.
6) Serve and enjoy.

Nutrition Information:
Calories: 463; Carbs: 44.1g; Protein: 17.9g; Fat: 23.8g

Tangy Orange-Choco cake

(Servings: 8, Cooking Time: 35 minutes)

Ingredients:
- 100 g Self Raising Flour
- 110 g Caster Sugar
- 50 g Butter
- 20 g Cocoa Powder
- 1 Tsp Cocoa Nibs
- 1 Large Orange juice and rind
- 1 Tbsp Honey
- 1 Tsp Vanilla Essence
- 2 Medium Eggs
- 50 ml Whole Milk

Frosting Ingredients:
- 50 g Butter
- 100 g Icing Sugar
- 50 ml Orange Juice

Directions for Cooking:

1) In blender, blend all wet Ingredients. Add dry ingredients and blend until smooth.
2) Lightly grease baking pan of air fryer with cooking spray. Pour in batter. Cover pan with foil.
3) For 20 minutes, cook on 330°F. Remove foil and cook for another 10 minutes. Let it stand in air fryer for 5 minutes more.
4) Meanwhile, mix well all frosting ingredients in a bowl. Once cake has cooled, spread on top of cake.
5) Serve and enjoy.

Nutrition Information:
Calories: 284; Carbs: 41.0g; Protein: 3.0g; Fat: 12.0g

Amazing with Every Bite Fried Bananas

(Servings: 4, Cooking Time: 12 minutes)

Ingredients:
- 4 Ripe Bananas, peeled and sliced in half crosswise and then in half lengthwise
- 2 tablespoons All Purpose Flour (Maida)
- 2 tablespoons Rice flour
- 2 tablespoons Corn flour
- 2 tablespoons Desiccated Coconut Powder
- 1 pinch Salt
- 1/2 teaspoon Baking powder

Directions for Cooking:

1) Make the batter by mixing coconut, salt, baking powder, corn flour, rice flour, and Maida in a bowl. Add bananas and cover well in mixture.
2) Lightly grease air fryer basket with cooking spray. Add bananas.
3) For 12 minutes, cook on 390°F. Halfway through cooking time, shake basket.
4) Serve and enjoy.

Nutrition Information:
Calories: 192; Carbs: 32.0g; Protein: 2.1g; Fat: 6.2g

Blackberry-Goodness Cobbler

(Servings: 5, Cooking Time: 20 minutes)

Ingredients:
- 1/4 cup white sugar
- 1 tablespoon cornstarch
- 3 cups fresh blackberries
- 2 tablespoons melted butter
- 1-1/4 cups all-purpose flour
- 3/4 cup white sugar
- 1-1/2 teaspoons baking powder
- 1/2 teaspoon salt
- 1 cup milk
- 1-1/2 teaspoons vanilla extract
- 2 tablespoons melted butter

Directions for Cooking:
1) Lightly grease baking pan of air fryer with cooking spray. Add blackberries and drizzle with 2 tbsps. melted butter.
2) In a small bowl, whisk cornstarch and 1/4 cup sugar. Sprinkle over blackberries and toss well to coat.
3) In another bowl, whisk well salt, baking powder, and ¾ cup sugar. Stir in 2 tbsps. melted butter, vanilla, and milk. Mix well and pour over berries.
4) For 20 minutes, cook on 390°F or until tops are lightly browned.
5) Serve and enjoy.

Nutrition Information:
Calories: 429; Carbs: 76.4g; Protein: 6.1g; Fat: 10.9g

Appetizing Apple Pound Cake

(Servings: 6, Cooking Time: 60 minutes)

Ingredients:
- 1 cup white sugar
- 3/4 cup vegetable oil
- 1 teaspoon vanilla extract
- 1-1/2 eggs
- 1-1/2 cups all-purpose flour
- 1/2 teaspoon baking soda
- 1/4 teaspoon ground cinnamon
- 1/2 teaspoon salt
- 1 medium Granny Smith apples - peeled, cored and chopped
- 2/3 cup and 1 tablespoon chopped walnuts

Directions for Cooking:
1) In blender, blend all Ingredients: except for apples and walnuts. Blend thoroughly. Fold in apples and walnuts.
2) Lightly grease baking pan of air fryer with cooking spray. Pour batter.
3) Cover pan with foil.
4) For 30 minutes, cook on preheated 330°F air fryer.
5) Remove foil and cook for another 20 minutes.
6) Let it stand for 10 minutes.
7) Serve and enjoy.

Nutrition Information:
Calories: 696; Carbs: 71.1g; Protein: 6.5g; Fat: 42.8g

Sugared Doughs with Choco Dip

(Servings: 10, Cooking Time: 24 minutes)

Ingredients:
- 1-pound bread dough, defrosted
- ½ cup butter, melted
- ¾ to 1 cup sugar
- 1 cup heavy cream
- 12 ounces good quality semi-sweet chocolate chips
- 2 tablespoons Amaretto liqueur (or almond extract)

Directions for Cooking:
1) Roll the dough into two 15-inch logs. Cut each log into 20 slices. Cut each slice in half and twist the dough halves together 3 to 4 times. Place the twisted dough on a cookie sheet, brush with melted butter and sprinkle sugar over the dough twists.
2) Lightly grease air fryer basket with cooking spray. Add dough twists in a single layer. Cook in batches for 8 minutes at 390ºF. Halfway through cooking time, shake basket and brush with butter. Once done cooking dip in a bowl of sugar.
3) Meanwhile make the dip by heating cream in microwave. Stir in chocolate and heat again until melted and thoroughly combined. Stir in amaretto. And set aside for dipping.
4) Serve and enjoy.

Nutrition Information:
Calories: 469; Carbs: 51.1g; Protein: 5.7g; Fat: 26.8g

Appealingly Coconut-y Cake

(Servings: 8, Cooking Time: 40 minutes)

Ingredients:
- 1 cup gluten-free flour
- 3/4 cup white sugar
- 1/2 cup flaked coconut
- 1/4 cup chopped walnuts
- 1-1/2 teaspoons baking powder
- 1/2 teaspoon baking soda
- 1/2 teaspoon xanthan gum
- 1/2 teaspoon salt
- 1/2 cup coconut milk
- 1/2 cup vegetable oil
- 2 eggs
- 1/2 teaspoon vanilla extract

Directions for Cooking:
1) In blender blend all wet Ingredients. Add dry Ingredients: and blend thoroughly.
2) Lightly grease baking pan of air fryer with cooking spray.
3) Pour in batter. Cover pan with foil.
4) For 30 minutes, cook on 330ºF.
5) Let it rest for 10 minutes
6) Serve and enjoy.

Nutrition Information:
Calories: 359; Carbs: 35.2g; Protein: 4.3g; Fat: 22.3g

Cranberry Bread Pudding

(Servings: 4, Cooking Time: 45 minutes)

Ingredients:
- 1-1/2 cups milk
- 3/4 cup heavy whipping cream
- 1/4 cup and 2 tablespoons white sugar
- 2-1/2 eggs
- 3/4 teaspoon lemon zest
- 3/4 teaspoon kosher salt
- 1/8 teaspoon ground cinnamon
- 3/8 vanilla bean, split and seeds scraped away
- 3/4 French baguettes, cut into 2-inch slices
- 1/4 cup golden raisins
- 1/2 cup cranberries1 teaspoon butter

Directions for Cooking:
1) Lightly grease baking pan of air fryer with cooking spray. Spread baguette slices, cranberries, and raisins.
2) In blender, blend well vanilla bean, cinnamon, salt, lemon zest, eggs, sugar, and cream. Pour over baguette slices. Let it soak for an hour.
3) Cover pan with foil.
4) For 35 minutes, cook on 330°F.
5) Let it rest for 10 minutes.
6) Serve and enjoy.

Nutrition Information:
Calories: 581; Carbs: 76.1g; Protein: 15.8g; Fat: 23.7g

Luscious Strawberry Cobbler

(Servings: 4, Cooking Time: 25 minutes)

Ingredients:
- 1/4 cup white sugar
- 1-1/2 teaspoons cornstarch
- 1/2 cup water
- 1-1/2 cups strawberries, hulled
- 1 tablespoon butter, diced
- 1/2 cup all-purpose flour
- 1-1/2 teaspoons white sugar
- 3/4 teaspoon baking powder
- 1/4 teaspoon salt
- 1 tablespoon and 2 teaspoons butter
- 1/4 cup heavy whipping cream

Directions for Cooking:
1) Lightly grease baking pan of air fryer with cooking spray. Add water, cornstarch, and sugar. Cook for 10 minutes 390°F or until hot and thick. Add strawberries and mix well. Dot tops with 1 tbsp butter.
2) In a bowl, mix well salt, baking powder, sugar, and flour. Cut in 1 tbsp and 2 tsp butter. Mix in cream. Spoon on top of berries.
3) Cook for 15 minutes at 390°F, until tops are lightly browned.
4) Serve and enjoy.

Nutrition Information:
Calories: 255; Carbs: 32.0g; Protein: 2.4g; Fat: 13.0g

Air Fryed Churros with Choco Dip

(Servings: 12, Cooking Time: 30 minutes)

Ingredients:

- 1/2 cup water
- 1/4 teaspoon kosher salt
- 1/4 cup , plus 2 Tbsp. unsalted butter, divided
- 1/2 cup (about 2 1/8 oz.) all-purpose flour
- 2 large eggs
- 1/3 cup granulated sugar
- 2 teaspoons ground cinnamon
- 4 ounces bittersweet baking chocolate, finely chopped
- 3 tablespoons heavy cream
- 2 tablespoons vanilla kefir

Directions for Cooking:

1) In small saucepan, bring to a boil ¼ cup butter, salt, and water. Stir in flour and lower fire to a simmer. Cook until smooth and thickened and pulls away from side of pan.
2) Transfer dough to a bowl and stir constantly until cooled.
3) Stir in eggs one at a time.
4) Transfer to a pastry bag with a star tip. Chill for half an hour.
5) Lightly grease baking pan of air fryer with cooking spray. Pipe dough on bottom of pan in 3-inch lengths.
6) For 10 minutes, cook on 390ºF. Halfway through cooking time, shake. Cook in batches
7) In a small bowl mix cinnamon and sugar. In another bowl, place melted butter.
8) Brush cooked churros with melted butter and then roll in sugar mixture.
9) In microwave safe bowl, melt cream and chocolate. Mix well and stir in vanilla.
10) Serve and enjoy with dip on the side.

Nutrition Information:
Calories: 159; Carbs: 12.0g; Protein: 3.0g; Fat: 11.0g

Out-of-this-World PB&J Doughnuts

(Servings: 6, Cooking Time: 30 minutes)

Ingredients:

- 1 1/4 Cups all-purpose flour
- 1/3 Cup sugar
- 1/2 Teaspoon baking powder
- 1/2 Teaspoon baking soda
- 3/4 Teaspoon salt
- 1 Egg
- 1/2 Cup buttermilk
- 1 Teaspoon vanilla
- 2 Tablespoons unsalted butter, melted and cooled
- 1 Tablespoon melted butter for brushing the tops

Filling Ingredient:

- 1/2 Cup Blueberry or strawberry jelly (not preserves)

Glaze Ingredients:

- 1/2 Cup powdered sugar
- 2 Tablespoons milk
- 2 Tablespoons peanut butter
- Pinch of sea salt

Directions for Cooking:

1) In mixing bowl, whisk well all wet Ingredients. Mix in dry Ingredients: and beat until thoroughly combined.

Roll dough to ¾-inch thickness. Cut into 3.5-inch rounds.
2) Lightly grease baking pan of air fryer with cooking spray. Add doughnuts in single layer. Cook in batches at for 10 minutes at 330°F.
3) Meanwhile, make the glaze by mixing all Ingredients: in a bowl.

4) Fill each doughnut with filling and spread glaze on top.
5) Serve and enjoy.

Nutrition Information:
Calories: 243; Carbs: 37.6g; Protein: 5.7g; Fat: 7.7g

Enchanting Coffee-Apple Cake

(Servings: 6, Cooking Time: 40 minutes)

Ingredients:
- 2 tablespoons butter, softened
- 1/4 cup and 2 tablespoons brown sugar
- 1/2 large egg
- 2 tablespoons sour cream
- 2 tablespoons vanilla yogurt
- 1/2 teaspoon vanilla extract
- 1/2 cup all-purpose flour
- 1/4 teaspoon ground cinnamon
- 1/4 teaspoon baking soda
- 1/8 teaspoon salt
- 1 cup diced Granny Smith apple

Topping Ingredients:
- 2 tablespoons brown sugar
- 2 tablespoons all-purpose flour
- 1 tablespoon butter
- 1/4 teaspoon ground cinnamon

Directions for Cooking:
1) In blender, puree all wet Ingredients. Add dry Ingredients: except for apples and blend until smooth. Stir in apples.
2) Lightly grease baking pan of air fryer with cooking spray. Pour batter into pan.
3) In a small bowl mix well, all topping Ingredients: and spread on top of cake batter.
4) Cover pan with foil.
5) For 20 minutes, cook on 330°F.
6) Remove foil and cook for 10 minutes. Let it stand in air fryer for another 10 minutes.
7) Serve and enjoy.

Nutrition Information:
Calories: 279; Carbs: 41.4g; Protein: 3.6g; Fat: 11.0g

Pumpkin Pie in Air Fryer

(Servings: 8, Cooking Time: 35 minutes)

Ingredients:

- 1 (15 ounce) can pumpkin puree
- 3 egg yolks
- 1 large egg
- 1 (14 ounce) can sweetened condensed milk
- 1 teaspoon ground cinnamon
- 1/2 teaspoon ground ginger
- 1/2 teaspoon fine salt
- 1/4 teaspoon freshly grated nutmeg
- 1/8 teaspoon Chinese 5-spice powder
- 1 9-inch unbaked pie crust

Directions for Cooking:

1) Lightly grease baking pan of air fryer with cooking spray. Press pie crust on bottom of pan, stretching all the way up to the sides of the pan. Pierce all over with fork.
2) In blender, blend well egg, egg yolks, and pumpkin puree. Add Chinese 5-spice powder, nutmeg, salt, ginger, cinnamon, and condensed milk. Pour on top of pie crust.
3) Cover pan with foil.
4) For 15 minutes, cook on preheated 390°F air fryer.
5) Remove foil and continue cooking for 20 minutes at 330°F until middle is set.
6) Allow to cool in air fryer completely.
7) Serve and enjoy.

Nutrition Information:

Calories: 326; Carbs: 41.9g; Protein: 7.6g; Fat: 14.2g

Easy 'n Delicious Brownies

(Servings: 8, Cooking Time: 20 minutes)

Ingredients:

- 1/4 cup butter
- 1/2 cup white sugar
- 1 egg
- 1/2 teaspoon vanilla extract
- 2 tablespoons and 2 teaspoons unsweetened cocoa powder
- 1/4 cup all-purpose flour
- 1/8 teaspoon salt
- 1/8 teaspoon baking powder

Frosting Ingredients:

- 1 tablespoon and 1-1/2 teaspoons butter, softened
- 1 tablespoon and 1-1/2 teaspoons unsweetened cocoa powder
- 1-1/2 teaspoons honey
- 1/2 teaspoon vanilla extract
- 1/2 cup confectioners' sugar

Directions for Cooking:

1) Lightly grease baking pan of air fryer with cooking spray. Melt ¼ cup butter for 3 minutes. Stir in vanilla, eggs, and sugar. Mix well.
2) Stir in baking powder, salt, flour, and cocoa mix well. Evenly spread.
3) For 20 minutes, cook on 300°F.
4) In a small bowl, make the frosting by mixing well all Ingredients. Frost brownies while still warm.
5) Serve and enjoy.

Nutrition Information:

Calories: 191; Carbs: 25.7g; Protein: 1.8g; Fat: 9.0g

Sour Cream-Blueberry Coffee Cake

(Servings: 6, Cooking Time: 35 minutes)

Ingredients:

- 1/2 cup butter, softened
- 1 cup white sugar
- 1 egg
- 1/2 cup sour cream
- 1/2 teaspoon vanilla extract
- 3/4 cup and 1 tablespoon all-purpose flour
- 1/2 teaspoon baking powder
- 1/8 teaspoon salt
- 1/2 cup fresh or frozen blueberries
- 1/4 cup brown sugar
- 1/2 teaspoon ground cinnamon
- 1/4 cup chopped pecans
- 1-1/2 teaspoons confectioners' sugar for dusting

Directions for Cooking:

1) In a small bowl, whisk well pecans, cinnamon, and brown sugar.
2) In a blender, blend well all wet Ingredients. Add dry Ingredients: except for confectioner's sugar and blueberries. Blend well until smooth and creamy.
3) Lightly grease baking pan of air fryer with cooking spray.
4) Pour half of batter in pan. Sprinkle half of pecan mixture on top. Pour the remaining batter. And then topped with remaining pecan mixture.
5) Cover pan with foil.
6) For 35 minutes, cook on 330°F.
7) Serve and enjoy with a dusting of confectioner's sugar.

Nutrition Information:
Calories: 471; Carbs: 59.5g; Protein: 4.1g; Fat: 24.0g

Made in the USA
San Bernardino, CA
03 January 2019